AN INDIAN SOJOURN

*One woman's spiritual experience
of travel & volunteering*

Ellen Besso

ELLEN BESSO

First Edition published January, 2013

Editor, Jill Crossland
Cover design & book formatting, Suzanne Doyle-Ingram

Printed in the United States of America
ISBN: 978-0-9812381-2-8

"This is a rather unique book. Ellen seamlessly weaves together a saga of personal spiritual journey, useful travel tips for India, poignant documentary about the lives of Tibetans in exile, an honest look at the realities of foreign country volunteering, with its blessings and challenges, and the ongoing story of grief and loss about a parent with dementia. The story is told with a light and elegant touch in a highly readable style; it's one of those books that keeps you up reading through the night. Her sense of humour shines through, along with a clear eyed honesty. Her attention to detail makes you feel you are right there in India, with its smells, sounds and sights. The people she meets come alive, through the small but intimate details of her daily interactions.

"I want to say bravo, bravo!"

~ Rose Clarke, Counsellor & Art Therapist

"Ellen Besso leaves the blue herons that fly over her home in British Columbia and travels to India. Journeying from Delhi to Panthankot in the Punjab, Ellen's destination is McLeod Ganj, Dharamasala; the home of the Dalai Lama where she and her partner, Don, plan to work for a while from the Kirti Monastery Guesthouse as volunteers to the Tibetan community there.

Ellen draws deft brush strokes of the minutiae of her life within the community as she acclimatizes to the changing rhythm of her days. She glimpses the inspiring presence of the Dalai Lama and forges lasting friendships as she listens to the harrowing stories of Tibetan refugees escaping persecution in their own country. *An Indian Sojourn* is both a factual account and an emotional and spiritual journey through India. Ellen is searingly honest and admits with humour and humility when she is out of her comfort zone and her love affair with the country temporarily palls.

Her tolerance of a patriarchal culture where poor women are invisible and often abused and middle class women confined by their gender tests her feminism to the core. Visceral moments, such as when Ellen sees a lone woman pacing up and down a small rooftop like a caged animal eloquently illustrates her ability to conjure the vivid colours, shimmering sensations, atmosphere and contradictions of India.

At the beginning of her book Ellen says, "Wherever you go, there you are". I think this captures the truth and the heart of *An Indian Sojourn*. We are changed and enriched by our exposure to other cultures. We need to carry those experiences forward in our hearts into the lives we have. I believe Ellen, back with her blue herons, has achieved this."

~ Sara MacDonald, Author of *Another Life* and *Sea Music*

CONTENTS

INDIA

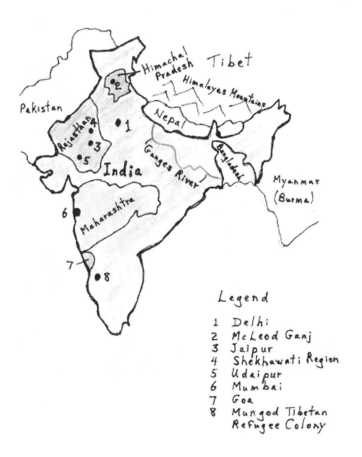

Legend

1 Delhi
2 McLeod Ganj
3 Jaipur
4 Shekhawati Region
5 Udaipur
6 Mumbai
7 Goa
8 Mungod Tibetan
  Refugee Colony

"All journeys have secret destinations of which the traveller is unaware"

...Koala

INTRODUCTION

"Whatever you think or say, you're wrong; it's the opposite," said our 14 year-old guide as we walked the lanes of Varanasi. Attempting to describe this multifaceted nation and my relationship to it is impossible. India is a country of paradoxes where extremes are at play.

Writers often apologize for not being able to clearly explain the intricacies that make up this country of over one billion people, where the middle class now constitutes one quarter to one third of the population and English is the common language in cities and tourist areas.

India's draw is complex; we can't understand it within the frame of reference of our Western minds, and that is part of what pulls us in. Once our constant internal analysis abates, we're more open to flowing with what is unfolding around us. To say that the environment there is over stimulating would be an understatement. People, vehicles, cows, even the colours are de trop, but my approach has been, "bring it on". I was thirsty for India after waiting for her so long and I wanted to soak in every tiny little detail.

India is very rich and very poor, spiritual yet also extremely material, beautiful but also ugly. The welcoming hospitality we felt everywhere helped to counteract the overload, the frustrations and the oxymorons of the country.

For as long as I can remember I've had a preoccupation with India and its people, feeling drawn to go there. Life intervened, and my first visit did not take place until I was well into midlife. It was worth the wait, and I viewed it with different eyes than I would have at a younger age.

I've always felt quite certain that numerous past lives have been spent in India, and my immediate affinity and strong connection to the country and to the Indian and Tibetan people living there pointed to this. Later a friend, a talented professional psychic, confirmed this for me.

My partner Don and I are very fortunate to be on the same page when it comes to travelling. With our childraising years over and career transitions underway, my desire to see India overtook my homebody routines, and our first six week trip to the Indian continent was in 2007. The adventure was so successful we decided to return two years later for a longer period of time, one that would involve volunteer work as well as travel.

For three months we lived, volunteered, soaked in the culture and breathed the often arid, dusty air of the country. India turned out to be everything I imagined it would be...and more. The women and men we met, almost without exception, in both the North India Tibetan and Indian communities and in South India, embraced us with their warmth and friendship, and a sincere desire to understand more about our country, our lifestyle and us as individuals.

Every section of *An Indian Sojourn* is its own unique vignette, describing the adventures and personal connections made in each place visited or volunteered in.

The first part of the book is about the McLeod Ganj Tibetan refugee community, the home base of the Dalai Lama. It is the story of their culture and of the struggles and joys of the men and women who became my friends.

The second and third parts of the book follow Don and me as we explore other areas of India that attracted us. Part 2, Rajasthan, will introduce you to the ancient "outdoor art gallery" of Shekhawati, where the repression of women and the unusual energy disturbed me; to Udaipur's relaxing, European-like atmosphere and abundant market; the city of Jaipur, the access point for both Shekhawati and Udaipur to the south; and a brief interlude in the British hill station of Mount Abu.

Finally, in Part 3, we enter the chaos of the 20 million large city of Mumbai, where Don loved riding the rails, and we had the privilege of touring Dharavi Slum, a mind-altering experience. The final rejuvenating vacation in the South Indian Goan community of Benalim was our last destination, before other adventures on the return trip home.

Over the years I've read about India sporadically and absorbed the overall geography of the country, so I had a feel for it. Certainly we can develop a sense of India's beauty, colourfulness and congestion from reading descriptions of it, looking at pictures and watching movies. But for me, to appreciate it more fully, I needed to feel the country first hand.

I invite you to join me on my journey, through the ups and downs of travel and volunteering, meet the people we developed strong friendships with, and enjoy the fascination and wild rides that are India. This book is also about the heartfelt stories of refugees, fellow travellers and the Indian people themselves and the effort of trying to understand cultures very different from ours. Ultimately though it is the moments when we are not so far apart that defines *An Indian Sojourn*.

PART ONE

THE TIBETANS IN INDIA

Breaking Away

The trip will be a long one, three months, so preparations are extensive. My mother's needs must be planned for; herbal tonics and whatnots stockpiled at her care home, extra visits from friends scheduled and new knee socks purchased to keep her warm during the winter months.

As a life coach with a private practice, it's essential that I take care of innumerable business projects that require my attention; three of the internet radio shows I'm booked into are within a month of our departure. My friend and her daughter are both deteriorating from breast cancer complications, and it's hard to part company after closely supporting the mother over the past six months. Finally there's the actual trip prep itself; I try, a tad obsessively admittedly, to plan for any eventuality, impossible of course. I've never made so many excursions to our local one-stop-shopping pharmacy.

The tasks feel so relentless that at one point I actually question whether the trip is worth it. Staying home would be much easier. But there is a purpose behind this voyage and I'll never know what experiences have been missed if my partner Don and I do not go.

I fret less this time about leaving my mother than on previous trips, satisfied that she's in capable, loving hands at Totem Lodge. I'll think about those left behind while we're gone, but the great distance gently buffers my worrying.

My sense is that I have begun the process of detaching from my mother lately. Intermittent dreams during Mom's long process of aging and deterioration from dementia have centred on taking care of her. Often we were pulling her out of deep water to save her from drowning. Now the dreams are shifting to reflect a letting go, in preparation for what is ultimately to come.

It's common to have doubts before embarking on an expedition like this; I always do. Many of us wish to travel, but somehow life intervenes and we never get around to it. Our doubts make it hard to break away from the routine of daily life…what will people think, will we lose our hard earned place on the career track, how will we find the money, and so on.

My daughter says when she shaved her head at age eighteen, part of her rite of passage, women of all ages approached her saying, "I've always wanted to do that." "I know they never will", Bronwen told me. Travelling is a bit like this – the yearning must be strong enough that we're able to override the voices of doubt and do what it takes to put our dream into action. Leaving family, friends, jobs or businesses involves complex arrangements, but when the will is there, it's doable.

A journey of this nature is something we nurture within ourselves, then plan for, often years in advance. I waited thirty years for my first trip to India, finally the timing was right and the pieces came together in 2007.

Intention is the first step towards doing anything important in life. When one is clear about wanting to travel, volunteer or work abroad, even if we can't articulate why, our mind becomes focused around this idea, we begin to envision it happening, both consciously and unconsciously, and then we move to make it a priority.

Most of us need to give ourselves permission to enrich our lives. The voices need to be put to rest, the external and the internal ones, the judgements and criticisms. When one's intent is clear and passion is strong, the doubts and limiting thoughts can be processed and we begin to feel free to move ahead.

It's remarkable how creative individuals can be once a plan is formulated. We begin to think outside the box and the blocks to moving forward gradually work themselves out. "Once you make a decision, the universe conspires to make it happen", Ralph Waldo Emerson said.

My co-worker at a social service agency had twenty percent of her pay withheld for four years, then took one year off to work at a monkey sanctuary in South Africa, a lifelong dream. While this would not have been the fantasy for the rest of us, we thoroughly applauded her brave actions.

Everyone feels differently when it comes to travel; we've met families with young children trekking, volunteering or living as expatriates in both Mexico and India. Child raising held me back. Being a Taurean with a strong nesting instinct meant I needed a stable home for my family; the idea of travelling extensively and volunteering in developing countries with a young child made me nervous. Our lifestyle may have been different had we been childless.

Initially we made our home in Southern Ontario, then, after falling in love with Gibsons during a visit, we put down deep roots in this small community on the West Coast of Canada. I knew intuitively our lives would be different here.

The move from Ontario to British Columbia in our early forties, at the beginning of our daughter's second decade, gave us a new lease on life in many ways, as the culture of the West Coast offered everyone new opportunities for growth.

Over the years I've supported women, also some men, as a social worker, counsellor and as a bodywork therapist. A helping spirit and a desire to uplift others seem to be at the core of who I am. This journey is an extension of my work, with an added spiritual and social justice component, and in many ways I have a lot riding on it.

I have no idea how the next three months will unfold…whether it they will be as rewarding as hoped…as spiritually uplifting. What I do know is my journey to India feels like the right thing to do, to challenge myself to explore life's meaning in a different way.

Launch Time

It's now mid-October, and a kind hearted neighbour packs us, bag and baggage, into her aging Land Cruiser and makes the ten minute trip to the ferry terminal, where we walk on as foot passengers. Our home is left alarmed and in the capable hands of Alan, who looks after houseplants, mail and banking whenever we're away; his friend, who is now en route from Quebec to BC, will live in the house during our three month absence.

With everything finally in place, we begin to relax, and enjoy the 40 minute sail into Vancouver, ride the crowded express bus downtown, then hop onto the new skytrain that runs right to the airport. Our daughter steps on the train along the way, connecting with us at the airport. We know the drill and the whole process is becoming quite routine, on this third extended trip.

After a short visit with Bronwen we board the flight to Hong Kong, the longest leg of the journey, at 12 hours. New seats, recently installed by Cathay Pacific Airlines, are uncomfortable for sleeping; their backs do not recline, this allows the airline to cram more seats into each plane. The sound system is a treat though, state-of-the-art, with current movies plus TV shows.

Once in Hong Kong we stroll around the airport, then try to rest; I lie down but my body objects to the slanted, molded plastic seats and sleep does not come. Then the plane takes off for Delhi, arriving in the middle of the night. Our bodies have adjusted to long distance flying over time and the trip passes relatively quickly; nevertheless we're pretty tired on landing. It's surprising how well the human body can function on so little sleep.

Shortly before the plane touches down in India an announcement is made, then air attendants wearing masks come through the cabin, spraying lavish amounts of insecticide into the air above our heads. The fine mist is particularly toxic for very young, old or sick individuals, but India requires that inbound planes be treated to prevent the spread of disease. We now know a flimsy mask can be requested; another helpful approach is to get into a bathroom during the actual proceedings.

Since we've arrived during the night, the usual hustle and bustle at Indira Gandhi Airport is noticeably absent. Passengers flow easily through immigration, health check (a questionnaire that attempts to identify people with H1N1 virus), then baggage pickup quickly and without misadventure, very helpful when one has been up for over 30 hours.

Cutting in is an old-fashioned art in India. No power struggles occur tonight though, as in the long lineups during the congested daylight hours. The last time we passed through this airport, as I waited to purchase a taxi voucher a man pushed in from the side, attempting to work his way into line. Determined that this rude bully would not succeed, I pushed my baggage cart forward, inch by inch, gently nudging his buggy and blocking him from entering. A couple of grumbled words were exchanged, but it was satisfying! In Varanasi I witnessed a young, modern looking Indian man dress down another male for this behaviour, but most people passively accept it.

Our Prince Polonia Hotel driver is waiting, ready to sweep us away and deliver us to our lodging, where we settle in for a much needed nap. The hotel taxi service is new; previously we had to make our own way there by either expensive public taxi or by engaging the government run service, whose drivers do not speak English and cannot read the hotel address on the card. This was always a challenge since no one can ever find the Prince Polonia, buried in the warrens of Paharganj, just past Old Delhi.

Delhi Once Again

With a population of 16 million, Delhi is the most polluted city in India. Although the air is cleaner than in the seventies, the situation is worsening daily, with cars now being the main culprit rather than industry. Over the past five plus years the city government has done much to reduce emissions, even switching its bus fleet from diesel to compressed natural gas, but the situation is still spiralling out of control.

The city boasts a state-of-the-art metro service, with stations and trains reminiscent of BART in San Francisco, but the expanding middle class likes to own private vehicles. The number of cars in Delhi has increased 50 percent over the past five years and there are over four million in the city, many with diesel engines, cheap but toxic.

Try to stretch your mind around this; as manufacturers churn out affordable small vehicles, 1000 new cars hit the streets of the city each day, leading to unimaginable congestion. Tata Motors, India's largest automobile manufacturer, released their tiny *Nano* in the spring of 2009, selling at the unbelievable price of approximately $2,500 or one Indian *lakh*.

Despite the madness, I like it here; it feels good, like visiting a favourite relative or friend. As long as you don't attempt too much in a day, staying in Delhi can be an enjoyable and stimulating experience.

During our first trip in 2007, we stayed at Wonghden House in Majnu-ka-Tilla, New Delhi's Tibetan refugee colony, as the guidebook reported it was quiet and off the beaten track. This was an understatement as it turned out. Once installed in the cloistered settlement you're stranded, with little to do other than stroll through the exceptionally narrow, dirty laneways, perusing the few market stalls. Encountering the area's beggars in the confines of the cramped lanes can be disturbing, particularly in the sad case of the mother with her hydrocephalic infant.

Walking outside the gates is not an option as safety is an issue on the teeming roadway, and with each step there's a tout, (more about these 'store agents' in the next chapter), auto rickshaw or taxi driver shadowing visitors, badgering them to purchase their services.

This settlement, home to 2,500 Tibetan exiles and their Indian born offspring, was built in the sixties on the banks of the Yamuna River, one of India's sacred waterways.

The stone and cement buildings and the dark, narrow laneways, unnavigable by car, make the community seem older than its 50 years. Buddhist monks in yellow-trimmed wine-coloured robes and women in traditional attire roam the pathways, but the Western clothes and haircuts of the younger Tibetans and the many internet cafes add a modicum of modernity to the place.

The hotel itself was a positive experience. The nourishing vegetarian Tibetan fare gently helped ease our systems into the new culture, we encountered many monks in the peaceful atmosphere of the inn, and our assigned room was decent, except for a few random baby roaches in the bathroom and the skinny, solidly-packed horsehair mattress.

Although staying in Majnu-ka-Tilla is not an experience I'm in a hurry to repeat, clearly it was predestined. We had no idea when we booked the hotel just how important the Tibetan connection would be for us, or that we would later become volunteers in the northern colony of Dharamsala. An interesting introduction to Tibetans in India, the refugee settlement was a convenient place to embark on our brief side-trip to Dharamsala from.

Prince Polonia Hotel (Photo: Don Smith)

There's something comforting about familiar surroundings, and that's how I feel about the Prince Polonia Hotel in Paharganj, a working neighbourhood near both Old Delhi and New Delhi's touristy, upscale Connaught Square. The hotel was recommended by a Varanasi cafe owner and we were welcomed and caringly looked after here once before.

The word that comes to mind when I think of the Paharganj neighbourhood is folksy. Its unpretentious, down to earth simplicity and friendly shopkeepers make it a comfortable place to stay awhile.

Brij, the hotel owner, grew up here; he's a second generation vegetable vendor, university-educated, and now the owner of a variety of businesses. His old cargo auto rickshaw is always parked outside the hotel, a reminder of his roots. A devout Hindu with a strong social conscience, Brij puts his money and abilities to work as a philanthropist and volunteer. Currently the head of a large national charity, he sponsors several businesses in the basement of his hotel; a computer lab, dressmaking school, doctor's office and after-school tutoring class.

In 2007 Brij drove us to an ashram that houses orphans, one of his charity's programs. In the abandoned babies room we saw a dozen children, all girls except for one little boy, since girls are viewed as inferior in India. There was also a 10 -year-old mentally handicapped girl in residence; she was not receiving the stimulation she would get in a Western facility, but she was one of the lucky ones, safely away from the streets, well loved and her physical needs taken care of.

During the 1980s Don and I attempted to expand our family by adopting a girl from India through Families for Children, a Toronto-based non-profit, a sister for Bronwen. We cancelled our application after a couple of years when we discovered that not only did India dislike sending girls out of the country, the current magistrate in charge of international adoption disapproved of any Indian children being raised in a foreign country, making only one exception for an orphaned child with relatives in Canada. Brij told us that the aim of his charity is to have all the children adopted, and only Indian couples are allowed to do this, thus bearing out the problem we had during our process.

Brij is in the lobby today, dressed in the traditional male white tunic and loose pants; he remembers us from two years ago. For some time he's been planning to move his family out of their apartment on the second floor of the hotel and into a house across the street, but they are all still firmly ensconced in the Prince Polonia. Passing their open door I get a warm feeling, knowing that kindly Brij and his family are close by.

This time around, a bit more knowledgeable and wiser, I view matters here somewhat differently, but am aware that I'll never really "get" the mindset of this country, influenced by both its Hindu and Muslim religions and the vastness of both its population and cultural diversity.

The workings of the system are marginally clearer to me now; for example, several workers perform various aspects of a single job, so when water is requested, our call to the front desk is relayed to the restaurant upstairs, then room service delivers it to the room. If we run up to the restaurant to get the bottles of water the employees are deprived of much needed work. This requires an adjustment for me as an independent Western woman, brought up by a Welsh immigrant mother whose own mother worked as a scullery maid for a wealthy English family at the tender age of 14.

It feels good to settle into this agreeable hotel and spend a few enjoyable and restful days before heading north to McLeod Ganj and our unfolding adventure.

Settling In

"Wherever you go, there you are"

Jet lag from the 30 hour trip hits me on the first night and I lay awake staring the ceiling. After a while I get up, move to the couch at the end of the large room, and with camping light atop my head, stretch out and read. After less than an hour, I'm able to go back to sleep.

Apart from the obvious problem of one's body being out of sync with waking and sleeping times in the new environment, severe jet lag can make one almost ill, physically and mentally. Recovery time is about one day for each one to one and a half time zones crossed (12 zones between India and Western Canada.)

Travelling eastward, as we do returning home, shortens your day and is therefore a greater adjustment. Recuperation is an all encompassing experience for me, and includes the reverse culture shock of re-entry into Western life.

Once the jet lag stage is passed it's tempting to go flat out, touring as we would in Western countries, but here where everything is more challenging, less is definitely more. The additional aggravation of a virus, no doubt picked up on the plane, hits us in Delhi and remains for several days after we reach McLeod Ganj.

Dreams are at the forefront for me during this trip; I've included a sample of them in this book, at times with an interpretation. In the early morning hours one presents itself. An impasse has been reached with a group facilitator, when she refuses to sell me her book unless I take the training, given in a Church. I feel the book itself will offer me enough.

Questions arise out of this dream: What part of me does the trainer represent? … a person with knowledge and gifts to share with others, the ability to help women catalyze their change? (When we *gestalt* a dream, as above, we become each person or inanimate object.) Why does the training take place in a Church? Churches represent spirituality; most are rather conventional for my needs, hence wanting to "read the book myself".

The quote that begins this chapter, attributed to both Buddhism and Christianity, is so fitting. As the adjustment to being in India continues I await the unfolding of my purpose here. The transition from homebody to volunteer and traveller abroad is a work in progress. Still attached to

Canadian life, I'm not yet fully engaged with my Indian journey. Not knowing what the next months will bring makes it harder to close one door to allow another to open.

We've come to India with no volunteer jobs in place, hoping to teach beginner level English and offer tutoring to Tibetan refugees in Dharamsala, North India. Last spring we took a six-day Teaching ESL course in Vancouver. Surrounded by sharp young university students seeking paid work abroad, I never felt entirely comfortable in the class, and found that the experiential teaching method lacked specifics. It became apparent from the final test results, however, that we did learn quite a bit.

After the course I applied to the main volunteer clearing house in McLeod Ganj, Dharamsala; they acknowledged receipt of my application, then made no other contact with me. All the NGO's (Non-Governmental Organizations; non-profit groups that provide social services), are short-staffed, but I couldn't help wondering if my application fell through the cracks because I did not ask to be met at the airport, delivered to a hotel, then put on a bus to McLeod Ganj the next day, an option that provides income for the NGO.

Don enjoyed the course, but decided not to apply anywhere, feeling nervous about his new role of teacher and shy about standing in front of a group of people. I took my non-job as a sign and we both decided to simply go there and wing it.

One part of me is unsettled and somewhat disconcerted to find myself on the ground in India, another part knows it's alright. Leaving one's life behind and stepping into another, very different one for a few months is a transition that requires time. Every so often I think of the comfortable cocoon called home, and wonder why we've come here, unable to picture what our sojourn in India will look like, how our days will unfold. Perhaps we've made a mistake.

Then the internal talk begins…the questions about whether I have the right to do whatever I choose. This is where Byron Katie's exercise is helpful, turning my doubts around to "I do have the right." Self coaching, I push through them, telling myself to be patient, not to fret. My goal is to open to whatever unfolds.

From moment to moment I'm aware of how my every experience of this foreign culture is filtered through my library of knowledge acquired as a Canadian. I frequently and consciously remind myself to be flexible and not try to impose rules about how things should be done in India. That only leads to anger and frustration.

As I tentatively begin to get a feel for the country once again, the process of temporarily releasing the deeply engaged home life continues, to make room for the journey that is unfolding. My Western self is merging with the Indian part of me...connecting with an aspect that was available on the last trip... an energetically softer one, more attuned to what's around me, more alive.

Rediscovering My India

In the daytime the anxieties and the "not knowing" of the night recede and I enjoy visiting tourist sights. Our first choice is a market in an upper class neighbourhood not visited before, but we cannot arrange a taxi for the long trip across town, as drivers work, not by the hour, but by the day or half day. Instead, we make a return visit to Connaught Circle, the upscale shopping area only one metro stop from the Old Paharganj district, walking round the huge inner circle a couple of times, then stopping for coffee.

Security in the country has increased due to the Mumbai terrorist attacks in November of 2008. In a corner of each Delhi metro station an armed soldier stands behind a sandbag bunker. Seeing this token display of power for the first time gives me an eerie feeling.

Old Delhi Street (Photo: Don Smith)

On our second full day we visit the Red Fort in Old Delhi, then take a ride through the markets of the old town in a bicycle rickshaw. *Lal Quila*, as the octagonal structure is called, was built in 1639 when Delhi became India's capital and was the most beautiful of all the palaces in its day. Surrounded by massive red sandstone walls, some as high as 100 feet, it was originally decorated in marble, gold and precious stone mosaics, and is made up of palaces, gardens, halls, monuments and mosques.

Old Delhi is the original city and the heart of Delhi's Muslim community, a chaotic area of shoppers, workers and vehicles of all descriptions. Its dilapidated, aged buildings and narrow lanes give it the appearance of a foreign community within a larger city, the atmosphere very different from all the other neighbourhoods. Bicycle rickshaws play a vital part in moving people and goods through the narrow lanes of this district. Some operate in Paharganj also, but the communist government of Kerala in the south has outlawed them on humanitarian grounds, considering them inhumane for drivers.

We bring our outing to a close with lunch at a guidebook recommended restaurant, populated mostly by locals. My excitement at being here gives me energy, despite only four hours of sleep.

Delhi has its share of beggars and touts; they're here in Paharganj and in the neighbourhoods we travel to by metro or auto rickshaw. I prefer beggars, who are usually quite upfront, while touts, on the other hand, are canny and not to be trusted. In small towns or cities it's easy to strike up an acquaintance with beggars, but in Delhi the opportunity doesn't present itself in the same way, due to the volume of hardcore, aggressive types. A tourist learns quickly when giving out rupees to have the money ready in hand and make tracks afterwards, or risk being surrounded and hounded by a mass of beggars.

Often charming and engaging, sometimes heavy handed, touts are agents for stores and services, receiving a commission for each tourist sent by them, whether or not that person buys merchandise. Even the government craft stores have touts on their payrolls.

Their basic modus operandi is to engage and keep the tourist in conversation, with a goal of eventually convincing them to buy into whatever they're promoting. They attempt to woo a person by becoming their friend, throwing out opening lines such as; "Are you from (fill in the blank)", or "That's a beautiful scarf you're wearing"; they then invite the visitor into a store and apply pressure when they decline.

I thought my tout radar was pretty good, having gone through trial by fire immediately after arrival in 2007, when we were pursued for a mile or so in outer Connaught Circle by a string of cell phone carrying touts, until the tourist police ran them off. Normally I don't engage beyond "hello", and never stop walking, but today, just one block from our hotel, a tout fooled me on the way to the metro. His smile was so nice and he said "Namaste", a different, gentle approach that initially took me in. Of course I was quite jetlagged, plus I'm a sucker for that traditional greeting of well wishes, at least that's my story.

The social structure is quite different in India, more gender based, and has its foundation in the old caste system. Males are more prominent everywhere, in the streets and the retail stores, while women perform a secondary role. The Prince Polonia Hotel now has a female desk clerk and she adds a positive dynamic to our time here. Some family women live in the owner's apartment but we never see them; the younger ones say hello at the Diwali party Brij hosts, but do not mix.

India is very proficient when it comes to service; the philosophy is more formal, staff are here to serve, not to interact with you. Our male desk clerk tells us: "Your problems are my problems", and he sincerely means it.

Diwali: Festival of Lights

We've come to Delhi during *Diwali,* the festival of lights, signifying the victory of good over evil. It's a five-day celebration of life, this year from October 17th to 21st, and the entire country is illuminated by fireworks and small oil filled clay lamps that burn all night. All the celebrants wear new clothes and share sweets and snacks with family members and friends.

There are various legends about Diwali's origin; some believe it to be the celebration of Lakshmi and Lord Vishnu's marriage, (Lakshmi, my favourite Goddess, helps us with life purpose and overall happiness); in Bengal the festival is dedicated to the worship of Mother Kali, the dark goddess of strength, while Lord Ganesha, the elephant-headed God, symbol of auspiciousness and wisdom, is also worshipped in most Hindu homes on this holiday.

The downside of Diwali in Delhi outweighs the upside for me. It sounded like an exciting, magical interval in the city; I think for most Indians it's a lively party time, an opportunity to step out of their daily routine, to get together with family and friends and celebrate.

Excitement is in the air, that part's fun, but the increasingly crowded streets and the gratuitous noise from fire crackers is taxing and often downright risky. Indians are proud of their fire crackers, said to have been invented in this country, although several other countries also claim this. They go off from dawn to midnight over the five days, in a never-ending series of explosions. As we walk along the street, I jump nervously as the "bombs" burst mere inches away; it feels quite unsafe to walk past them, particularly as some of the people setting off the pyrotechnics are small boys (supervised by Dad, but still…).

Thinking Diwali would be a good time to have a celebratory henna hand painting, I walk through Paharganj's main market, where several young men offer that service. But they fight over me, shoving plastic covered photographs in my face. Irritated, I push them away and walk on. This is not what I have in mind at all; I'd prefer to have a woman paint my hands anyway. Back at the Prince Polonia, I discover the in-house hairdressing salon provides the service, so I make plans to go there in a day or two to relax quietly while a female esthetician decorates me. But the next day I begin to sicken so it doesn't happen.

Our hotel has its own unique form of Diwali chaos. Early one evening, we climb the stairs to the restaurant deck; we've been invited to attend Brij's party. The decorations are beautiful; fresh marigold garlands hang from the stairways, votive candles burn at the top, centred within complicated flower designs, everything looks lovely. Smiling staff greet us, appetizers in hand, and offer alcoholic drinks from a nearby table (an unexpected surprise; it's the only day of the year liquor is served at this traditional Hindu hotel). Brij's entire family is in attendance, including grandbabies; the family and staff are gracious and the other guests friendly.

We have assumed that the restaurant, high above the street, would be a safe haven, but when we arrive Brij, our gracious middle-aged host, is joyously setting off loud firecrackers in a small space at the open end of the deck. He's thoroughly enjoying himself, howling with laughter like a schoolboy each time one explodes!

I've looked forward to participating in this party, but the loud eruptions hurt my ears. An Israeli guest and I take inventory; we notice a heap of fresh firecracker boxes stacked on the floor, just waiting for Brij. We know we must leave to preserve both our hearing and nerves, so we escape back to our respective rooms, asking to be called when dinner is served.

Well over an hour goes by with no word, so I return to the deck. The scene that meets my eyes is a curious one: several guests have red marks on their faces and various other body parts, including Don, who has been hit in the forehead by a firecracker gone AWOL.

Brij himself, closest to the scene of the crime, so to speak, has received an injury near his eye. One woman's leg is bleeding and at least six guests are hurt in all. Apparently one of the firecrackers was a dud and exploded, sending bits of hot material through the air to land on the bystanders. This has never happened before, Brij assures the group.

Everyone was very fortunate, the injuries could have been much worse. But what surprises me the most is that so many people remained on the deck, even the injured ones.

Dinner was served much later, by then even Don had called it a night.

The next day, Sunday, the city is much quieter. We walk out early and see very few people on the street. The revellers are resting.

As we recover from the trip, the bulk of our time has been spent relatively close to the hotel, resting, eating, and exploring the familiar haunts of the neighbourhood. This lively, colourful community is a delight to be in, but our experience merely skims the surface of life in Paharganj. As an observer, not a participant in daily life, one can't really expect much more.

Our time of acclimation is coming to an end. Rife with anticipation about what will emerge in McLeod Ganj, I'm also apprehensive about embarking on this volunteer experience. We're working without a net, so to speak, with no advance plans other than accommodation, a necessity in the popular Dharamsala area.

Perhaps I'm over thinking; letting go of the outcome may be an important lesson. Deep down I sense that my experience in McLeod Ganj, Dharamsala will be a major one, that a significant shift will take place within me. This is, in fact, exactly what happens; the healing energy of the town allows me to transform, to move into a deeper part of myself.

The theme of opening to the experience has come up twice in my journal in under a week. The idea of baring myself is unnerving, and makes me want to give up and go home. But in truth I seldom quit anything once I begin.

All these thoughts percolate in my foggy and overstimulated brain as we prepare to leave for McLeod Ganj tomorrow night.

Odyssey from Delhi to McLeod Ganj

The initial plan is to stay in Delhi for four days to regroup, and then travel to McLeod Ganj, Dharamsala, the home of His Holiness the Dalai Lama over the weekend. First class sleepers are not available on the heavily booked trains when we want to travel, so we leave Delhi on the evening of October 20, a Tuesday. The hotel staff have pre-booked our tickets as we were unable to book them from home. The India Rail website was continually overloaded in the brief hours available to us with the time difference.

The extra days in Delhi have proven helpful because they gave us time to mend. Centred in my head, the virus creates a dizzy sensation and by Friday evening I'm sprawled head down on the table of the hotel restaurant with what at first feels like low blood sugar. Moving as little as possible proves the best plan.

Indian Train Station (Photo: Don Smith)

24

Finally the evening arrives when, ready or not, it's time to leave, and we take a proper taxicab, rather than an open auto rickshaw, to the nearby train station in Old Delhi. It's a pleasurable ride amidst the traffic chaos and the cab arrives in plenty of time for the 10 p.m. train. Two porters in red uniforms carry the luggage on their heads from the front door of the gigantic station through the main building, along an overpass, then down the long stairway to the track where the Pathankot train will arrive. At first I'm unsure if they have deposited us and the bags at the right place, but the signs indicate the train will pull in here.

Everywhere there are people strolling about or sitting on the ground in small groups. The trains are very long and I wonder if there will be enough time to reach the assigned car once ours arrives. Don is not worried.

After a one-hour wait that feels like three, the train bound for Panthankot in the Punjab enters the station, and we haul ourselves aboard, bag and baggage. About two minutes later I begin repeating the mantra I have invented silently: "Be Flexible." For when we enter the private, first class sleeper car, the one that matches the number on the ticket, there are three other people already there! At first I think there's been a mistake and someone is in the wrong car, but it's soon revealed that the car is meant to be shared. (First class cars on some trains really are private I'm told, but not on secondary routes.)

Once I recover from my initial shock and nervousness about sleeping in the same cabin with this apparently nice family of strangers (a fortyish married couple and their aged mother), I look around at my surroundings; the compartment looks fine. Then a burly Sikh man enters and once again I'm thrown off kilter. He's the one who's meant to be our sleeper car mate, along with the mother of the couple; the family booked late and couldn't get three beds together.

Again my recovery time is quick, I'm proud to report (my mantra must be working); after a brief moment I adjust to sharing *our* car with the large male stranger. The turban atop his head initially makes him seem much bigger than he actually is. He appears to be a gentle man, polite and respectful, and has brought his dinner along with him in a takeout container.

25

Don and I are assigned to the two lower berths, with the Indian woman and the man on the uppers. The woman's son asks if Don or I would mind trading beds with her because she's too old to climb up to the top bunk and Don graciously agrees to this.

In conversation the next morning, we discover that the woman is close to our age, however working class people seem to age faster in India, having harder lives on the whole, living in an unforgiving climate, working long hours and often without the benefit of adequate health care.

Since it's late when we board the train, the beds are already made up with white sheets, pillows and blankets, so there's not much opportunity to visit before lights out. When I turn off the ceiling light after checking with my three cabin mates, the Sikh man says "Good night sir, good night madam" most politely, as though this is an everyday occurrence. It may well be for him; to me it's a bit like adult camp.

We settle in for the all-night trip; my one-inch mini camping mattress, on top of the thin India Rail one offering a bit of extra cushioning. Cool air blows into the cabin through the ceiling air vents all night long. Although it is now October it's still quite warm.

The forward movement of the train combined with its sideways sway feels soothing and the rhythmic clicking of the wheels is a meditation of sorts. I'm aware that strangers are sleeping a couple of feet away, but feel quite comfortable in the narrow bed and probably would have slept well, but the jiggling makes me acutely aware of every ounce of urine in my bladder.

The door of the cabin slides open, then bangs itself shut repeatedly, the lock is broken. Once it's propped open and the curtain pulled across for privacy, things are much quieter.

The solicitous treatment of our *elderly* cabin mate by her family throughout the journey is similar to the way we look after my Mom; two or three times during the night her daughter-in-law enters the cabin to make sure she's alright.

In the morning I tidy up in the tiny washroom down the hall, at the far end of the next car, a second class sleeper. The sight of the two long rows of curtained bunks down each side of the car and the legion of people sleeping, quietly talking, listening to music or working on laptops makes me very happy to be occupying our small cabin with only two others. While the train waits on a side track before completing the journey into Pathankot, we enjoy a quiet conversation with our roommates and their family.

The train arrives at eight in the morning. We walk out of the station and hedge our bets by asking two different groups of people standing outside when the bus leaves for Dharamsala. Each party tells us it will come soon, as the schedule indicates, a positive sign. Time passes and it grows warmer in the parched bus yard but I'm able to find a bit of shade to stand in, keeping a close eye on the bags. The bus arrives after a thirty or forty minute wait and we're given a good seat at the front of the freshly hosed down vehicle.

The cost of the almost daylong trip from the Punjab to McLeod Ganj in Himachal Pradesh is only eighty-five rupees each, less than two dollars, cheap even by Indian standards. Everyone can afford to ride the government-subsidized trains and buses in India.

Although billed at four hours, the trip actually takes seven. We've forgotten that estimated times are just that – conjectures. An excellent rule of thumb is to automatically double the expected length of time from point A to point B.

When we meet our Tibetan doctor friend the next day, she says: "You should have hired a car in Pathankot instead of taking the bus". Locals know what travelling is like in India and realize we may not be up to the rigors of it. It's tough for them too, but often they don't have much choice in the matter due to finances.

There are few people on the bus at this point and at first the trip is exciting. The cross-country ride in the midst of chaotic traffic, frequently bumpy, rutted roads and colourfully dressed people makes me feel like I've really arrived in India. Early in the journey an auto rickshaw stops right in the middle of the road in front of our bus, and somehow six people squeeze into it.

As the hours wear on, what was initially captivating becomes tedious, then tiring, and finally overwhelming. As we drive onward towards our destination, the bus becomes jam-packed with people of all ages and descriptions; it's like a bottomless container on wheels. From time to time a few get off as we near a town, but they're replaced by others and the vehicle is packed for at least three-quarters of the trip. Sitting in an aisle seat you become used to people pressing against you as they pass each other in the narrow aisle or when they sit close to you on the crowded seats.

We all have our limits, and near the end of trip I reach my point of overload. Normally a pleasant person, I become quite irritated with the noise, the jolting of the bus, the constant honking and the frequent stops. Now the aisles are full of high school kids on their way home and their bags are inadvertently hitting me. Finally a loaded knapsack thumps me in the back of the head; I speak curtly to the young guy wearing it and he moves it away apologetically.

Finally the bus arrives at the bus station in Lower Dharamsala, a typical small Indian town. We're both out of sorts, me from the intermittent virus and interrupted sleep of the previous night, Don from a head cold that has gradually worsened as the day wears on. (He doesn't tell me this until now.)

By now it's late afternoon. The stop in Lower Dharamsala will be half an hour, we're told, and then the bus will motor on to McLeod Ganj. The wait is longer, why am I not surprised? Disembarking and taking a taxi up the hill would be best at this juncture, but we're now in that somnolent mode that overcomes weary travellers, past the point of making decisions.

Not anatomically blessed like our male friends, women tend to drink little on bus journeys because there likely won't be a toilet available when needed. By Lower Dharamsala, it's time for a washroom. On arrival at the scuzzy, dark toilet building, I find my purse empty of change so I am unable to leave a tip for the attendant. After using the facilities I indicate this to the custodian in English and by signing, then leave. He exudes an aura of displeasure, but by this point it's immaterial to me. That is, until I look up to find this very determined, rough looking guy standing beside me on the bus; he's hunted me down after noticing me buy a snack at the kiosk. I ask "How much?" He demands thirty rupees (sixty cents), an exorbitant amount. Unwilling to give this seedy character one extra rupee, also knowing I won't see the back of him until he gets his money, I look around for assistance. A South American man across the aisle kindly makes change for me.

In writing this, the arrogance and unkindness with which I treated the poor man becomes clearer to me. The fair thing on my part would have been to go back and pay him after receiving change at the kiosk, but his attitude, interpreted by me as obnoxiousness, got my back up.

Eventually the bus chugs its way up the winding roadway to McLeod Ganj, the driver navigating each sharp switchback without needing to reverse once for an oncoming bus or truck, nothing short of a miracle. Arriving in town, we discover that the buses now end their trip a couple of hundred yards downhill, no longer stopping and turning around in the small town square as they did previously.

After a fifteen minute delay, Don thankfully locates an auto rickshaw driver who delivers us, dusty and travel weary, to the Bhagsu hotel a couple of kilometres away. We arrive at Spring Valley Resort around dinnertime. Our room is on the fourth floor and there's no elevator. Climbing the stairs, we settle into our small, cozy room, with its large shared balcony and panoramic view of the hills and tiny town below.

The altitude of the Bhagsu-McLeod Ganj area is under 2,000 metres, (6,000 feet), not that high, but for folks used to being at sea level, it seems that way, and it has a negative effect on me. After an hour has passed I begin to develop an odd migraine headache. It's likely that the combination of higher elevation, four-flight climb with no pause, tiredness, plus the head virus have put me over the edge.

Using Ibuprofen judiciously, I recline on the bed propped against pillows, keeping my head very still. After a couple of hours the headache has subsided enough to allow me to lie flatter; I'm then able to sleep and consider myself fortunate that the elevation sickness is of a minor nature.

As I rest, the emotions begin. My system is overstimulated from the illness, residual jetlag, plus the journey here. In the night my body vibrates gently to the movement of the train; it thinks it's still en route.

The journey to McLeod Ganj has not been easy, however I feel happy to be in this special place that has occupied my dreams since I first set foot in it two years ago. Our plan is to explore the town, then find an NGO that is a good fit for us, a place to help Tibetan refugees learn English.

For now though we will take some time to acclimate ourselves in preparation for what lies ahead.

View from Bhagsu Hotel (Photo: Don Smith)

Coming Home

"Places have power – not only the physical power of sheer presence, but the emotional clout to alter our moods…"

Martha Beck

And so it is with me and McLeod Ganj. I have a sense, a precognition that immediately on arrival in town, an internal meltdown will begin, with all my emotional and spiritual baggage suddenly unpacking itself. Perhaps the brief but debilitating elevation-related headache yesterday is the beginning.

McLeod Ganj

After two attempts I'm able to assume a vertical position on the bed. My strange headache is gone, thankfully, but the sleeping sickness-like virus remains, along with leftover jet lag. Don is too ill to get out of bed and I promise to bring him back some comfort food.

Creeping slowly down the stairs to the dining room, I stop to rest on each landing to acclimatise to the elevation. What must hikers experience at truly elevated heights if I feel like this at under 2,000 metres?

Through the window two donkeys can be seen trotting down the trail, and a boy runs joyfully down the path on his way to school, arms spread like small wings.

Air is light here in the mountains…thin…noticeable even in the hotel room. The energy feels delicate, almost ethereal, quite different from what we're accustomed to.

It's Thursday, our first full day, and we're staying in Bhagsu until the apartment at the Kirti Monastery Guesthouse is available. Ten years ago, His Holiness the Karmapa, the reincarnation of a high Buddhist lama, was hidden in a hotel in this town after being smuggled out of Tibet.

Bhagsu is a quiet little offshoot of the main town and this four-star Indian resort in the mountains is a good place for us to recover. The hotel was tricky to book and did not come cheap. Our room is a premium one, no doubt at a special foreign visitor rate. The other residents, all Indian, line up in the dining room at mealtime for an Indian buffet, which was not part of our package.

I know coming downstairs this morning is the right choice when I meet a lovely young Indian couple from *Kolkata*, formerly Calcutta, seated at the next table. During an interesting conversation, they disclose that they've been married about a year and he works for a subsidiary of General Electric, while his wife has the traditional role of homemaker. The husband's business takes him abroad frequently and he has been trained in intercultural communication. He tells me Westerners speak at a rate of about 60 words per minute, while Indian speech is more than twice that, explaining certain challenges that arise from time to time.

As the world shrinks due to internet communication, and flying is more affordable, intercultural communication grows in importance. Neophyte Western visitors often experience what sociologists term ethnocentrism; we assume our own cultural way of doing things is correct. This patronizing attitude diminishes our experience and often leads to unhappy interactions with locals.

I work hard at monitoring my judgmental reactions, particularly strong in the early days of a trip, before a level of comfort in a country is reached. These responses also occur when unpredictable, stressful events challenge me. I think of it as "Seeing the world through my Canadian eyes". Misunderstandings can easily occur when we come from such diverse backgrounds, so the safest thing is to assume that everyone's thoughts and actions are *not* like ours, thus reducing the frustration level for members of both cultures.

The message that appears repeatedly on this trip is a very practical one: "Be flexible". At this first meal at Spring Valley, my scrambled eggs have sugar in them, quite unappealing to my tastebuds. My Indian neighbours notice my scrunched up face and ask what's wrong, helping me to cue myself, and I articulate aloud that I am working on being adaptable.

In the midst of the breakfast conversation, a soft voice beside me says "Excuse me". Looking up, I see Dekyi, our Tibetan doctor friend, standing at the table. Leaping to my feet, I fling my arms around her in a big hug. If she's taken aback by this joyful greeting, she makes a quick recovery. (Tibetans are warm people, but more formal than us.) It's a reunion of heart and spirit to see Dekyi again. Although our acquaintance was brief in 2007, we've grown closer over the past two years of e-mail and telephone conversations, sharing many personal details. By the time our visit here is completed we will know each other on a deeper level and I will come to think of her as my Tibetan sister.

When Dekyi hears about Don's illness she says, "I must come upstairs and take his pulses." After I quickly finish my breakfast, we go up to the room, where she carefully checks him, then gives us each a white silk prayer scarf, called a *khata*, as a welcome and pulls a paper bag of juice and cookies out of her backpack. We both feel better wearing the scarves, blessed by a high lama, and keep them on all day.

The bestowing of khatas is perhaps the best known Tibetan custom. Given to those arriving or leaving on a journey, they also signify one's love and respect for another. Traditionally white or ivory to symbolize purity, goodwill and compassion, they can now be found in yellow, gold and even red, blue and green.

We wear our khatas to the Dalai Lama's teachings the next day, but quickly sense that they're not meant to be worn on a regular basis as scarves. Dekyi confirms this.

On our departure from McLeod Ganj we each receive ten khatas, which will give you some idea of the depth of attachments formed during our time here.

Something Strange is Happening to Me

As I sit on the deck at the Spring Valley Resort the sky is clear, hawks soar nearby, and the mountains appear close enough to reach out and touch. The edge of a high, snow-covered peak, barely visible behind the green hill, triggers a faint memory, and for a split second I am transported back to another time when I was a Tibetan living in the Himalayas.

My heart is very open here in the tiny town of Bhagsu. I feel so much sadness... what is it? Not someone who cries often, I give myself permission to let go and the tears flow briefly, leaving my heart a little lighter. Whatever is arising from deep within me feels very old. Perhaps the potent spiritual energy of this land is allowing me to open and to release grief from both the present time and lost lifetimes here...for what was but is no more. I wonder to myself why it has taken me so many years to (re)discover it.

I'm uncertain what my relationship is to the place, whether I am a stranger, here on my first visit, or if something deeper and more profound is taking place, beyond everyday understanding. How many lifetimes have I spent in McLeod Ganj, North India and in Tibet itself? Perhaps many tourists are unconsciously drawn to the area because they are reincarnations of Tibetans or Indians. None of us will ever know for certain. But what I do know is that this place is calling to my spirit.

Later, back at home, I work with Alma Anderson, a powerful psychic, to flesh out my sense of McLeod Ganj. Alma's guidance and support have been a helpful part of my personal journey for twenty years. In her McLeod Ganj reading, she validates the powerful feelings I experience, saying "It feels like an absolutely amazing town, there's a lot of light there. It has transformational ability." Alma affirms that McLeod Ganj is a very important place for me and that I have spent a number of lifetimes in the area.

My belief in reincarnation began at age nineteen, when introduced to the concept of *The Wheel of Nirvana*, the Hindu reincarnation wheel, by my radical English teacher in a Toronto highschool.(Her brother hosted a cable television show on UFO's, surprising for Toronto in the sixties). The concept of reincarnation intrigued me, it felt natural and right.

Although not my permanent home, this may be the part of the world where I'm most connected with spirit, mine and the greater one. In British Columbia, tuned into nature, particularly to the blue herons and eagles that fly over our house, I'm able to align with spirit, but have never experienced anything remotely similar anywhere or at any time during this lifetime.

Unable to properly describe the experience, I seek out the dictionary and find a description that fits what is happening to me: ineffable - too intense to be expressed in words, too sacred.

Mid afternoon Dekyi returns to the hotel, arriving unexpectedly with her eldest son, age ten. They bring Tibetan medicines and more food, fruit this time, perfect for housebound folks. Dekyi explains that her husband, also a physician, has urged her to get Don started on his medicines today, as he is quite ill, rather than waiting until tomorrow, as planned.

Her attentions are to become a pattern, with Dekyi plying us with food on each visit during our time in McLeod Ganj, and offering medical consultations at her clinic. As a natural healer, doctoring and nurturing is her way of being in the world, as well as natural Tibetan hospitality.

We plan to meet in the morning outside the temple, *Tsuglagkhang*, for the final day of the Dalai Lama's teachings; hopefully we'll be well enough. My virus comes and goes, while Don steadily improves over the next week with the help of Dekyi's ministrations.

Himalayan Mountains (Photo: Don Smith)

On Friday October 23 I awaken at five a.m. to a dream of my brother telling me Mom has died. Now that Mom is moving farther away from us mentally my connection with her is changing. Memories from an earlier time have begun to surface and I'm beginning a review of our relationship, seeing her as a younger, vital woman.

This morning, feeling anxious and out of touch, I begin to feel sorrowful about "My Little Mommy", as she is now experienced in dreams, and shed a few tears. This is the first time I've allowed the sadness an opportunity to surface; previously the distress has been channelled into moving forward, doing the practical things necessary to keep Mom healthy and happy in the care home. I've hidden the grief under anxious busyness.

Making the commitment to care for my mother has allowed our issues to resolve themselves in a natural way over time; resentments have melted, translating to compassion and closeness.

Dreams about losing Mom began several years ago when she began to depend on us more. In them Don, our daughter and myself were called on to save Mom from drowning. My unconscious has been processing her gradual departure, preparing for her physical death. Recent dreams foreshadowing my mother's actual death help me feel peaceful about what will come down the road.

The spiritual environment of McLeod Ganj seems appropriate for this releasing work. For almost a thousand years, Buddhists, particularly Tibetans, and their Hindu brothers and sisters have focused on their dreams. *Lucid dreaming*, or the awareness that one is dreaming, is viewed as a spiritual discipline.

Many Tibetan Buddhists believe that the experience of the soul after death is the same as what we refer to as dreaming. My personal belief is that our waking world and our dreaming one are moving closer together, just as the veil between those in body and those in spirit is merging.

Testing young monks at the Dalai Lama's Temple (Photo: Don Smith)

Dekyi meets us at the gate of the temple at nine and her son, on holiday from residential school, accompanies her. We separate, the two of them standing in the Tibetan lineup, while we join the one designated for foreigners snaking along the outside passageway and up the stairs. Males go through a men's checkpoint while women are frisked by female security. All attendees receive a full body and bag search. Don is barred from entering because he's brought his camera and is sent to a nearby store to have it checked in.

The upstairs courtyard and the inner temple area where His Holiness sits are filled with registered attendees, while in the downstairs courtyard enrollment is not necessary. Dekyi mentions that all volunteers in McLeod Ganj are required to register at the Tibetan government office, but we forget to do this and the Tibet Hope Center does not ask about it.

The Tibetan line grows too long after a time, and a group of monks are sent to the foreigners' line. As we wait in the fresh morning air, I gaze at the mountains in the distance; the tears come again, I know we are in the presence of something holy.

The body search over, the crowd swarms upward towards the courtyard. Dekyi's son waits for me at the top of the stairs, but we miss each other. Huge tables are laid out to one side, in preparation for the lunchtime feast, contributed by the Taiwanese Buddhist sponsors. I stroll slowly around the enormous compound, searching the crowd for signs of Dekyi and son, locating them at the back, under the trees after a few moments. Don joins us.

Colourful banners wave high above the courtyard as we sit in the filtered sunlight. It's still quite warm during the day in the third week of October. Hundreds of people of all ages - families, individuals, monks and lay people - are seated nearby. Though the atmosphere is quiet and respectful, the air of expectancy is palpable. Doing a rough crowd count, I estimate that 10 percent of the attendees are Westerners.

Many of the elders patiently turn mini prayer wheels in endless circles, whispering the prayer "Om Mani Padme Hum", the mantra for love and compassion. This is an ancient mystical practice meant to assist practitioners on their journey to enlightenment; also it is believed to bless the environment, transform bad luck and promote healing.

Desiring to do everything possible for our comfort, Dekyi has brought along padded cloth mats to sit on; we later discover they've been rented from a nearby store. She also brings back some pasta in mid-morning, trying to tempt us with familiar food; we eat a little to please her, but we're not very hungry. Healthy food is an important part of the Tibetan lifestyle and we appreciate Dekyi's good care during our illness.

An older British woman sitting nearby watches as Don sits down on a mat and imperiously inquires whether he knows "that woman", pointing at Dekyi. In her inept way she's trying to stop what she fears is exploitation of a marginalized Tibetan woman by an entitled Western male. (If she only knew what a powerful woman Dekyi is in her own right!).

His Holiness speaks in Tibetan this morning, ending with a brief English statement. While he talks we listen to an English translation through an FM radio band, using the tiny, old transistor brought from home for this purpose.

Time morphs into *kairos* or natural time, also referred to as sacred time; one hour feels like two. Being in close proximity to His Holiness the Dalai Lama in his home temple has a profound affect on me.

The messages are fundamental ones; he teaches that we can rid ourselves of painful thoughts and feelings by achieving internal emptiness, and that loving ourselves is important, then we're able to love others. Balancing the two is imperative because over-focusing on self causes pain.

It has been said the essence of the truth expressed by different religious and spiritual leaders is similar. The Dalai Lama's messages of loving kindness to self and others are akin to those of other schools of thought. In late November during the Russian teachings he will address these similarities.

His Holiness ends the session by speaking of what he terms "life after life", saying that some of us are imprinted for reincarnation. Descending the steps of the temple, he walks along the cordoned off pathway beside the seated crowd. The Tibetans bow and toss khatas towards him. In my awe, I spontaneously wave, the only person to do so!

Afterwards monks walk through the crowd carrying huge pails of food, serving a meal of rice and dahl to everyone who wants to partake of it.

Dinner at Dekyi's

Later in the day we take the five-kilometre auto rickshaw ride down the hill to Dekyi's residence, halfway between McLeod Ganj and Lower Dharamsala. It's part of the Men-Tsee-Khang Tibetan Medical and Astrological Institute complex. The road from the temple onward is unbelievably washed out, having deteriorated severely in our two year absence. Bouncing around in the flimsy auto rickshaw, I imagine my internal organs repositioning themselves.

Some feel the Indian government puts too little money into the infrastructure of McLeod Ganj, while an Indian taxi driver tells us it looks after the roads well; it all depends who you talk to. One week later this entire stretch of road has been repaved.

Men-Tsee-Kang, part of the Dalai Lama's organization, is a small community, housing the medical clinic, Tibetan Medicine and Astrological School, staff residences, an internet café, a bookstore and variety store. The complex is community centred; the parents and youngest child come home for lunch each day to a meal prepared by the matriarch of the family.

Dekyi practices medicine at the clinic, along with two other "lady doctors", as she terms them. She sees all English speaking patients as her language skill is high, and her husband Khenrab teaches Tibetan medicine in the nearby school.

Men-Tsee-Khang was established in 1961 to promote Tibetan medicine, astronomy and astrology, and to provide accessible health care to everyone. The care is free for the poor, monks, nuns, new arrivals from Tibet and those over 70 years of age. The organization also produces medicines in an environmentally sensitive manner.

The business buildings are located at higher elevation, while the residences are built into a terraced hillside of flowering bushes and trees, while the apartments are accessed by descending multiple flagstone steps.

We climb the stairs to the second floor apartment, where Dekyi's 76 year old mother, Sonam, awaits us with a laughing "Tashi Delek", the everyday Tibetan greeting used to say "Hello", "Good luck" or, my favourite, "Blessings". Their unit has two doors, one near the stairway, the other at the opposite end of the narrow apartment, opening onto a large communal deck. The view from the deck is pastoral, overlooking a grassy slope where a handful of cows graze. More than 30 other Men-Tsee-Khang families live in the residential complex.

Their apartment is small, yet comfortable, about 600 square feet in size. The couch and easy chairs in the small living-dining room are covered with Tibetan rugs, a cultural convention, and the walls display pictures of the Dalai Lama. A large flatscreen television transmits messages from His

Holiness. The family is well nourished with Tibetan food cooked in the compact kitchen, clothes are washed and everyone is kept clean, all with no hot running water.

Sonam laughs frequently and uproariously over the smallest things. Most Tibetans have a great sense of humour. Even Khenrab's brother Karpe, who does not speak English, jokes about Don's hairy white guy arms by pulling on the hairs!

The children are full of vim and vigour, each very much their own person. The atmosphere in the home is relaxed, laissez-faire with respect to child raising. Over the course of our visits I saw one or two kids yanked by their Mom when they overstepped boundaries, but no one was ever hit.

For dinner Karpe, a cook, serves us a flavourful feast of cheese *momos*, (dumpling-like diet staples), green beans, a veggie stir-fry, chicken and rice. We're urged to eat vast quantities of food. Don gladly complies; unfortunately I'm able to have only a small serving myself.

After dinner we offer the gifts brought from home. Sonam seems tickled by the wine coloured fleece snuggle blanket for damp winter evenings; oddly it resembles a monk's robe. Everyone else seems pleased with their presents and Dekyi translates that her small daughter likes her English book. This precocious child aspires to attend an English school rather than the Tibetan one.

It's now dark, time to leave, and Khenrab, erring on the side of caution, decides to accompany us home, explaining that their part of town is quiet at night and tourists can sometimes be targets. We try to pay for the roundtrip cab ride, but he beats us to it by prepaying; he and his brother drop us off at the bottom of our lane. It's clear that the family feels a sense of responsibility for our welfare during our visit, particularly in the early days; once we've settled in they relax in the knowledge that we are happy and safe.

On weekends I don't see much of Dekyi; she often works Saturday or Sunday, as Men-Tsee-Khang Medical Clinic is open seven days a week. The weekend is also the time for housework; the cleaning, cooking and time consuming laundry work for the household.

I would like to interview Dekyi about her life as a doctor, mother and Tibetan woman living in Dharamsala, but somehow the time is never right. Most significantly, I'm reticent about asking questions due to her apparent reluctance to talk about herself.

A Little About McLeod Ganj

The Dhauladhar mountain range, part of the Himalayas, surrounds McLeod Ganj with *Hanuman Ka Tibba*, well over five thousand metres high, lying behind the town. Dense pine, Himalayan oak, rhododendron and deodhar woods outlie the settlement.

McLeod Ganj, or Upper Dharamsala, is part of the municipality of Dharamsala and it's centre lies ten kilometres below. Dharamsala, or "rest place for pilgrims", is situated along the lower edges of the steep slope, while McLeod Ganj is built higher up. From the upper town, the view of the Himalayan foothills and the Kangra Valley below is breathtaking.

Set on narrow, densely packed laneways, the row housing of the core area creates the impression of an older town. Houses are precariously perched in the surrounding hills, later additions stacked on top of existing homes.

Named after Sir Donald McLeod, Lieutenant-Governor of the Punjab during the nineteenth century, McLeod Ganj was built as a British hill station, a summer retreat for tea plantation owners, government officers' families and the princes who ruled the District.

There's an interesting story behind the Dalai Lama's decision to settle in McLeod Ganj 50 years ago. In the town square sits a very old general store called Nowrojee and Son, the name of a Punjabi family that arrived in the late nineteenth century. The large back part of the store, full of old wooden display units, is bare, only a small area at the front is now in use, offering Hindi and English language newspapers and snacks.

When the Dalai Lama decided he must leave Tibet, he began searching for a place for himself and his people. Nowrojee wrote to Pandit Nehru, then Prime Minister of India, offering his land to His Holiness and the Tibetan government in Exile. The land the Dalai Lama's residence and Namgyal Monastery sit on was once owned by this remarkable man, who passed away in 2000.

Lower Jogiwara Road near Tibet Hope Center (Photo: Don Smith)

If you visit McLeod Ganj it may not feel like India. Little Lhasa, as the town is fondly called, after the capital of Tibet, is permeated with the atmosphere of the Dalai Lama's presence, his sacred temple, plus the thousands of refugees who live here.

Upper Dharamsala has evolved into an international crossroads, where travellers, Buddhist monks and nuns walk the streets daily alongside the local Indians and Tibetans. Hundreds of thousands of visitors from all over the world journey to this small, remote town annually to attend the teachings of the Dalai Lama and to soak in the energy of this Buddhist centre.

Eateries have sprung up catering to those drawn here. All serve excellent food, without exception, even Japanese and Korean meals are available. Visitors on a budget will find the Tibetan restaurants, particularly the monastery run one, stretch their money farther.

Life is comfortable for travellers. In addition to the variety of cuisine, meditation and yoga classes, trekking, sightseeing and of course volunteering are on offer.

Tibetan souvenirs such as *singing bowls*, (made of a combination of metals, they vibrate up to seven tones, their sound powerful for centering the mind and body), prayer wheels, musical instruments and silk *thangka scrolls*, (rolled paintings with Buddhist designs done on cotton, canvas or silk, originally carried by travelling monks), can be purchased in McLeod Ganj, while the Lower Dharamsala market offers Indian products and fresh produce.

Long distance calls are easy and inexpensive, as is sending e-mails, purchasing airline, train or bus tickets or booking a car and driver. Mobile phones or phone cards can be purchased with proper identification. With Khenrab's old phone we can keep in touch with the family down the hill easily.

Reflections Ten Days In

After ten days the challenge of allowing myself to simply be still persists, although to a lesser degree. I continue to self-coach by tracking the mental messages and modifying them, to be present in each moment as it arises.

Our recovery period in Bhagsu has been a gentle time, just what we need. Bhagsu is a tiny but busy town. The work here is of a labour-intensive, assembly line nature; transport donkeys carry dirt and gravel up and down hills in heavy saddle bags, while women collect rocks in wheelbarrows and men hand-mix cement with supplies they've lugged to the job site, filling potholes in the road.

From our deck we have a panoramic view of the mountains, other resorts and the activities taking place in the town. About a dozen hotels and guesthouses are visible and many more are hidden in the hills. Vegetable and grain crops grow on a series of plateaus built into every available bit of land.

I'll miss watching the activities of the town from the balcony, but we're ready to move to the monastery, where we'll be part of a new, equally fascinating scene.

Boundaries are different here. The personal and the public merge, as much of life takes place on the street in this crowded, communal culture. We've grown tired of the shared deck; unfortunately, the glider is in front of our window and at times we find ourselves irritated by people sitting there, overhead lights blazing, when we're in bed or dressing.

Saturday our search for volunteer opportunities takes us to McLeod Ganj, where we will research NGO's. It feels good to have a change of pace from the tiny village and hotel room where we've spent the bulk of the time since arriving.

On the street we meet a young Swedish woman who asks us to sign a petition to reduce atmospheric carbon dioxide. It will be sent to Stockholm as part of the World Environment Day campaign. She kindly offers us the names of several volunteer organizations, saying that she worked with the Tibetan Welfare office for a few days.

We stroll around the village looking for the NGO's mentioned and locating some others, but it's Saturday so they're all closed. A poster on a downtown wall announces an English-speaking group once a week, while a sign beside The Tibet Hope Center door says volunteers are needed to edit articles and partner with refugees for English tutoring, both activities I'm interested in.

Beside the Hope Center is an association for former political prisoners, one of two in the town. Louise Lefebvre, a teacher from our home community, spent five months teaching ex prisoners at a residential school in McLeod Ganj in early 2007, the year of our first trip. She wrote a fascinating book about her experiences, called *An Indian in India.*

As we wander on, the home for retired nuns catches my eye. I've always had a soft spot for old folks and the idea of helping here resonates. The organization that intuitively stands out for both of us is The Tibet Hope Center, off Lower Jogiwara Road. Someone once said: "It's all in a name" and this name resonates, it feels uplifting. We decide to go there Monday morning and meet with the staff.

Pleased with our progress, we locate a third floor deck restaurant in the town square, with a sweeping view of the mountains. Over soup we surreptitiously watch three young, upper middle class Indian couples from Lower Dharamsala, as they eat, drink beer and smoke tobacco hookahs. These tall, glass-based pipes cool and filter smoke by passing it through water. Popular in the sixties, they are back in fashion as a group recreational activity.

The Mehndi Ripoff

Our last meal in Bhagsu is an excellent Mexican breakfast at an outdoor cafe near the hotel. While eating I notice a woman and her small children sitting on the pavement, surrounded by what appear to be carved boxes; during the meal she repeatedly signals me over.

After breakfast I cross the road to look at her goods, wanting to support this friendly, poor-looking woman. The "boxes" are actually *buntas,* stamps used to apply henna designs called *mehndis.* Since I missed my opportunity in Delhi, I let her paint both my hands.

Perhaps not as guarded in this small town as in the city, and more accustomed to slick male entrepreneurs, I break a cardinal rule and neglect to negotiate the price beforehand. After she has decorated my hands, the woman asks for Rs 700, about $15. Hearing this I'm incensed, feeling that she has lured me across the street in order to use me.

The negotiating begins, after the fact. In response to "That's way too much money", the woman's counter offer is "Rs 650". My intuition tells me Rs 250 to 300 is the right amount, but the gap between asking price and what I'm willing to pay is enormous, so I seek input from someone in the know. One of the waiters affirms that my amount is fair. Coming in at the low end, I give the woman Rs 250. After one last attempt to extort a bit more money she becomes silent, seeing the set look on my face.

I mock myself for being a bleeding heart liberal. Having a soft spot for marginalized women, my desire is to support her and her kids, but it seems hers is to exploit a rich Western woman. But now, in the fullness of time, I realize the woman was just doing whatever she could to survive in life.

Moving Day

Ellen, Kirti Monastery Guesthouse Deck (monks residence to her left)
(Photo: Don Smith)

It's Sunday of the third week of October. Moving day has finally arrived and we're anxious to settle into Kirti Monastery in the heart of McLeod Ganj. The luggage is piled into a cab and we're driven the two kilometres to the monastery, near the bottom of Temple Road. Our driver takes one look at the steep, narrow lane leading to the monastery and parks near the temple gate. At our request, he helps us cart our bags up the hill to the front door of Kirti.

The main building is perched on the side of the hill at the top of the lane. From this point on, the road becomes a restrictive walking path, winding uphill between Kirti buildings, a nunnery, private homes and guesthouses. Inside the front door of the monastery are several offices. From there stairs lead downward to a courtyard surrounded on three sides by walls.

The monks' lodgings take up much of the building and two large decks, where the men and boys spend their free time, are located above and in front of the rooms. The guesthouse is situated underneath and to one end of the main building, and consists of three levels of single rooms and several suites.

A monk named Kunchok meets us at the door and helps us down the steep stairway to the guest residence. A mature thirty-three year old, he is the manager of this large monastery, a busy and demanding position. Kunchok has the peaceful, sensitive face of an aesthete and a lovely, mild energy.

With a combination of simple words and gestures, he indicates that our suite is being cleaned, and seats us comfortably in the window of a single room overlooking the mountains. After a short time we're shown to our apartment. It's small and lovely, with a magnificent view of the mountains and Lower Dharamsala in the valley below. We sense we'll be very happy during our time here.

From the narrow communal porch outside our suite we have a view of the monks' deck on the left. To the right is a lawn and a metal roofed building, both are used daily for lectures, chanting, prayers and debating practice.

Dekyi located the guesthouse through her network when Don requested a place with cooking facilities. (I myself had no plans to cook.) By Canadian standards the apartment is rough, but it's relatively luxurious accommodation for McLeod Ganj, and affordable at an equivalent of 10 dollars a day. Electricity and hot water are available around the clock, except for occasional storm outages. The suite is bug-free, always a surprise in both north and south India, where one anticipates tropical beasties.

The door of the narrow apartment opens onto a cozy sitting room with a wide window. Behind is a small bedroom with large curtained windows on the living room side, providing both light and air, then at the back are the washroom and kitchen. The tiny refrigerator in the livingroom works after a fashion, but the freezer is defective and as the weeks go by the useable portion of the fridge shrinks because the food freezes.

The cold water kitchen's location at the back of the apartment is not an ideal situation. Added to this, the rusted exhaust fan over the propane stove is broken; at times the odour of singed oil creeps into our rooms and we suspect that other fans are also defective. We happily make do, using the facilities to prepare cooked cereal with fruit salad most mornings and sandwiches accompanied by steamed vegetables for lunch. We eat dinner out each day, due to a combination of kitchen fumes, laziness and our enjoyment of an evening outing after conversation group. Before we leave we have one final hurrah in the kitchen, brewing up a huge pot of vegetable soup for our friends.

My favourite area is the sitting room, warmly furnished with an old, but attractive wine coloured couch and easychair, purple curtains, a coffee table and an old television set that displays ghostlike Western shows (oddly, my favourites like Grey's Anatomy). I'm to spend many happy hours in this room, gazing at the valley below, reading and tutoring our new friends.

Sunday is the day of rest for monks and some are sitting in the shade on their deck. Two small boys play a game together at a table under a tree. Birds twitter, hawks soar in the sky and voices filter down from a second deck above the guesthouse. From the Dalai Lama's nearby temple the deep, haunting sound of Tibetan horns resonates.

The energy is magnificent here at Kirti Monastery, light and uplifting. This "monk energy", as I come to call it, built up over time, comes from the heightened state of consciousness achieved over years of disciplined practice.

While the bags are being unpacked, Khenrab arrives unexpectedly with his brother and oldest son, to ensure that we're settling in comfortably. From our supplies I manage to produce British-style tea (not Tibetan, made with boiled milk), and cookies, devoured by the boy, as boys will do. Khenrab assures me they often drink their tea the English way. We have a short, but pleasant visit, then they're off so he can drive his son back to school.

Late in the afternoon the monkeys visit en masse; leaping quickly through the grounds of the monastery, then playing on the lawn below the prayer building. Great fun to watch, they can be a real menace, and sometimes the Indian staff throw empty water bottles at them to chase them away.

You do not want to get in their way when they're at work. Upending the garbage cans on the deck, the big monkeys can be quite nasty. Don takes one on, his rationale being: "I'm bigger than he is, so I can scare him". In a humorous attempt to run the blighter off, he spreads his six-foot wingspan and shouts loudly. The creature simply stares at him, then bares his teeth and hisses!

The monkeys around here are rhesus macaques. On Temple Road there are a few Japanese macaques, nicknamed "snow monkeys" because of their attractive white neck ruffs.

Later, on our way to dinner, we see a number of people sitting on a low platform opposite our lane. A banner informs us that a twelve hour sit-in is in progress, a protest against the murder of four young nuns by Chinese soldiers several days ago, as they attempted to flee Tibet.

As darkness falls a moving scene unfolds before us. Chanting monks lead an assortment of Tibetans and Westerners in a long candlelight procession down Temple Road, culminating at the temple. My heart aches for the women, their families and for the suffering of all Tibetans.

Don expresses the sentiment well when he says, "It's important that the Chinese are embarrassed by this". Many murders of escaping Tibetans are not recorded because they are unseen. About a year ago, a group of American trekkers witnessed two young nuns being shot and killed; that time the Chinese were forced to admit their crime.

McLeod Ganj: Accident or Synchronicity?

Some would say our discovery of McLeod Ganj in 2007 was an accident, but it was synchronicity (a coincidence of events that seem to be meaningfully related). Don had been successfully treated for a health problem when our chiropractor, a long time practitioner of Tibetan Buddhism, told us that in Dharamsala we could consult a monk who was also a doctor of Tibetan medicine. Intrigued by the idea of visiting the Dalai Lama's home, we tentatively decided to travel up north.

As we prepared for that trip a psychic acquaintance said, "I don't think you know why you're going to India". My reply was: "After a 30-year wait, I just want the experience". Her comeback was: "You're going to meet a healer there."

In another conjunction, on that trip we chose Majnu-ka-Tilla, the Tibetan refugee colony in northeast Delhi, as our city base. Once there it became clear that the distance between Delhi and Dharamsala was considerable, entailing a long trip through the mountains. But a few days of Delhi's unfamiliar chaos led us to reassess, and not knowing exactly what we were getting into, but feeling quite enthusiastic, seats were booked on the night bus from Majnu-ka-Tilla to McLeod Ganj.

Twelve hours on a creaky bus along bumpy roads. The vehicle broke down during the trip, but surprisingly I did not find the conditions bothersome. Daybreak marked our ascent into the mountains, motoring uphill on winding switchbacks, with the occasional entertainment of a troop of monkeys along the way.

Sunrise found us eating a hearty breakfast on a deck high above the town, overlooking the Himalayan foothills. Then, with luck on our side, a room was obtained in the tiny octagonal-shaped Cheryton Guesthouse, run by an Anglo-Indian couple.

The next day we went in search of the Men-Tsee-Khang Medical Clinic and a doctor-monk, walking several miles in the heat searching for the centre. Eventually someone directed us to the clinic where, instead of a monk, Dr. Dekyi Tsomo was on duty for consults in English. I knew as soon as Dekyi put her hands on my bloated belly that she was a powerful healer - she was the one we were meant to meet in India.

McLeod Ganj felt very "other" to me...mysterious and enticing. Although our entire visit spanned only sixty hours, the place made a deep, lasting impression. I departed feeling strangely drawn to the small Tibetan enclave in the Himalayan foothills, the community the Dalai Lama and thousands of Tibetan refugees call home.

Tibet is a country of widely differing provinces: the central area of U-Tsang is called "the cradle of Tibetan civilization"; high-altitude Amdo in the northeast, the home of the Dalai Lama, is mostly nomadic; while Kham in the southeast offered the fiercest resistance to the Chinese invasion of Eastern Tibet.

Ngari, in the sparsely populated southwest, is the site of the fifteen thousand foot high Mount Kailas, Asia's sacred mountain. Known as "the navel of the world" it is holy to Buddhist, Hindu, Jain and Bon pilgrims.

The author of *The Sacred Mountain of Tibet*, Kerry Moran, *circumnambulated* (the act of moving around a sacred object), Kailas ten times. She writes eloquently that the mountain is "Where the temporal and the eternal unite, and the divine takes physical form".

Our friend Dekyi was born in a small village not far from Mount Kailas; her family escaped from Tibet and settled in India when she was four years old. The Tibetans who fled the country following the Dalai Lama were placed in settlements all over India, with others from their region. Dekyi and her family lived in Mungod, South India for many years; it's the largest colony, housing almost 20,000 people.

For centuries Tibet was self-governing, with the Dalai Lama and his descendants acting as spiritual leaders. This all changed when China became communist, and in 1950 the army began infiltrating the country. The agricultural system could not support its own citizens plus the thousands of Chinese soldiers stationed there, and serious famine resulted.

Non-violent revolts against the occupation became common and the Chinese army retaliated by bombing and pillaging Tibetan monasteries, torturing and executing monks and guerilla leaders. The occupation continues today, wreaking havoc on the simple, peaceful country and violating human rights. Hundreds of thousands have been killed.

Tibet had never joined the United Nations, preferring to keep itself isolated from the world to maintain its traditional nomadic Buddhist lifestyle. As the Chinese slowly overtook the country and appropriated its natural resources, it did not get the help that was expected from UN countries.

In 1959, when a Chinese plan to kidnap the Dalai Lama was uncovered, His Holiness knew he must leave, and fled into India, eventually settling in McLeod Ganj. Eighty thousand Tibetans followed him into exile and tens of thousands more fled the country over the next fifty years.

The myriad refugees who dwell in India do not have citizenship; each holds an identity card, usually renewable annually. My understanding is that the original Government in Exile feared the loss of Tibetan culture and religion if Tibetans became Indian citizens.

Buddhism plays a prominent role in the life of the refugees. One young female friend seeks the comfort of the temple whenever she feels upset.

When loved ones die, 100 butter candles are lit in a special room beside the temple, to speed the soul on its way. Our friends have done this for us several times, both asked and unasked.

The Buddhist tradition of mindfulness helps its practitioners awaken to what actually is, and to live from that understanding as fully as possible. Most Tibetans we know have suffered greatly, but they have positive, engaged attitudes that help them in their daily lives.

Although warm and gracious, Tibetans are private people in many ways. After reading The Dance of Seventeen Lives by Mick Brown, I have more insight into why Dekyi deflects some of my personal questions. When interviewed by Brown, Tai Situ, Head of Sherab Ling Monastery outside Dharamsala, told him that in Tibetan culture they never talk about themselves; but since Westerners are curious to know about Tibetans, both Tai Situ and the previous Karmapa made exceptions, offering personal details.

First Day

Khenrab predicted that the weather will hold until the end of November and we planned our visit accordingly. Fall may be the best time of year to visit McLeod Ganj with respect to both weather and crowds. In the hot spring months the streets of the town are elbow-to-elbow with visitors anxious to see His Holiness the Dalai Lama. One must be vigilant to avoid being pushed into oncoming traffic or falling into deep runoff ditches missing top grates. As fall deepens, there are fewer and fewer visitors remaining, with the exception of the two brief periods of the Dalai Lama teachings.

This morning we discover Moonpeak, a popular café owned by a progressive Indian man and run by young Tibetans. After an excellent breakfast of muesli, curd and fruit, we connect with the director of The Tibetan Hope Center, (THC). Warm and welcoming, Kusang takes my hand in both of his, inviting us to sit down in the office. In his early twenties, Kusang founded the Center three years ago with Tseten.

Kusang was sent out of Tibet by his parents as a little boy, in the care of a guide, to have the chance of a better life. He lived and was educated at the Children's Transit School, a boarding school for Tibetan refugee children and young adults near Dharamsala. Later he studied at a university in South India. Kusang has strong beliefs about the power of young Tibetans to sustain and spread the word about their culture, and puts his education, intelligence and talents to work helping educate others and sponsoring cultural events. We arrange to begin our work this evening at the THC Conversation Class.

After connecting with Kusang we wander around town, passing the Reception Center for new arrivals, those who have left their country for personal as well as political reasons. Each new arrival is personally greeted by the Dalai Lama. Many say that meeting His Holiness changed their lives.

Our brief visit to McLeod Ganj two years ago helps us to quickly become comfortable, and we enjoy renewing our acquaintance with the town. Time feels unbroken as the days flow one into the other.

Sometimes I wonder if the McLeod Ganj sojourn could be an illusion…something created in my mind…or perhaps a dream. Tibetan Buddhists say all life is illusion.

Strolling down the main street, we spot the entrance to the yoga centre where we attended a sitar concert two years ago. Passing under the wooden sign, "Meditation Class, free, eleven to twelve and four to five daily", we go down the steps to discover that not only has the centre vanished, but the entire building is under construction, with new rooms being carved out of what was once the outer courtyard. In my mind's eye, however, the scene from two years ago remains vivid; the sitarist plays his instrument while the audience sits around him on the carpeted floor.

The intensity of my experience is disconcerting. Writing this more than a year later, once again I feel the energy of the place within me, distilled only fractionally by the passing of two years. What took place there is still very much alive; it's as if time and space have compressed themselves.

I have a strong sense that I have lived in this town before. It was darker then, there was no electricity. Later when I speak with Alma, whose spirit guides are Tibetan, she validates this and adds significant details.

Some believe that everyone we meet in life is someone we've had a relationship with before, a close one or perhaps just a fleeting acquaintance. As my friendship with Dekyi develops, the strong sense that we have shared past lives grows. This fits with their beliefs as Buddhists, she says. Both she and Khenrab feel that we must have past life connections because of our kindness to their family, before we even knew them well.

Alma's reading and suggestions from another intuitive confirm my own sense that Dekyi and I have been both sisters and brothers in past lives, as Tibetans in India and in Tibet, and that our families are intertwined.

Living in this environment is changing some essential feature deep within me, and I feel a subtle vibration throughout my being. I decide it's time to give myself permission to be joyful. It's okay and it is possible, even with Mom deteriorating and my friend and her daughter terminally ill, and all other past and present life challenges. As my spirit is lifted up, the jumble of emotions and the deep sadness I felt on arrival in Bhagsu have lost their hold on me. It's safe to let go here.

English Conversation Group

In a little valley near the bottom of Jogiwara Road, not far from the Korean Restaurant, The Tibet Hope Center makes its home on the main floor of a damp, decrepit building. The Center consists of four small rooms, each with a Tibetan-style curtained door. The space houses an office with missing window panes and metal safety grates, two classrooms and a library with several shelves of yellowed, dampish books, the product of two annual rainy seasons, lack of proper heating and the Center's location down in the valley.

We've decided to begin slowly with the evening English conversation group, the backbone of the English studies, Kusang tells us. Each Monday to Friday Western volunteers lead groups of three to six refugee students in the front yard of the Center. Participation is on a day-by-day basis and group size depends on the ratio of Tibetans to volunteers on any given day. Although many women attend the daytime classes, males outnumber females by at least five to one in the evening, with over a third of the participants monks.

For one hour a particular topic is focused on, with subjects varying widely from Buddhism to politics, life and love, and the Tibetan New Year. After our discussion we come together in a large circle, and as we warm ourselves around a bonfire, one Tibetan from each group reports on their topic as part of their English training.

As December draws near I pile on more and more layers of clothing before going to the Center and even Kusang begins tying an Indian wool blanket around his legs. The monks wear their robes even when it's cold, but some add fleece vests or jackets; this is verboten inside the monastery, except for the young or old, who wear fur lined wraps.

Entrance to Tibet Hope Center (Photo: Don Smith)

THC Bonfire After Conversation Group (Photo: Don Smith)

Only three years old, the Tibet Hope Center is very active. It became an official NGO one year ago, and there's a back story behind this registration. The directors are very poor, so they do not own land in the area, as required to apply for NGO status. The lawyer for THC, an Indian man in his mid thirties, was sent to the Tibetan Children's Transit School by his father, also a lawyer and active supporter of the Tibetan community. The family are well-off landowners, and the son was able to apply for the Center's NGO status. We later meet him at the home of a student.

THC volunteers work the streets regularly, handing out small flyers with the dual purpose of promoting cultural and political events, and seeking additional volunteers for conversation groups. A constant influx of assistants is needed; although a few of us stay for many weeks, most attend only once or twice, either passing through town or shopping around for a Center to work at.

Update from a political speech at the film festival on October 27, 2012:

- 100,000 Tibetans are in exile
- 6 million are still in Tibet
- 1 million have died

This evening I meet three men and a quiet, statuesque woman named Dolma. Their sophisticated conversational English comes as a surprise; although all levels are taught here, few beginner or low-intermediate students attend these groups, perhaps finding them intimidating.

Some students are worldly and well travelled, and we learn a lot from them. Tibetan refugees are creative about finding sponsors and obtaining visas to visit European countries; North American visas are tougher to get. One monk travelled to Singapore with a spiritual teacher as a Tibetan-Chinese translator. Another student, Brinchen, is an artist hoping to go to France soon, where his teacher lives, for his first exhibition. Also in my group is a man who has visited Thailand and currently awaits his immigration papers to join his brother in New York.

Over time I become friends with Dolma and enjoy tea with her and Pema, another THC student. Twenty-five years old and a middle child of eight, Dolma is the first in her family to leave Tibet, as is the case with most refugees we meet. Approximately 70 percent of Tibetans still in the homeland are nomads, and the first twenty years of Dolma's life were spent in this way; in town during the winter and on the move the rest of the year with the family's myriad yaks, sheep, goats and cows. Her parents were not able to teach their children to read, having themselves descended from illiterate nomadic families.

Dolma has a light, calm energy and it's easy to picture her walking gracefully through the mountains. The family is comfortably off, and like other prosperous Tibetan families, sends money to India to support members abroad, not the other way around, as we supposed. Dolma has been in McLeod Ganj for four years and has learned to read and write in both Tibetan and English, initially at the Tibetan Transit Boarding School. If she has the opportunity, she would like to become a translator.

A Crisis of Confidence

The advanced English levels and sophistication of some THC students are almost intimidating that first evening. English is second nature to us; we speak and write it automatically, having done so since childhood, but find it difficult to articulate complex verb tenses in particular, when tutoring in written work.

The next afternoon we begin tutoring a friend from the monastery. Lobsang gives us a shortened version of his personal story. He escaped from Tibet eight years ago, in his mid twenties, in a mixed gender group of thirty people, ages fifteen to fifty-five. Fewer Chinese patrols are present in winter, but the weather is nasty and the trip out treacherous. The group walked through the snowy mountains at night to avoid detection; by day they rested, but the extreme cold made it difficult to sleep. From time to time they replenished their supplies by buying food and tea from nomads. The refugees reached Nepal after twenty-eight days.

The three of us enjoy our time together and are pleased with the outcome. Lobsang is a mid-beginner level English student but his enthusiasm and intelligence make him a quick study. He comes to the sessions well prepared, bringing three books, including a Tibetan-English dictionary, helpful when any of us become stuck. We do some role play, then review verbs and nouns.

Tired from the uphill climbs all day long, I'm not looking forward to walking to the Center tonight and almost skip the second conversation group. Auto rickshaws may not park at the bottom of the lane, and it doesn't feel right to take expensive taxi rides such short distances. We try a couple of different routes to THC, settling on an indirect one, a good twenty-minute walk from our place.

The effort of getting to the Center is well worth it; by evening number two I'm more relaxed and competent in my role of group facilitator, enjoying the curious questions and upbeat energy of the young Tibetans.

Kusang and I talk about possible editing work and private tutoring; he agrees to both. We never do pick up tutoring students at THC as we find them on our own. While in McLeod Ganj I begin the long process of editing student refugee stories, completing the project six months later at home.

Tobias is in the group this evening and he becomes one of my favourites. A gentle, sweet monk, thirty-three years old, yet ageless, his facility with English is astounding; after studying for only a year and a half, he speaks the language at an advanced level.

It's clear that Tobias is unique, a highly evolved being, and we seem to have a special connection. I later receive the impression that we have shared previous lifetimes together in the monastery. At group he greets me and says goodbye by taking my hands and looking deeply into my eyes; his spiritual presence is palpable.

When asked about him, Alma tells me Tobias barely touches the ground energetically; "This monk is three quarters of a foot above the earth, really joyful. Tobias is pure love", she says. "The man has amazing wisdom and awareness of humankind. He's like an ambassador on earth."

Like most Tibetans we meet, Tobias wants people to understand the situation in his country. He left 18 months ago with a group of other monks, walking to Nepal, because the repeat visitations of Chinese soldiers to the monastery became intolerable. The monks were ordered over and over again, on pain of torture, perhaps death, to denounce His Holiness the Dalai Lama.

The trek out was very difficult, taking almost five weeks, Tobias tells me. (Most refugees know the exact number of days their expedition took). His feet were ruined after one month. They ran out of food and had only water to sustain them for a while. Having a guide helped a lot, as he was able to purchase a sheep from some nomads, so the group was once more nourished.

In writing this, after more than a year away from McLeod Ganj, I suddenly understand that it was no accident that I became acquainted with so many male Tibetans while there. "You've been a man in many lifetimes in that part of the world", Alma tells me.

As my first tutoring week draws to a close, there are four in Friday's group: Dolma, her friend Pema, one monk and one layman. The topic this evening is friendship and we enjoy a heartfelt discussion on the subject.

Pema, whose warmth and sweet face I take an immediate liking to, tells me she's been in McLeod Ganj for four years and met Dolma at the Tibetan Transit School. Her English is excellent and she works several hours a week at the private International School as an English tutor.

It was March when Pema left Tibet at age twenty, and there was still a lot of snow in the Himalayas. Unlike Dolma, whose journey by vehicle then on foot took little more than a week, Pema's trip to Nepal took two months and five days. She describes her pant legs freezing solid in the extreme cold and the difficulty of walking. At times people would fall through the crust of thin ice into holes in the ground.

Pema recounts how, on another trip, a woman fell into a deep pit and her fellow travellers were unable to save her, despite their best efforts. The line thrown down to her, fashioned from pieces of rope and clothing, broke, and she fell deeper into the abyss; they could do nothing more to help her, so sadly and reluctantly they moved on, leaving her to her snowy grave.

Life at Kirti Monastery

Our day begins with an attempt to call Dekyi down the hill, but the borrowed cell phone doesn't work. It's been dropped and there's no signal even after charging it all night; we discover later that it's run out of credits.

The English newspapers are gone before noon if you don't grab them early on. We take a stroll and pick one up, along with papayas and bottled water. Most Indians drink bottled water now; the urban poor avail themselves of free, lightly treated drinking water from public taps on the streets. In 2007, a water filtration system plus sterilization pills were part of our supply kit; Don was thinking of the India of thirty years ago. Still, one must be cautious about the supplier of the water.

With no plan in mind, we enjoy meandering around the community, then relax in our apartment. In the evening, THC's weekly event is a documentary on the life of the Dalai Lama, shown at the public school. Kundun is a high budget film, directed by Martin Scorsese, two and a half hours of powerful, moving scenes. Three boys play the role of the Dalai Lama at various ages; the youngest actor stands out for me because he captures the incredible joy so evident in the being of His Holiness today.

Many people in the west, not having a particular discipline or leader, search hungrily for spiritual sustenance. In some ways I envy the Tibetans, with their wise Dalai Lama; they follow him, not blindly, but with love and devotion.

It's been said that those who visit or live on the same grounds as a master will themselves be transformed if they are in tune. Enveloped day and night by the spiritual energy of the monks and their Rinpoche, we ourselves are changing, adapting to the higher vibration.

In this atmosphere, the pressure to perform gradually lessens. I sleep well despite the absence of eleven inches of memory foam beneath me, topping the thin, hard monastery mattress with a tiny blow up camping pad. Life has become simpler yet ultimately more meaningful and satisfying.

We have access to nearby food supplies and a coffee shop for my morning coffee ritual. The comfortable apartment works well for us, and after a couple of weeks of climbing the steep stairs and walking several miles each day, my body is stronger, my stamina greater.

Our routine has become intertwined with the rhythm of the monastery. For the monks each day, except weekends, is structured, beginning with chanted prayers at five thirty each morning. The soothing sound lulls me back to sleep most days.

Around noon debating takes place. An important part of this skill is to unbalance your opponent by stepping towards him and clapping both hands together. The younger monks go about this in a very enthusiastic manner, loudly and vigorously slapping their hands. Those unfamiliar with the practice might think a violent argument is taking place!

Weekdays at four, the younger monks, the boys and teens, receive teachings in the building beside our guesthouse; from the balcony we hear the instructor's guttural voice followed by the repetitions of the young ones. Many evenings after dinner we arrive home to chanting, followed by more loud debating sessions on the lawn. This activity usually stops before 8 o'clock; we become accustomed to it, but the chanting is the most pleasant to listen to.

From Saturday mid-afternoon until Sunday evening all the monks have free time to relax or walk about the town. The repetitiveness and ritual of monastery life puts me in mind of the Ganges River in Varanasi; there is constancy, an eternalness to life in both places and the same lifestyles have survived, with surprisingly little change, over thousands of years.

The Subtext of Tibetans in India

We've been told that Indian residents of McLeod Ganj tolerate the Tibetan presence because of the Dalai Lama, but what will happen after His Holiness passes remains an unknown. Tibetans are extremely concerned about this and some have chosen to make a pre-emptive strike, applying for visas to leave the country now.

Although the Indian government is supportive of the Dalai Lama, issuing him visas to travel around the world at will and allowing him free access to most parts of the country, it is sensitive about offending China. In mid November of 2009 The Times of India reported that despite saying it would not interfere with the Dalai Lama's visit to Arunachal Pradesh, near the Indo-Chinese border, state officials did, in fact, ask His Holiness to modify his program, speaking only about Buddhism, not politics. They also banned reporters who had already received permission to cover the event.

Kusang at the Hope Center tells us he personally experienced racism at university in South India, when one professor deliberately refused to treat the Tibetan students as individuals in their own right. For three years during roll call this teacher disparagingly said: "The Tibetans stand up".

In April of 1994, anti-Tibetan rioting took place in Dharamsala, moving from the lower town uphill to McLeod Ganj, after a young Tibetan man fatally stabbed an Indian youth. Tibetans stood by without retaliation as their property and shops were looted and destroyed, some by fire. What happened once could happen again.

There are somewhat mixed accounts about Indian acceptance of the refugees in Dharamsala. The Dalai Lama is quoted as saying that, in general, relations between the two groups are good, however, in late '99 His Holiness did briefly consider moving his residence and some administrative offices to Haryana, the state south of Himachal Pradesh, "As the growing tension between the locals and the Tibetans is becoming a cause of worry".

Reports from both the Canadian and U.S. governments in 1999 and 2000 say that despite random and isolated incidents, Tibetans are able to lead peaceful lives in India. Thubten Samdup of the Canada-Tibet Committee emphasizes that India is a tolerant and compassionate country that has gone out of its way to accommodate Tibetans.

These accounts demonstrate to me that although relations are peaceful on the whole, the potential for volatility exists at any time and Tibetans are right to be concerned about what will unfold down the road.

As the days pass, we come to know more about the Tibetans we live and work in close proximity to. There are four men in the group I facilitate tonight, including Rinzen, on a "working holiday" from an eminent monastery in Mungod, South India, in McLeod Ganj to learn English and computer skills. Don arranges to tutor him in Beginner English at our apartment.

Most Center students are relatively new arrivals, but one member of tonight's group is different; he arrived in India with his family at age seven, travelling on legal passports.

The politically astute students inform me that the Chinese government gives extra power and self autonomy to Tibet's more radical states, and residents there obtain Chinese passports more easily. It comes as a surprise that the totalitarian Chinese government would demonstrate such savvy. My friend Michael later explains that this approach is a way for citizens to let off steam; it was called "repressive tolerance" by Herbert Marcuse.

The students we meet seem relatively confident in their abilities, but from their questions and comments I infer that they compare themselves to Westerners like ourselves, who have more education and financial resources, minimizing their own exceptional life experiences. Hoping it will help them recognize and honour their own amazing strength and bravery, qualities that have blossomed out of adversity; I initiate a discussion about "no formal qualifications versus life qualifications" in the group.

Pema tells me it's harder for them to connect with foreigners, as we have no shared life experience. The male students relate in a rather functional way, asking many practical questions, while I believe Pema is speaking of a more personal connection. The young Tibetans at THC and our doctor friends seem open and trusting, but our lives are poles apart. However, we all keep trying to understand each other.

Rinzen's Story

A monk's life is a demanding one of spiritual discipline and deprivation. While the home monastery provides the basics of food, shelter and clothing, monks receive almost no money, so they must find creative ways to obtain funds to travel and achieve other goals, frequently relying on Western friends.

This is the case with Rinzen. He was admitted to a monastery in Eastern Tibet, near his home, at age fifteen. "For two years I studied the basic rituals of Tibetan Buddhism", Rinzen says, "Until the Chinese came for us". He decided to flee Tibet as part of a group of forty men, monks and some laymen. Their guide was a woman.

After driving several hundred miles out of Lhasa by truck, the group crossed the Himalaya Mountains on foot into Nepal. Many times they came close to military outposts, once crawling on hands and knees to get around one. Once over the border they felt out of harm's way, but the Nepalese military broke into their safe house and arrested the whole group, later releasing them, a confusing and frightening experience.

After reaching India, Rinzen studied for six years at in Mungod. But his parents, growing old, longed to see their son again, and asked him to return home. Family loyalties won out and he returned to Tibet, where he was welcomed back at his old monastery. There he did his best to serve, but the harsh policies imposed by the Chinese government, coupled with the life experience he had gained in India, made his life difficult and unfulfilling. His family understood, and in 2005 he again escaped to India and continued his studies in the south.

But having seen and heard much while in Tibet, Rinzen was now politicized. In March of 2008, he joined the peace marchers walking from India to Tibet to protest the brutal crackdown on peaceful demonstration there. Though the Indian government halted them, Rinzen's involvement in the march had a profound effect on him. "It changed me as person, as a citizen of this dying nation", he says. "I realized that even as a Buddhist monk, I must live for a greater cause; this is part of Buddhism as well". He joined Sera, a political NGO for monks and has taken part in further demonstrations and hunger strikes through the organization.

Rinzen's lack of English was holding him back; as there are few opportunities to learn English in South India, he took a leave from the monastery. Now most of his time is spent in Dharamsala, learning English and computer skills.

Feeling very restive, Rinzen is impatient to leave India and tell the world what is taking place in Tibet. He now wants to visit Europe if an opportunity arises to accompany a lama who is teaching there.

In his desperation to move forward Rinzen has a hard time accepting these limitations. He seems to believe that our resources are endless, and we have been forced, due to repeated requests, to set clear boundaries about the amount of support we are able and willing to give.

Wherever You Go, There You Are

We've been in Dharamsala for close to three weeks, including the Bhagsu days. The twelve days at Kirti Monastery feel longer, because we are existing in kairos time. As I slowly relax, space is freed up inside for a new peacefulness to enter; I'm becoming empty, the route to freedom from suffering, according to His Holiness the Dalai Lama. My dreams are indicative of this relinquishing of control, an organic way to process unfinished business.

The Tibetan pills religiously crushed and imbibed three times a day are beginning to do their internal work. In under a week my digestion is on the mend, my sinuses, congested from the air pollution, somewhat clearer and there are other improvements, falling under the category of "too much information". My body uses lots of energy to go through this change, and I do feel tired at times.

I'm pleased with the results of this powerful medicine that works in psychological and physiological ways as well as spiritually, having been blessed by high lamas. "The remedies are quite good for organ repair", Alma later tells me. I sense that they work better when taken in McLeod Ganj, and she confirms this.

I'm also told that I feel quite healthy to her overall, about eight years younger than my chronological age. Back at home, one of the women in my dream group says to me; "Over the eight months I've known you,

you're younging; I know there's no such word, but that's what it is". This, I believe, is the result of the potent formulas and the changes brought about by spending time in McLeod Ganj.

Kunchok has agreed to inquire at the nunnery next door on my behalf about tutoring students, but it seems he's forgotten. I have a yen to work with nuns, feeling something of an affinity with them.

Unwilling to wait any longer, I stroll up the walking path to Jamyang Choling Nunnery, behind the Kirti Monastery monks' residence. Concerned about intruding, I cautiously climb the stairs, following signs indicating that the office is up here. Fragrant cooking smells drift out of a third floor room. In the corridor is a sophisticated looking nun with short, dark hair; her spoken English is perfect. She explains that the nuns are studying for Buddhist exams this month and are not available to learn English. However, three new students from Tibet need help badly and if interested, I can meet them now.

She takes me through a doorway into a small two-room apartment to meet two women; they have special permission to live in the nunnery as one woman's sister is a nun here. Choden is thirty years old and arrived from Tibet one year ago, leaving her two children in the care of her parents, while Dechen is a feisty eighteen-year-old who came four years ago. The third student, Nima, is a monk from South India; he's been in South India since 2003 and is staying at the Dalai Lama temple while studying in McLeod Ganj.

We agree to begin our work together tomorrow afternoon at their apartment. After the first session I suggest we work at Kirti instead, as their rooms have a mouldy smell. My initial impression is that the three are beginner students, and I plan accordingly, however, their books indicate intermediate level. They're much shyer than the THC students, but as our sessions progress it becomes apparent that they are low intermediate, with Nima having had the least exposure to English.

After working with a few students one begins to grasp the basics of assessing English levels, but at first it's tricky. Women are frequently shy and their knowledge may exceed their oral output. Some are adept orally, but their reading and writing level is basic, like my Thai student in Canada who has spoken English daily for many years.

As our days become full we post a schedule on the wall, to keep track of our commitments. Sunday is a self-appointed day off and we go out for breakfast, a change of pace from Don's weekday ritual of oatmeal and fruit salad, this meal being important to him. Although we enjoy eating together, I thirst for the street activity, as well as my morning Americano, and am often restless by the time he's ready to leave the apartment.

Today it's a full breakfast at Jimmy's Italian Restaurant; tomato, onion and cheese omelette with salsa and rice, buns with butter and jam, and not one, but two Americanos. Jimmy's is where Westerners go for familiar foods and Indian beer (not for breakfast though). There are ten British teens here wearing T-shirts displaying an NGO logo.

Hike Day

Playing Tibetan Games on Annual Hike (Photo: Don Smith)

It's Saturday in early November and Don's up with the birds for the annual Hope Center hike to Triund, with the Directors, students and some volunteers. I opt to stay behind, having already done my share of climbing just getting around town each day.

After Don leaves I drift back to sleep, awaking calm and refreshed after a dream about white rats. The setting for the dream is a guesthouse on the grounds of a large hotel in a foreign country. After spending one night here, I discover that there are many white rats living in the porous old wooden house. Changing rooms is not an option as the bedrooms in the main house are all occupied.

In the afternoon, when my Tibetan guests arrive, I tell them about my dream. They feel intuitively, as I do, that the white rats are a positive message. Later research indicates that white rats signify help coming from unexpected sources; they are telling the dreamer that beneficent forces or entities are around her, offering protection. The soft energy of Kirti Monastery seems to reinforce this idea. After this dream I feel more grounded within myself.

Relaxing on the deck, my preferred way to start the day, I relish the warmth of the sun. The sky is clear and the mountains so sharply defined that the individual trees and houses stand out. Lower Dharamsala can be seen at the bottom of the valley, a bit hazy from smoke fires.

By eight-thirty it's too hot to sit outside and I leave; at nine I'm sitting in my usual spot outside Moonpeak Café, eating a veggie omelette and drinking Americano. This omelette may be the best I've ever eaten.

It was so hot at the apartment that I've made the wrong wardrobe choice for my outing, forgetting how damp and cool it is lower down in the morning; it's just a few hundred yards away, but almost a different weather pattern. The extremes of temperature in the Himalayan foothills far surpass the varying climate beside the Pacific Ocean at home. I'm wearing a long-sleeved jersey, no jacket, not even a scarf, plus it's earlier than usual; I hang in for an hour and a half at my table in the shade, eating and working, soaking in the street ambiance.

Then off to the internet café next door to catch up on blogging, facebook and e-mails. Our friends have sent a note announcing that their baby boy was born two days ago; I later post his picture and that of my new great-nephew on the blog.

Playing computer catch up every two or three days is not a good idea, too time consuming and energy draining. After sitting for so long my body wants to move, so I stroll through town, rediscovering a street from two years ago, off the Jogiwara-Temple Road intersection. In a small Kashmiri gem store I find a turquoise necklace, just right for our house rental agent, who tried unsuccessfully to find a short term tenant for us.

On the way home I stop in for milk for afternoon tea with my two friends, and the shopkeeper patiently explains how to make Tibetan milk tea. Chocolate puffs from Moonpeak Cafe complete the menu; the staff assures me that my guests will like chocolate.

Back home I inspect my laundry on the railing and find it's almost dry. In another 20 minutes, when the sun is off the deck, I'll be able to sit outside again. Yesterday's leftovers from Chonor House make a fine repast when reheated. Before my company arrives, I relax and read Shantaram, a fantastic epic loosely based on the life of an Australian armed robber and prison escapee who takes refuge in Bombay, becoming the medic of a colossal slum next to the World Trade Center. Later in our trip we visit the bar where he passed many hours with other expatriates.

When Pema and Dolma arrive, the coffee table is adorned with a wide red scarf to create a festive atmosphere, and soon we're all drinking the milk tea Pema has helped prepare, and eating the puffy chocolate cookies. They're a hit.

The women stay for about two hours, talking about their lives in McLeod Ganj. Both continue to study English and attend conversation classes at the Tibet Hope Centre. Pema tells me she enjoys her part time

Tibetan teaching job, helping many Mexican students at the International school.

After assuring me not to worry if Don returns late from the hike, the two friends leave. They found it a very long day when they participated last year. Don's in good hands with Kusang and the rest of the Center crowd, so I enjoy my own company until he returns shortly after dark at six-thirty.

It was a memorable day, Don tells me. The group of twenty-four met at daybreak in the town square and went by taxi to Dharamkot, where the hike began. The two hour, often rocky and steep climb, took them slowly uphill on a trail used by donkeys.

The younger men were concerned about Don's wellbeing; he was the oldest member of the group and they were not used to a 60-year-old being so fit, as Tibetans are considered old at this age. Despite his age difference and not being acclimated to walking in the mountains, Don managed to keep up with the others, and he enjoyed hearing about their personal experiences and discussing politics with them as they hiked. They presented him with a beautiful hand carved walking stick, purchased in a small store enroute. We transported this stick for many miles, in cars and on buses, until one day near the very end of our trip; we inadvertently left it behind on a plane.

Ashes to Ashes

I'm beginning to say goodbye to my mother and have been doing an ad hoc review of memories lately, seeing Mom in the days when she was vital and engaged with life. My dreams are more available to me here, and early this morning I awaken to a powerful one about Mom disappearing. It brings to mind the words above; they originate in the Christian bible.

We're at home and Mom is tired and lays down on our bed, wearing a flowing purple silk gown. A family arrives at the door with their children, the mother with a pregnant belly. I ask Mom if she wants to say hello, and always the social butterfly, she says "Yes" and sits straight up, feet dangling over the edge of bed. "Don't rush", I say, and walk into the front hall to speak with the family.

When I return, Mom has disappeared, only her purple clothing remains in a pile on the bed. In place of her, on a small cot alongside the wall, lies a small baby. Then the baby also vanishes, leaving behind its clothes. Finally, on the cot lies a small, red rectangular Chinese silk pillow.

My sense is that the dream is a metaphor representing my mother's essence returning to the source; first she changes into a very young form of herself, a baby, then regresses further to a state invisible to the average eye.

At the Center we talk about families often and some of the Tibetan women have told me I'm lucky to still have my mother. Each of these conversations, as well as time spent with Dekyi's mom has entered my subconscious.

Premature Rainy Season

The weather favours us with thunderstorms all morning; the temperature is much cooler now, and we're not sure if winter has begun or not. It's so beastly out I skip my morning café visit, drinking two cups of strong tea in the hopes that my coffee-dependent brain will survive. We relax, read and talk, a pleasant change from the usual routine.

At three we venture out for coffee and to stretch our legs. The town feels different, subdued and uninhabited, even though a few people walk the streets. The staff has crammed the outside tables and chairs into the café and our body heat makes the room comfortable.

On the street a woman passes by licking a popsicle, an odd choice of refreshment on this cool, wet day. Monday store closures on Temple Road add to the deserted feeling. After coffee, cake and perusal of outdated English-language newspapers, we wander up to the health food store to replenish our cheese, tuna and rolled oat supplies. I treat myself to a half-bottle of Indian wine, expensive and not all that appealing in the end.

Back at Kirti, Don says he feels guilty about skipping conversation group. "It will be awfully cold and uncomfortable sitting around outside today," he justifies. "Tomorrow will be a new day and perhaps sunny."

Heavy rain, thunder and lightning disturbed my sleep in the night, but by this morning it's lightened considerably. I shower and eat breakfast in preparation for my group. The three come through the door, a little bolder than before. As we work on verbs, it's apparent the students are really intermediate level, as their textbooks indicate. All are more confident today, less concerned about mistakes.

On my way to the Center for an early start on editing, I pass two Indian women dragging enormous bundles of branches, collected from the side of the road; they're goat food, I later find out, not firewood, as suspected.

Today by chance, Don encounters a group member outside Kirti Monastery and he shows him a more direct path to the Center than walking along the main streets. An intriguing man, he says that his home monastery, in the hills outside McLeod Ganj, permits him to live in town in order to study English. Unlike other monks on sabbatical, he never wears robes, and his manner is more aggressive.

You never know who you'll meet at the Center or what will unfold. The small NGO now serves 200 students, and 1,300 volunteers have passed through its doors since its inception in May of 2007. Today it's buzzing and the office full; all four computers are in use and a French tutoring session is taking place in a corner of the room.

Later, over a tea time chat, I discover that the tutor is a French psychologist, researching a book on psychic phenomenon. He's leaving McLeod Ganj tomorrow unfortunately; had we met sooner, we could have shared pleasant hours of conversational French and English, as we're both interested in improving our language skills.

Although it's a bit like the Gong Show here at times, somehow all the bits and pieces come together. THC accomplishes a tremendous amount with few resources beyond the enthusiasm and passion of the people who run it and the work done by transient volunteers. Tasks appear to be accomplished with little co-ordination; this system gives volunteers a great deal of autonomy to work on their projects. Kusang and Tseten have a deep appreciation of all that is done and trust that we have the best interests of the refugees at heart.

Despite the cold and extreme damp in the hollow, a crowd of forty is in attendance this evening, with a record volunteer turnout. I'm barely warm enough in two pairs of pants, hat, coat and gloves. The bonfire go-round at the end is a creative one; each participant takes a miniscule piece from the single chocolate bar passed around, then says "I want to share this piece of chocolate with my friend...", naming someone from a different culture. This simple, fun exercise connects us.

Morning Reflections

Indian Countryside (Photo: Don Smith)

It's beautiful and sunny again, but there's an absence of heat in the sun's rays now. Both the surrounding mountains and the valley below appear hazy. Small white eagles with black-tipped wings fly by, a beautiful and rare sight. A Kirti worker sweeps and washes the deck; after it's dry I walk outside to listen to the melodic harmony of the morning chants coming from inside the monastery.

The sudden weather change has affected our health. Everyone sounds like heavy smokers in the morning; I can barely swallow, and a few people have colds. Horrid hawking sounds come from neighbouring rooms, as the men clear their sinuses and lungs using a particular Indian technique that helps the respiratory system in this dusty country. We're glad of the Tibetan sinus medicines.

Anyone can stay at Kirti Monastery, but most people are unaware of its existence. At this time fellow guesthouse residents include visiting monks, and two new female Asian guests downstairs. A Tibetan couple, on their annual pilgrimage from Bangalore for the teachings, stay next door to us.

While Don is tutoring I head out for coffee, quite an amusement this morning. First there's a murmur on the street as six or eight snow monkeys swing through the trees overhanging the gully across the road. Magnificent looking, with white ruffled faces, they're an infrequent sight; some are almost as big as the rude monkeys at Kirti.

Each time one leaps from one tree to the next, a black dog races up and down the road, quivering with silent excitement, curiously not barking. The troop of monkeys hang around for a while entertaining us; pictures are taken and fun is had by all.

Just up from Moonpeak Café, I then notice a small white car on the side of the road, with three enormous, cotton-wrapped packages on the roof, completely lopsided and askew. It's a cartoon-like scene, where the little car looks like it's going to topple over at any moment.

The entertainment concluded, I return to editing. After being away from the stories for several days, I've lost some of the emotional immunity built up against the sadness inherent in each tale. The first one today, dictated by a woman whose brother was tortured in jail, is heartbreaking. I feel the weeping deep within me once again, but don't shed any tears.

The editing has become a significant part of my McLeod Ganj experience; it deepens and adds another dimension to my growing awareness of the refugee situation. Most stories are told by men because more male refugees have escaped and also because men play a more assertive role in the culture, though traditionally it was a matriarchal one. Women find telling their stories even more difficult emotionally than the men; Louise Lefebvre writes in *An Indian in India* that she discovered this when she asked her class of ex-prisoners to do this exercise.

Next trip I will focus on Tibetan women in my work, as contact with them has been limited during the time here. The plan is to interview females of mixed ages about their lives, in their own country and now as exiles in India. As she neared the end of her time in Burma, Karen Connelly, author of *Burmese Lessons*, realized that she had spoken to male revolutionaries almost exclusively, not capturing the feminine voice in any significant way.

The days are busy, but when I relax into the activities and let the moments flow, one into the other, it doesn't feel like efforting. Beginning the day slowly, tutoring at home, these things make a difference. The Tibetan medicines are doing their job, and I feel more balanced now.

After a short break we're off to the Center again, this time using the quicker route. The path travels uphill along the narrow walkway between Kirti and the nunnery, winds between houses and tiny shops, then makes a sharp right at a guest house before descending a stairway. The words Jogiwara Road in large letters on the wall let you know you're on the right track. After that it's a simple stroll along a path, at one point within a foot of someone's front door, then a final set of stairs lead down to Jogiwara Road, emerging a few steps from THC's entrance.

There's an upbeat, collegial atmosphere in the office during group today. I pause in my typing to speak briefly with an interesting young Polish man about Europe. The sounds of singing float in through the broken window from the bonfire area, each melody beautiful.

After the bonfire Don brings a woman into the office. Desperate for relationship counselling, she's decided Don and I can help her, since we're in a long term marriage. Out of his depth, Don turns her over to me, it's more in my line of work, he reckons. The woman reveals that during their nine month marriage the couple has quarrelled daily and he has hit her on several occasions. Later I learn from the Secretary of the Tibetan Women's Association that domestic violence among young new arrivals is a serious issue.

While we're talking, Don relaxes in the office, discussing politics and economics with the Polish volunteer. A tall, thin Tibetan man, a little older than most, serves us chai in colourful, oval-shaped china cups. With minimal English skills, this is his contribution to the community.

A few days later I would meet Amy again in a café. She tells of growing up in an upper middleclass family in an urban area of China, and later meeting her husband in McLeod Ganj. This enterprising couple earns a good income, but spends more, leading to friction and violence in the relationship.

My sense is that there are vast cultural differences between them, however Amy does not agree. She is seeking advice on improving her marriage, wishing to remain with her partner and start a family. I speak with her for a while, but do not feel I'm of much help.

For our evening meal we return to the Shangri La Restaurant, the best place in town for inexpensive, high quality Tibetan food. Tonight it's a nourishing dinner of spinach and tomato in a sauce, eggplant, chow mein with tofu and Tibetan bread spread with melted butter, (similar to a large, soft English muffin). We usually see someone we know there; this evening it's one of the THC students.

Our feast comes to a grand total of 80 rupees, about $2; at these low prices the restaurant is practically a soup kitchen. The monk at the front desk confirms that the food is priced affordably for people with little financial resources; food service is part of their work.

After dinner we purchase two large brownies at a kiosk near the square, enjoying them while watching a blurry Grey's Anatomy. After this first breakdown we crave regular infusions of sweets, but walk the calories off around town!

The monastery staff adjusts the TV cable strung over the balcony railing as needed for their Hindi programs; I never think to ask them to change it for the English ones. It's surprising that a monastery guesthouse would supply a television as monks are allowed to view only news, nature shows and documentaries about Tibet, nothing commercial, the monastery manager tells us. Some of the younger ones watch different shows and play computer games outside the monastery, they tell us.

TV soap operas are often in *Hinglish,* a combination of Hindi and English, amusing to listen to, but a bit disconcerting also; when you lose the story line the dramatic gestures and dances give you the general idea of the plot, though.

Commercials are unsophisticated, over the top and silly. Produced Bollywood style, they epitomize the perfection of romantic love. They are also the opposite of what we would expect in a sexually repressive country where female modesty is highly esteemed; products not normally advertised in the West are shown, such as the Morning After Pill. Parliament has debated whether to allow this type of advertising, deciding against regulating it, perhaps because of India's great entrepreneurial focus.

Stood Up Twice

It's a quiet day, sunny and fairly warm for mid-November. My tutoring group is conspicuous by its absence. After a time Dechen pops in to say she's ill and must go to the hospital; she will be accompanied by her two friends.

I take this found time to roam around town, have coffee, then draft blog posts. Next is a visit to a little side street near the Temple-Jogiwara Road intersection, where an excellent used bookstore is located, run by an outspoken dissident, a former member of the Government in Exile. In a previous conversation this man told us that he does not approve of the government's *Middle Way* of non-violence, a moderate position that advocates preserving Tibetan culture, religion and national identity, while giving China security and territorial rights over the motherland.

His plan for bringing the Chinese occupiers to their knees is a curious one; a series of non-violent actions would be carried out in Tibet, such as sabotaging the electrical system of the country and pouring water into mailboxes. These activities would be performed, not by those living there, but by exiles, smuggled back into the country for that purpose. This dangerous operation would, without a doubt, result in imprisonment, torture and death for many people and trouble for the families still living there. Later back home, I see the man on TV, part of a documentary about Tibetan issues.

Back at the apartment, Lobsang arrives 45 minutes late for his tutoring session, looking quite different with a freshly shaven head, a monthly event, he tells us. In his hand he carries a new florescent light to replace the burnt out one in the bathroom; clean towels will come tomorrow.

Lobsang lingers for a while, he seems to enjoy hanging out and practicing his English; for our part, we appreciate his calm, sensitive, yet energetic temperament. He won't be continuing with his tutoring, he informs us, as his monastery responsibilities are keeping him too busy.

Back in Canada, a Western Buddhist with an intimate knowledge of McLeod Ganj explains that Kirti is one of the most conservative monasteries. Its monks are not allowed to fraternize with laypeople or to learn English. This prohibition against the expansion of one's knowledge and therefore their world bothers both Don and I.

Don leaves to do errands while I sit outside reading *Shantaram*; I'm halfway through its nine hundred pages. From the deck I notice slews of monkeys swarming the roofs, the balcony below and the lawn, where they busy themselves digging up grubs for lunch. The two o'clock gong rings next door, signalling the beginning of classes for the young monks.

I gaze at the peaked mountains and rolling hills that end in the Lower Dharamsala valley below, and the birds gliding high on the air currents. The hills exude a feeling of peace and the energy of the monastery enfolds me securely. My spirit and consciousness are able to soar in this environment. In this town high in the mountains, an openness to possibilities exists at all times, and increasingly, each day is lived in the present moment.

Before group today I speak with Tsoeson, one of the few active females at THC, and also a board member. Each evening she assigns speaking topics to each group and keeps track of the students reporting at the bonfire.

Tsoeson tells me her parents sent her out of Tibet with a group of adults when she was nine years old. Alone in the world, she lived and studied at the Children's Transit School, cradled in the hills outside McLeod Ganj; later her older sister joined her.

The staff at the school always showed kindness to each child, Tsoeson says; "But basically we were on our own; there were way too many children for the staff to look after. We all had to care for ourselves, even washing our own clothes." This sensitive, intelligent young woman is 19 years old now, with the maturity of a much older person. Since completing school some years ago, the sisters have lived together in an old apartment building in the centre of town. Currently Tsoeson's sister is studying nursing in Delhi. She plans on returning to the Dharamsala area afterwards.

Norbulingka Institute

Ellen in Front of Norling Guesthouse
(Photo: Don Smith)

The intensity and richness of the first weeks have given way to a comfortable predictability. Our established daily routines and the sense of belonging here and of contributing to something bigger is growing. When we pull together, the whole really is larger than the sum of its parts.

Time to take a vacation from tutoring, conversation group and editing, and our plan is to visit the Norbulingka Institute, the cultural division of the Dalai Lama's organization. At the bottom of the lane we engage a waiting taxi and travel downhill, through Lower Dharamsala's markets, to Sidhpur, seventeen kilometers below. Although the driver maniacally propels his bouncing jeep along the windy road, it still takes a while to reach our destination as the traffic is heavy. "He's an average driver", says Don.

On arrival at the Norbulingka Institute at one in the afternoon, we pass through the Reception Centre. The polite desk attendant asks only what our nationality is, tells us free tours are available and points out the refreshment and washroom areas.

The Norbulingka, dedicated to expressing Tibetan values in the form of art and literature, was established 1988, once all basic government and social services were in place. Its location in the midst of an Indian town seems unusual, but the overcrowded slopes of McLeod Ganj could not offer the Institute space.

Strolling around the well-maintained grounds, we come upon the Norling Guesthouse, a charming, Tibetan style inn, its entranceway framed by brightly coloured, hand-painted carvings. A tiny deck overlooks the main door. The inn provides fifteen bedrooms on two floors. The foyer and upstairs atrium are decorated with paintings and appliquéd wall hangings, all produced by Norbulingka artists. Norling is beautiful and restful, as is the entire Institute.

The grounds of Norbulingka are pleasing to the eye in a minimalist Asian way. Flowering poinsettias abound and hibiscus trees dotted with partially opened red flowers border the pathway. Prayer flags hang from the larger trees and bushes. In the heart of the property, a stream of water runs under a walking bridge that leads to the temple.

As we enjoy the sights from the bridge, a group of tourists pass by on their way to the temple. Their guide, a gracious woman with excellent English, tells us that they are Vietnamese Buddhists. All but one wears street clothes. That person is dressed in the traditional grey costume of lay people who have *taken refuge* in a formal ceremony and received a Buddhist name; (refuge is a commitment to taking the Dharma, or the Buddha's teaching, as one's guide in life). Most Vietnamese are Buddhists, I learn from my research. Zen Buddhism emphasizes meditation, and is pursued by monks and nuns, while lay-people prefer the Pure Land philosophy, with a goal of rebirth in a paradise of enlightenment in the west.

It's time for lunch, and inside the restaurant a group of a dozen French-speaking visitors are enjoying a buffet lunch. Cheese momos and *thukpa*, a Tibetan soup of veges and chilies catch our eye; the thukpa is mild but tasty.

A monk and a European man take their place at the table next to us. This monk is one of the most radiant people I've seen during my time in India, a beatific smile fills his face and light emanates from his eyes. Tibetans are very curious about the world and many, particularly monks, have Western friends who act as sponsors and with whom they exchange political and cultural ideas. Some monks are sent to other countries by their monasteries to offer teachings or to raise political awareness about their homeland.

After eating we set out to see the workshops. In the metal shop Buddhas are being constructed from copper and brass, they range in size from tiny to enormous. Delicate carvings emerge before our eyes in the wood workshop. Women design and make colourful clothing, fabrics and quilted materials on industrial machines in the sewing room. Jewellery and thangkpa wall hangings are fashioned in other work spaces.

On the grounds of the Institute is The Norling Arts Shop, a showcase for the products made on-site by the talented artists. Here visitors can purchase books and cards, clothing, household accessories and other arts and crafts to take home. A brisk virtual mail-order business is also part of the service. Production of the intricate arts and crafts is very labour intensive, and the Western prices reflect this.

Navy blue quilted *chuba* dresses, jumper-like traditional garments, appeal to me. Falling just below the knee, they are simple and warm enough to be worn casually at home. I decide to treat myself to one, but our cash supply is low and the store does not accept credit cards. It's agreed that the dress will be sent to Chonor House this evening; it's nextdoor to our guesthouse, and also part of the Norbulingka Institute.

We continue browsing through the beautifully appointed shop, admiring elegant quilted bedspreads, silk appliquéd hangings, cushion covers and Tibetan boxes and chests. Wandering into a side room, we discover that it's entirely dedicated to Buddha and other god and goddess statues. A knowledgeable employee explains the origin of many of them.

There's more to see here, but on discovering that the Institute will be open for a couple more hours, we decide to visit the nearby Handicapped Children's home. A Norbulingka employee takes us through the gate at the back of the property, pointing in the direction of the home. After a ten minute walk through the quiet back streets of the tiny Indian village, we're feeling lost. A woman passing by kindly indicates that we're almost there; just a left turn down a laneway opposite an enormous poolroom.

At the home, named Nyingtob Ling, meaning "Realm of Courage", by the Dalai Lama, the female employees are pleased to see us. It's quite dark inside, lights are turned off as a cost-saving measure; the floors of the building are made of cement. Nyingtob Ling's founder, Mrs. Nawang Lhamo, a genial woman, is also a member of parliament for the Government in Exile. Mrs. Lhamo describes the facility's function and the students who live and work here.

Built in 1999, this small building initially housed the schoolroom, dining room, craft room and sleeping areas; there were eight children, a teacher, cook and a helper. Phase II saw a second, larger construction on the far side of the property, for dormitories and a dining room; that attractive building is accessed by a long, cleanly-swept walkway. The children have finished their work and are back in their dormitories this afternoon, so we do not meet them.

Nyingtob Ling provides training and employment opportunities for physically and mentally handicapped Tibetan and Indian children; the government has no services of this nature. The children enter the program between the ages of twelve and eighteen, with families in financial difficulties having priority, Mrs. Llamo explains. Thirty to forty students live in residence at any time. Children return home on holidays to maintain the family bond and, in theory, to make it easier for them to reintegrate later, but in actuality, students tend to stay at Nyingtob Ling indefinitely, with some over thirty years of age.

We're shown student craft projects, giving the background of each person. Sales of the work assist the Centre. An original painting of the Dalai Lama's residence in Lhasa, Tibet catches my eye; the artist is a twenty-year-old man who, although not mentally handicapped, is unable to function in the world due to a high level of dependency. The Chinese bombed the Potala Palace two or three times, but it was built securely and was not destroyed. Tibetans believe it was somehow protected.

Once again short of cash and Mrs. Llamo suggests that we take the painting and pay the manager of Chonor House, a friend of hers. Insisting on a down payment, we give her some cash. I'm touched by the trusting nature of both the Tibetans and the Indian shopkeepers who also work on the honour system. Mrs. Llamo gives each of us a khata for safe journey.

Bridge to Norbulingka Seat of Happiness Temple
(Photo: Don Smith)

The Seat of Happiness Temple, the spiritual centre and focal point of the Institute, is next on the Norbulingka tour. The main hall of the small temple is dwarfed by its high ceiling. Over 1,000 images of the Buddha decorate the room and other paintings portray his 12 deeds, the 14 incarnations of the Dalai Lama and countless other saints, sages and great teachers. At the back rests a gilded copper statue of the Buddha, fashioned by Norbulingka's statue master, Penpa Dorje, the largest Buddha of its kind in exile. Sculpted clay images decorate the arch behind the golden statue, and in the middle of the temple an enormous, breathtakingly colourful hanging stretches from floor to ceiling. Hundreds of candles burn in perpetuity. Standing quietly in the empty sanctuary for a few moments, I feel the pull of the energy on a visceral level.

Back outside, the keeper of the temple motions for me to tie my shoelaces, concerned that I may fall. As I sit on his old wooden chair on the porch, I notice an empty whiskey bottle tucked between the wall and chair; this is not part of Tibetan Buddhist practice.

The tiny Losel Doll Museum is last on our circuit, interesting in its own way. The only Institute display that charges admission, the fee is 20 rupees for foreigners and 5 rupees for Tibetans. The museum holds the world's largest collection of Losel Dolls, handcrafted by exiled monks at Drepung Loseling Monastery in Dharamsala. Begun in 1983, the project is meant to preserve the tradition of Tibetan costumes and give the talented monks a platform for their artistic heritage. Their handiwork, illustrating many aspects of the religious culture and traditions, is showcased in the U.S., Europe and Asia.

The dolls are very unusual looking, constructed of wire and papier maché, with cast metal hands and heads of clay. Their faces are painted, hair is attached and they're dressed in tailored clothes of cotton, wool and silk, depicting native costumes of different time periods from the country's four regions. Miniature diorama displays show scenes of nomads, monks, warriors, Lhamo opera and ritual dance. The oddest dolls are the feverishly dancing monks in their colourful costumes.

It's past five o'clock now and we pause for a moment in the Visitors' Sitting Room, before our journey home. Small and thoughtfully designed, it's a very restful place; we gaze at the picture of His Holiness mounted on the wall and peruse beautiful magazines about Tibet. Traffic is light and the trip back quick, darkness falls making the curvy sections of the route less obvious. It's raining when we reach the town square, so we duck into nearby Jimmie's for a light supper, then walk home to our cozy apartment.

We're broadening the landscape now, after many weeks of soaking up the richness and intensity of this spiritual centre and establishing an interim life here. Tomorrow Dekyi is taking us to another town to see His Holiness the Karmapa, a high lama.

The Weather Goes South Again

Now into the third week of November, it pours all Saturday. A good day to settle back at home, listening to the even tempo of the rain that began during the night. Dekyi calls to suggest that the Karmapa teachings be rescheduled to mid week, saying the trip down to Sidhbari would be difficult in this weather.

Don and I have a conversation about the standard of living and the lifestyles in McLeod Ganj and the country as a whole. Our apartment with its creature comforts is luxurious compared with that of our Tibetan friends. Almost any topic is fair game in conversation group, and if a curious Tibetan asks what I've paid for an item, I give them an honest answer even if it's a bit embarrassing; for example, my warm pants, purchased on Temple Road, might be the equivalent of two months rent for them. We're not rich as is assumed; in discussions we explain that although incomes and standard of living are higher at home, it's costly to live in the West.

Dekyi has some knowledge of Western lifestyles after treating many English-speaking patients. She asks if we have a car at home, and whether there will be pensions on retirement. We explain the various public and private pension options in Canada.

Living in the Dharamsala area is not inexpensive, and the cost of living is going up all over India now. An article in the Tribune English language newspaper last Friday said: "Rising prices change eating habits; vegetable parts usually discarded become part of poor man's diet". The story goes on to say that pulses, (split peas and lentils), a dietary staple, are now a luxury. In a country where the average person makes only 100 rupees per day, (just over $2), the rising food costs are creating an untenable situation. The government has plans to increase subsidies for basic items such as pulses, sugar, vegetables, oils, rice and wheat flour. It also has programs meant to supply poor people with food staples, however a good part of this aid does not reach the people it is meant for.

Venturing outside in the early afternoon, we inquire about clean towels, having already turned in the dirty ones. "This evening, this evening", the manager tells us; it's then we realize there's only one set of towels!

Dodging the raindrops, we travel the few yards down the lane to Chonor House, an eleven room Tibetan-themed boutique hotel. Climbing the stone steps to the restaurant, we enjoy a late lunch of Tibetan soup. Rooms here are affordable for middle class Westerner travellers, but most people prefer to spend much less than their rate of 2000 rupees plus per night for a double room ($50).

Beautifully decorated, with dark wooden floors and enormous, hand-painted wall murals depicting scenes of Tibet, the restaurant offers high quality, reasonably priced, mostly Tibetan fare. This peaceful dining establishment becomes our default eatery, a place to come when the weather is bad or when we're simply too tired to walk another mile of hilly terrain.

While we're here this evening, I'm able to give the hotel manager the 2500 rupees owed to Mrs. Nawal, and he assures me he will pass the money along to her in a few days. A tall, elegant woman eventually locates my chuba dress, tucked behind the restaurant counter; it arrived after store closing yesterday. Chonor House is one-stop service.

Since it's still pouring rain, the helpful manager allows us to use the hotel's internet service saying, "Just keep track of the time". This gives us an excuse to view the upstairs of the hotel, with its fabulous sitting room replete with Tibetan art and gracious bedrooms. We peek into open doors; each room has a different scene, painted by a Tibetan artist.

Needing some exercise despite the rain, we walk the circuit to the square and back; up Temple Road, then back down Jogiwara, an enjoyable walk when dressed for cold and rain. Don's wearing a travel rain poncho belonging to me, it's made from dry cleaning plastic; his soaking legs don't bother him. I carry a broken down umbrella and we both wear hiking boots.

The town has a different feel in this weather. A surprising number of people roam the laneways and their brightly-coloured umbrellas form a pattern of coloured dots all the way up the street. Teashop owners have built fires in large tin drums, keeping themselves warm under the roof overhang.

In our favourite miniature grocery store, Don stocks up on bananas and curd, while I focus on important details like hand cream. The shopkeepers look very content behind the counter, and peering over I see that their satisfied expressions stem from the warm heat blowing from a small electric heater!

It's interesting to watch McLeod Ganj evolve into a slower, more indoor town as the weather changes and more people move on. So far we've had three days of heavy rainstorms and cool temperatures, making us wonder about leaving a week early, but everyone assures us it will not rain everyday yet. They're right, not another drop comes down before our departure at the beginning of December!

December and January, on the other hand, are known for their miserable weather; rain, sleet, sometimes even snow falls, with temperatures dropping below freezing at times. Summer months are scorching, until the monsoons arrive in late June.

Surprise Tea Party

On Sunday there's a bit of blue sky showing and the sun's trying to break through the fluffy white clouds. Rather than settling the dust, however, the rain seems to have stirred it up. It's too wet to sit outside, but the clean, soaking wet towels that have been delivered are draped over the railing to dry.

In the afternoon Khenrab, his brother and eldest son make an unexpected visit, bearing gifts of food; much like Dekyi did on our arrival. This time it's a bit different, raw chicken parts and a heap of lettuce, a problem as we have only a couple of burners to cook on and the refrigerator deteriorates by the week. Khenrab had plans to make Saturday night dinner for us yesterday, but could not make contact as our phone was out of credits. Later we boil the chicken and eat a portion of it, trying to fob the rest off on the monastery manager, forgetting he's vegetarian.

The visit is an agreeable one, Karpe seems to enjoy seeing us despite the language barrier. Afterwards we join a group of Tibetans and visitors at the Korean Restaurant, while a refugee tells his life story, translated into English by Kusang. It quickly becomes apparent that the oral autobiography is a more detailed version of a story I've worked on; it's about abuse of power, torture for the sake of power over another. The spoken word is more powerful, harder to listen to.

This political prisoner and his comrades were forced to kneel in an icy yard during the winter and stand or work scantily clothed (naked in the case of one woman) in the searing summer sun. Their keepers told them the exercise was to build character. The man tells us that the food was so terrible some prisoners threw it in the toilet; they were then forced to eat it, whereupon they became ill immediately.

An Indian newspaper prints an article about a trendy restaurant in Hong Kong called The Modern Toilet Restaurant, where patrons sit on toilet seats and eat meals with names reminiscent of bodily functions, presented to them in miniature elliptical toilets. The juxtaposition of the prisoner's story and this one sickens me beyond words.

Author Karen Connelly, writing about Burma, emphasizes that torture is about wielding absolute power over a society, and that the particular individual represents the whole community. "...in the world of interrogation, the acquisition of information is almost never the point."

After the talk we meet our Australian friends for dinner at a tiny Tibetan restaurant on Jogiwara Road; we recognize it as one of our breakfast stops in 2007.

Their Finnish friend, who is meant to join us, appears partway through the meal with a dog in tow. We say, "Come in, sit down, eat", but Meri refuses, saying that there's a problem. Two hours ago this kindly woman acquired a stray dog that was bitten by another dog, and is planning to take the animal back to Finland with her somehow.

Once home I reflect on the day. The story at the Korean Restaurant was extremely moving. The question of why some people must suffer makes me wonder about karma; my mind goes back two years, to a basement office in the Prince Polonia Hotel in Delhi, where Brij, a devout Hindu, told us that it was due to good karma that our daughter was born as our child in the West.

Are We So Different?

The town is quiet, the vanloads of weekend tourists from Amritsar have come and gone. On the street the usual Tibetan craftspeople and Indian shopkeepers occupy their shops and kiosks, a few tourists still roam around, and some new visitors have arrived, several groups of nuns. They come from all over the world, many from Europe; they're allowed to stay for six months.

It's hard not to notice that after spending years abroad, the appearance of expats often goes through changes. They adopt aspects of the local dress and begin to look weathered and travel worn. A few Westerners wear the traditional dreadlocks of *sadhu* and *sadhvi* ascetics (wandering holy men or women), along with Indian clothing.

There's a type of traveller who comes for extended periods of time, staying over the winter, perhaps settling here permanently, like the older dreadlocked woman who's a fixture in the town. An opportunity arises to finally meet this interesting woman. A retired Australian, she's been in India for ten years, and has spent the better part of that time here in McLeod

Ganj, she tells me, as we chat on the deck of the café. She is working on an epic tale about her adventures.

In our THC breakout group we're asked to pick our own topic, and the students like my suggestion that we discuss free time activities. The conversation is telling as it soon becomes evident that most of the group, monks included, have addictive habits. One person plays computer games all weekend, someone else feels he's addicted to music, for me it's television and sugar. Another man watches sports as much as possible on his private television. It's an interesting interlude, I didn't expect monks to have addictions, but it seems they're not all that different from anyone else in many ways.

There are nine new volunteers tonight, typical of the days following flyer distribution on the street. The bonfire go-round takes a long time with so many groups and it's cooler and damper by the minute. The warmth of the fire helps if you can get close to it.

After the reports an Israeli volunteer is honoured for her seven weeks of service at the Center, and receives a gift and a prayer scarf to send her safely on her journey.

We meet Brinchen for the first time tonight; he left Lhasa, Tibet at Christmas time in 1997, when fewer patrols are out. At one point the snow came up to their waists during the 27 day trip to Nepal, and Brinchen lost all the feeling in his legs. He felt sure this was the end for him.

They kept him in the hospital in Nepal for 15 months, as the nerves in his legs gradually healed and feeling slowly returned. Ultimately only three toes were lost to amputation, including one big toe; it doesn't affect his balance much, he says. The emotional damage may have been greater for Brinchen, though; throughout the long dark nights, as he tried to rest, hordes of dogs panted closeby, once biting him. Our hearing is a powerful sense, and he still has occasional nightmares about the wheezing pack of wild dogs.

The Oldest Tibetan Buddhist Reincarnation

Moving towards our final two weeks in McLeod Ganj our schedule intensifies, as we attempt to fit in everything that feels important. Next week we'll attend the Dalai Lama's Russian Buddhist-sponsored teachings. Buddhism is one of Russia's traditional religions, part of their heritage, and its main form is Tibetan.

Today is our visit to the Karmapa's monastery. It's now after eleven and Dekyi has requested that we come to Men-Tsee-Khang earlier than planned. Rushing to the square, we have picture ID taken in the travel agency/photo shop, then attempt to register for the teachings at the Security Office, where we're told that only Buddhist initiates can enrol. This is untrue however, and is clarified the next day.

With time saved, we make a quick stop at the internet café to research hotels. New Years is a busy time in Goa, so bookings must be made early. I make a reservation for the final two weeks of our trip at an appealing resort in quiet Benalim, South Goa by telephone. The hotel manager surprises me by recognizing my accent as Canadian; she's hosted guests from our country in the past and has a good ear for voices; (many people here mistake us for British, not American, the more common error).

Speedwalking back to the guesthouse, we find there's not enough time for lunch, so I gather tangerines and nuts for the trip. A waiting cab drives us down the hill where Dekyi is standing outside the gate of the complex; her brother-in-law, Karpe, is coming too, she says. Dekyi and I take turns sitting on the edge of the backseat in the tiny car. She's missed lunch also, due to a patient emergency, so I share my food with her.

Sidhbari, the location of Gyuto Monastery, is only six kilometres past Lower Dharamsala, but it takes 30 minutes to make the trip. The drive through several small Indian towns is interesting, but just before we reach our destination, a disturbing incident takes place when a puppy darts out on the road and the driver, unable to stop, runs over it. I gasp, putting hand over mouth. No one in the car says a word, no feelings or thoughts are shared about what just happened; perhaps it's a different cultural response or maybe everyone is too shocked to speak.

On the way I learn from Dekyi that His Holiness, the 17th Karmapa, is a very high lama, occupying the third highest post in Tibetan Buddhism, after the Dalai Lama and the Panchen Lama. The Karmapa lineage is 900 years old, making it the oldest and most revered in Tibetan Buddhism.

During our first visit to McLeod Ganj we noticed a poster indicating that Tibetan authorities are still searching for the bona fide Panchen Lama, kidnapped along with his entire family in 1995, at age six, immediately after the Dalai Lama formally recognized him. Chinese authorities say the Panchen Lama was placed in protective custody; another boy was then appointed in his place. Recently I read that this lama is the person responsible for choosing each new Dalai Lama, so his absence becomes more serious as the current Dalai Lama ages.

The present Karmapa was himself recognized by China as a young boy. Unable to complete his Buddhist studies there and afraid he would become a puppet of the Chinese government, at age 14 he decided that he must leave Tibet, so his advisors smuggled him out of the country. During the dangerous winter trip, a man fell off the narrow cliff path, but the Karmapa reached out and miraculously pulled him to safety.

After the party's arrival in India in 2000, His Holiness was initially hidden in a hotel in Bhagsu, dressed as a simple Tibetan youth in jeans and a T-shirt, then later installed by the Dalai Lama in his own monastery.

The Indian government, under whose protection the Karmapa lives, will not allow him to reside in his official domicile, Rumtek Monastery, in the tiny Indian state of Sikkim, nestled between Nepal and Bhutan and bordered by China. Since Gyuto is not part of his lineage, he is unable to conduct many important religious rituals at the Sidhbari Monastery.

Although he has travelled in the past, even visiting Vancouver, Canada, his requests for visas to visit Europe and America have been turned down of late, for no plausible reason, with three planned teachings abroad cancelled.

During our time in McLeod Ganj we hear that the Karmapa is being groomed by the Dalai Lama to take over as spiritual leader when he passes on, but a recent article in the British Guardian claims that he categorically disclaims any possibility of succeeding the Dalai Lama. His own job carries enough responsibility, he says.

Arriving early, we sit on the steps of the temple. The temperature is significantly higher at lower elevation; here it is still summer, yet I'm wearing my usual multi-layered ensemble. Fortunately, once my fleece jacket and wool vest are removed, I'm comfortable in the remaining two layers.

After a short wait, the registration office opens; it has a busy Western wicket and a vacant Tibetan one. Dekyi marches up to the quiet window, speaks to the staff, then comes back and asks: "Where are your passports?". We've left them behind, we tell her, and offer photocopies instead. Back to the window she goes, returning shortly, saying that they actually need to see our Indian visas, stamped inside the passports. When Dekyi goes into action she's a force to be reckoned with, and the woman is persuaded to let us in, with a caution not to tell anyone. We consider ourselves very fortunate.

Everyone takes their shoes off and stows their bags on a rack outside the temple, water and coats are allowed inside. Security staff pat each person down before they enter. The room is magnificent, larger and wider than the Dalai Lama's twin temples. A giant Buddha sits in a place of honour at the back, beautiful hangings are displayed throughout and a white, padded armchair awaits His Holiness at the front of the room.

A mixed group of foreigners and Tibetans sit cross-legged on the carpeted floor, monks to the side. Three men arrive, two middle aged and one older; they wear black cotton chuba dresses with high black boots and one has a long braid over one shoulder in traditional Tibetan style. Walking to the front, they sit down ahead of those already seated. From the audience comes a murmur and some snickering; it feels disrespectful. Two security guards gently move the men further back and others make room for them. Later, in response to my query, Dekyi tells me they are new arrivals from Tibet.

A middle-aged Indian man in a white suit enters the room, the same man who watched as everyone was frisked outside. This gentleman walks over to the white chair and pats it down, unexpected and somehow disturbing. Don suggests that security is high because the Chinese are unhappy with the Karmapa as he dishonoured them by fleeing Tibet after their formal recognition of him.

Five or ten minutes later a group of ten men enter the room; with them is a monk In simple robes, he is the 17th Karmapa. A young man of twenty-four, His Holiness has a still presence and emanates a powerful, focused energy, very different from the Dalai Lama's soft, loving one. Guards stand on either side of him and others station themselves throughout the temple. The translator sits on a cushion nearby.

His Holiness begins his audience by chanting for several moments in a deep voice. When he stops, a column of peace vibrates through my being. Triangular-shaped, the energy moves downward from a point a few inches above my heart chakra, stopping at the base of it.

Paramahansa Yogananda, the Indian guru whose mission it was to bring spiritual teachings to the West, said: "To receive Christ means to feel his consciousness in you", as happened when the Karmapa chanted.

Ward Holmes, a Western follower of the 16th Karmapa, wrote: "If you have an inflated ego, the power of Karmapa to reach the heart is difficult." I have felt in turns humble, open and child-like in the presence of both the Karmapa and the Dalai Lama.

The Karmapa speaks for about fifteen minutes in Tibetan; we sit watching and listening to the tone of his voice, soaking in his presence. Afterwards the translator reads a one-page English teaching to us: "There are two ways in life", His Holiness says, "the spiritual path and the lay one". He speaks from the spiritual perspective as that is the one known to him, the translation goes on to say. Surprisingly, little distinction is made between the two paths. I have always believed, perhaps due to early religious upbringing, or maybe past life experiences, that the holy path of prayer and discipline is somehow more valuable than the secular one.

Today's message focuses on the idea that there are those who wait for things to happen and those who take action when necessary. After the reading, the Karmapa speaks to us in perfect English for a few moments, saying, "I always talk about action; I'm the action man." This gets a laugh from the audience. An article in Contact Magazine later describes his environmental activism.

The audience over, those in attendance line up, each one holding a white khata prayer scarf, with monks at the head of the line. Dekyi has provided us with scarves. Each person hands their khata to a monk, he puts it around our neck before we approach His Holiness, bowing. The Karmapa hands each of us a red silk protection string, to be tied around the neck or wrist. The entire process takes only a few moments, even though there are well over a hundred present.

As the line moves slowly past His Holiness, I notice that after a time he appears distracted, no longer looking at the individuals approaching him, handing the string to us while communicating with a staff member. This feels disquieting, dishonouring of the sacred process, of us, and perhaps of his position. Despite his elevated consciousness, the Karmapa is still a very young man.

Afterwards everyone walks slowly out of the temple into the warm sunlight and through the grounds. This has been a powerful experience, we tell Dekyi, and thank her for the opportunity.

With her Hindi skills she secures a roomy minicab. The trip back is uneventful, and nearing Men-Tsee-Khang, Dekyi invites us in for tea. Sonam is waiting for us in the family apartment; not one child is in sight, an unusual occurrence. Tibetan milk tea and tasty Indian digestive cookies are served by the women; more flavourful than the Canadian variety, they also have added fibre.

Dekyi never seems to sit in one place for long when at home; while she busies herself in the tiny kitchen making Tibetan bread, we interact with her mother nonverbally. The flatter version of the bread served today resembles pita. No matter the shape and thickness, Tibetan bread is always very tasty with a little butter or peanut butter on it.

By now it's late afternoon and the younger son, aged eight, arrives home; shy and with little English, he takes his snack to another room. By five o'clock, when no one else has arrived, Dekyi suddenly remembers she must return to her office for a phone number she's promised to pass on to a young woman patient. Her working hours apparently segue into family time, typical of a physician's job anywhere in the world.

We walk as far as the Clinic with Dekyi, then head in the direction of a taxi stand, encountering a dogfight on the way. An aggressive young dog fights with another dog and I'm initially afraid to pass them on the street. Most dogs are fine, but some are unpredictable, and although the community is pro-active about the disease, a few have rabies.

Our short drive back to the apartment is thankfully unexciting as both Don and I are tired but quietly content.

Venturing Further

Morning Has Broken

The sky is hazy today, but outside it's warm and the sun peaks through the clouds. A flock of blackbirds circles outside the residence; at the corner of the deck a monk talks on his ubiquitous cell phone, so common we initially thought they were monastery issue, when in reality they're often gifts.

A man I've not seen before steps onto the shared balcony from a side room to shake out a piece of clothing. He's wearing an undershirt and grey waffle long johns, (so that's how they stay warm on those cool evenings!).

The untended cosmos in the flowerbox on the railing remind me of the ones growing at home; lack of water makes these spindly however. Down below rose bushes bloom, each with a small flower or two; after a couple of days' rain, several new blossoms appear.

A long string of miniature prayer flags spreads across the width of the guesthouse below. A Tibetan man shouts down from the corner of our balcony and a woman's voice answers back faintly from that direction. He notices me sitting outside my door and says "Sorry".

The 9 o'clock gong rings. The first bell is at 5:30 a.m. for morning prayers, then they ring at set times throughout the day, ending at 10 p.m. when the monks eat their curd before going to bed; it helps them sleep, we're told.

One of the nice things about this town is that it has accommodation suited to everyone's budget; our apartment is 500 rupees, (about $10 dollars), while our friend Jolene was able to get a tiny single room with shared bath and a view of the sunrise for only 200 rupees at the Green Hotel.

When Richard Gere comes to town he stays at Chonor House next door; he was here two years ago, a taxi driver told us. Gere is a personal friend of the Dalai Lama and sponsored the building of Temple Road, sometimes referred to as Richard Gere Road. I imagine what fun it would be to meet him on the laneway.

A later newspaper report notes Gere is attending the Dalai Lama's December 2009 teachings at Bodh Gaya, near Varanasi, the holy place where the Buddha attained enlightenment. Several of our friends have taken the eighteen hour train trip there from Delhi.

In my usual place outside Moonpeak Café, I pause in my editing and notice a tiny woman coming up the steps onto the deck of the café, offering her handmade bracelets to restaurant patrons. She turns her miniature prayer wheel as she moves, sending prayers outward. This gentle woman, named Kelo, speaks no English; she has kind eyes and her face shows deep character. The printed English note she carries states that she is trying to raise funds to return to Tibet.

Whenever I buy bracelets from Kelo she says prayers and blesses me, and my heart cracks open a little more. Over the next weeks we become friendly through our frequent encounters on Temple Road, and once we see her volunteering at the temple. Her age is hard to guess due to her nomad-weathered face, later she tells me in an interview that she is sixty-two years old.

Today's story is about a boy whose mother died when he was a baby; he was raised by his father and older siblings. Life was harsh for the family of subsistence farmers, and he left Tibet as a young man seeking the education he longed for. As I go deeper into the biography, I realize it belongs to a man who is prominent at the Hope Center; his heartfelt commitment to the Tibetan cause and to uplifting individual men and women is not only impressive but touching.

Lower Dharamsala, Another World

Laneway in Lower Dharamsala
(Photo: Don Smith)

After five busy weeks here and a couple of passes through Lower Dharamsala on our way up and down the mountain, we finally visit the bazaar. Although the distance is only a few kilometres, travelling from one town to the other means going through a culture change. The narrow streets of the bustling market town are crowded with shoppers during the day, but volunteers find the evenings long in this commercial centre.

Dharamsala, Hindi for "sanctuary", lies in the upper Kangra valley, fifteen hundred feet below McLeod Ganj. Rolling hills of tea plantations, rice and wheat fields cover the valley. From our deck we watch the lights of the bigger centre twinkling in the distance each evening.

With a population of 20,000 people, the municipality qualifies as a city by Indian standards. Mcleod Ganj, where the area's up to 5,000 Tibetan refugees live, is within the municipality; other member towns are Bhagsu, Forsyth Ganj, home to an old Anglican Church, Sidhpur and Sidbari.

What makes Dharamsala different from other markets is its melding of two cultures; Indian residents work and shop side by side with Tibetan monks and lay people, who are shopping for fresh, low priced vegetables and other goods in the lower town.

At the entrance to the city a colourful signpost has been erected; on it arrows display the names and elevations of each nearby town and point travellers in the right direction. Sari-clad women, and Indian men arm-in-arm in intense conversation, stroll along the street.

Kotwali bazaar begins at the edge of town and occupies several blocks. A large market, it offers tourists a snapshot of the character of the town. The main attractions are vegetable kiosks, arts and crafts, carpets, electronics, household goods and clothing.

Passing through cement automobile barriers, we escape the confusion of the bustling main thoroughfare and walk down a path to a quieter laneway. Cars, but not motorcycles, are barred from entering the street. Multicoloured saris hang from the awning of a nearby store; a bit farther along small shops display housewares and electronic products. Winding our way through back lanes, we return eventually to the far end of the busy road, but have no luck finding a lunch spot.

We do locate a used clothing market with heaps of sweaters and pants piled on outdoor tables, reminiscent of mobile second-hand bazaars in Mexican towns. Two women from the Hope Center are shopping here, Tsoeson, who co-ordinates the conversation groups and the THC Director's Korean fiancée, a frequent presence in the office until her Indian visa expires.

We decide to return to McLeod Ganj together. Tsoeson secures a taxi after only a short wait; at the last minute a monk we don't know asks to join the party, and we share a ride back up the hill.

Women in India

Travellers, particularly females, must be vigilant about their physical safety in this town and in India as a whole. Pedestrians share the road with cars, trucks, buses and motorcycles, sidewalks, when they exist, are unnavigable in spots, (McLeod Ganj has no sidewalks).

Here motorcycles glide down the lanes with their engines turned off to save energy; perhaps the drivers enjoy startling people too. I've heard tales of riders harassing women as they drive by. Walking the streets is a greater challenge during peak tourist season than now. In this country I have become so habituated to jumping out of the way when vehicles pass by I find myself doing the same thing on the peaceful streets of Gibsons after returning home!

Women from both cultures dress modestly; it's a show of respect for visitors, particularly women, to do the same, also safer. Young Tibetan females often wear jeans and t-shirts, while more traditional ones, like Dekyi, wear simple cotton chuba dresses with blouses or sweaters underneath; multicoloured aprons over the dress signifies that a woman is married.

In smaller, more conservative centres, Indian women often wear saris, while city women dress in *salwar kameez suits* usually (pants with long overshirts) or Western clothing, in the case of younger women.

The great cultural and religious-based differences in this society often mean that the intentions of women travelling alone, making eye contact, and possibly revealing skin are misinterpreted. A blog post by Jeff, an American man, speaks volumes about the skewed attitude of certain male citizens. "My female friends have learned to be discreet, dress humbly and still expect to be harassed."

Indian men usually shake hands with Don only, in deference to the prohibition against touching non-family members; they always interact verbally with me in a courteous manner.

McLeod Ganj feels welcoming during the daytime, as I walk the main streets and follow the convoluted path to the Hope Center alone, concerned only about stray dogs. "It's a safe place for foreigners", Alma relates in our channelling session later. "There's a lot of light there, quite a bit of this due to the Dalai Lama's presence". There are not as many robbers and bad people in this town as in other places, her guides say.

Even so, bad things happen here from time to time. Being out alone after dark, particularly on side streets can be risky. Sophie, a young Australian acquaintance recalls her crash course in "Eve teasing", as it's called, when she slipped out to phone her mother one evening and was followed and taunted by young Indian males. She was close to home and was not assaulted, but it was an alarming experience. Young Indian women are harassed also, but less frequently.

The worst case scenario, rare, but shocking, is rape and murder. Louise Lefebvre describes noticing a terrible smell while walking between McLeod Ganj and Bhagsu, and later hearing that the decomposing body of a Western woman was found in a tree in that very area.

There is no such thing as perfect peace on earth. Karen Connelly words this well when she writes; "There is no pure place, no pure light".

I have been harbouring the idea that I am relatively protected from being bothered in this country, as an older woman, but in truth Don's frequent presence is a protective shield as we travel more around the community.

Friends, a group of three women and one man, were hiking on a remote trail in Northern India. One woman was repeatedly touched as she tagged along behind the others; the harassment stopped only when the single male in the party loudly and firmly told the man to stop.

Another friend speaks of a day trip to the beach from Amma's ashram in South India; the group was mixed gender, made up of Indians and visitors. Although the women dressed in a respectful manner, a group of Indian males surrounded them and there were tense moments before the Western men in the party convinced them to move along.

Indian males are often blamed for violence against women in this town, but it's a false generalization. Pema tells me that the Tibetan owner of a teashop by the main temple tried to rape a young woman from his country the previous day; fortunately the attack was interrupted. In a vigilante justice way, an announcement written in Tibetan is posted on the wall, with the man's name; this man has now been publicly shamed by his community for his actions.

Is She or Isn't She?

It's mid November now, and a warm day today. After editing at Moonpeak Café while Don tutors at home, I encounter a small black cow coming directly towards me as I climb the steep pathway. Veering to the other side of the lane, I'm careful not to step on the cow dung. Halfway up the hill, Don appears beside the walkway to Chonor House. Since the weather is suitable for eating outside, we decide to have lunch there.

The garden is an oasis of tranquility in the middle of the dusty town, esthetically appealing, with trees, bamboo and potted flowering plants placed on the black flagstone patio high above the street. From one end of the deck there's a view of our lane, and over the rooftops we see a monkey jumping around on the wall of the Dalai Lama's complex.

While lunch is being prepared a party of six seats themselves at a nearby table; two midlife American women, a Tibetan couple and older man, and a boy about ten years old, wearing a school uniform. One of the women looks a lot like Goldie Hawn.

Don says she looks too young, but the woman has blond hair, a similar build, and her wide grin resembles Goldie's famous smile. It's a challenge not to stare, but I rise to the occasion, glancing over at the other table only periodically. Maybe most of us have stars in our eyes; I find it difficult not to go up to her, but don't want to embarrass myself.

Once I've calmed down and the Tibetan soup, coffee and shortbread have been consumed, we sit awhile and soak in the peaceful warmth of the deck, becoming almost somnolent after a time.

May I Have Your Hat?

Ellen beside prayer wheels at Dalai Lama temple
(Photo: Don Smith)

It's damp this morning, I give in and move inside after only a brief interlude outside the cafe. Time here is drawing to an end, and deep within me there's a sadness.

While on a final visit to the main temple, we meet a family of Indian tourists touring the grounds. One teenage daughter accompanies them, perhaps in keeping with the current middleclass, small family trend. The woman requests a picture with us and we oblige. After the photo shoot she asks to have her picture taken wearing my Kashmiri hat, so I pass it over. She looks so good in it I suggest to her husband that he buy her one on Temple Road. These brief, simple encounters are golden moments to travellers.

Taking a cab down to Men-Tsee-Kang, we inexplicably become lost in the grounds. As we wander around we run into Khenrab, climbing the stairs from the staff residence. He guides us towards the clinic, and we recognize the short flight of stairs leading to it.

Inside it's quite busy, and there's a wait before Dr. Dekyi calls my name. She is in her office, bundled in a large white wool jacket with a heavy red sweater underneath. The weather is quite comfortable for us, but the body's response to temperature depends on the climate we're accustomed to.

As Dekyi patiently studies the pulses on my wrists, her colleague comes in for a brief consult; at other times, patients have dropped by. My digestion is a bit better, she tells me, but my kidney energy is lower; they've lost some of their warmth due to the cooler, damper weather.

She wonders if I'd like some "elixir of life", a powdered tea taken daily, and giggles when I ask if it will turn me back into a young woman. The tea seems like a good idea in the moment, but I carry it home unopened, hesitating to introduce yet another medicine into my body.

Don's kidney energy is also low and Dekyi prescribes kidney pills and other medicines for both of us, one week's worth, so she can reassess before we leave.

THC Men Playing Pingpong (Photo: Don Smith)

From the clinic we go directly to the Hope Center, where Don plays ping pong with the men on their homemade table, while I work on the computer. The bonfire activity tonight is dancing; it was Kusang's idea and I encourage him. Surprisingly, younger Tibetans can't or don't dance, he tells me. My response is: "Well, we'd better teach them".

Volunteers are asked to demonstrate techniques, but many are reticent. After a time we nudge most into action to show the locals some dance steps. Pema and Dolma are up and moving, but only dance as long as I'm right beside them, demonstrating. The women are just humouring me, and as soon as possible, they stop, one even hides behind a post! A great benefit of aging is not caring so much what you look like or what people might think of you. I sense that the young Tibetans are intrigued by my dancing.

The Tibetan men are a sight to behold; once started they really get into it, dancing around the fire in chain formation. Don, who does not view himself as much of a dancer, surprises me by joining in.

Cut off from McLeod Ganj

As we begin our preparations for departure in two weeks, I'm beginning to consciously disconnect from my surroundings, to minimize the wrench of leaving. Part of me is ready; after hearing so many sad stories one can begin to feel helpless, hopeless, maybe even angry at the injustice of it all. However, my spirit would like to remain forever in this place where I have attuned to myself in a deeper way, and made lifelong friends.

Of my three students, only Dechen arrives for tutoring this morning, saying she feels better now after seeing the doctor. They're doing well with their studies, continuing to attend Intermediate English classes. Choden, the oldest, is less shy than previously, Dechen assertive and thirsty for knowledge, while gentle Nima demonstrates focus in his work, as do most monks.

Dechen's ubiquitous cell phone rings and it's Choden asking to join us; she arrives at the apartment and we continue our work. Our progress is slower now, as Choden had no English on arrival a year ago. Today, over my objections, she sweeps the dusty living room floor. Conscious of potential hierarchal differences, at first I don't feel comfortable about this, but later consider that it's a way for her to give back for the lessons. A slatternly housekeeper, I haven't quite got the hang of daily sweeping in dusty India, but I'm working on it.

After my students depart Don and I leave the apartment to roam the neighbourhood. I've skipped breakfast, so we go to the upstairs cafe run by the Children's School. It's warm enough to enjoy the outside deck with a coat on and pass the time people-watching.

Several snow monkeys are playing in the trees. A telephone employee climbs a pole and attempts a repair on the hundreds of spliced wires drooping down. (An electrician friend from home was amazed at the wiring in India; he tells a story of wires that appeared to be holding up a wall, rather than the other way around!)

After lunch we investigate agencies on Bhagsu Road in preparation for research I'm planning on female refugees. Soaking in the town's atmosphere and locating agencies was exactly the right activity for me today, it helped dissipate the sense of separation.

It feels good to serve, everyone says so, including His Holiness the Dalai Lama.

When one helps others, dopamine is released, Dacher Keltner, author of *Born to be Good* writes. We are moved to awe, and our "helping part" becomes more prominent, while our competitive side is dampened, the author goes on to say.

Volunteers working abroad experience many stages; each person's reaction is personal, but there are commonalities. The progression I have noticed is spiritual opening; enthusiasm; a sense of stable routine; then overwhelm/compassion fatigue and finally, separation.

Debbie Leventhal, who studied volunteers working with street youth in Israel, identified formal stages similar to what I've experienced. Individuals become part of the greater purpose by on-the-job immersion. Through "reality shock", as Levanthal terms it, volunteers make sense of their experience. Shock was part of my experience; coming particularly in the form of the refugee stories edited.

After a time, the initial intensity of being in McLeod Ganj, reconnecting with Dekyi, with whom I share a rich past, meeting her family, developing friendships and working with students, began to fade. Events continued to impact me on a daily basis, but I no longer had the sense that they were coming at me headlong. Some internal mechanism activated and I began to adjust to my surroundings and to incorporate the vibration of the town into my own energy system.

When visitors stay a while, immersing themselves in the culture and activities, they gradually segue into an enhanced level of engagement. After a time, a deeply satisfying contentment developed in our routine of volunteering, editing and watching the weekend visitors arrive from Amritsar. Our doctor friends, busy with their daily cycle of work and family, make time for us when they can; once we're safely settled in they no longer call daily or turn up unexpectedly with bags of food.

A time comes when many visitors sense they're nearing the end of their sojourn. It's not just the arrival of winter, with its cold and dampness that leads us to feel this way, although that is a consideration.

I've reached the overwhelm stage in my volunteering experience, that feeling of never being able to do enough. Others have mentioned that they feel the same; it's a common reaction when there is a great need, as with this population. Underneath our life here, the work done and the precious connections made, runs a subtext; the knowledge that our lives are very different and that we cannot fully comprehend the Tibetan culture or life experiences.

Several rituals help complete the circle for us: a leave taking tradition at our last THC group; dinner with Dekyi's family, and lunch cooked in our honour by Rinzen from South India.

Don't let the same dog bite you twice*

After tutoring I meet Jolene, from the U.S, at Moonpeak Café; our Australian friends are seated at the next table and greetings are exchanged. The group is not leaving today for Jaisalmer as planned; Deb was bitten by a dog at the Tibetan Children's School yesterday. Ironically, we had a lengthy discussion about rabies with her just two days ago.

Although the dog had its shots, there's still risk involved. Deb received rabies immunization back home, but needs three additional inoculations now. The hospital 50 kilometres away has the necessary medicine, so it's not necessary to travel down to Delhi to receive it.

The staff at the school were upset about Deb's injury; later a veterinarian she met on the street expressed concern that a dog with that temperament would be allowed around young children. The very day Deb was bitten, another dog peed on her, *and* she lost her camera. She seems in remarkably good spirits despite all of this!

---

*   *Chuck Berry*

Local officials provide free neutering and rabies clinics for dogs annually; still what happened to Deb is unnerving. In the evening the streets farther from the square are relatively deserted, and when the humans go home, the dogs begin to gather in their night packs. The eerie atmosphere created when dogs outnumber people on the street makes being out after 10 o'clock an experience not to be looked forward to.

Afterwards Jolene and I talk for a long time about our philosophy of life and about memorable dreams during our travels. With our common interests of travelling and writing, the age difference of thirty years doesn't seem to matter much. Connections are made and released daily here in McLeod Ganj

We later walk to the Tibetan Settlement Office on Bhagsu Road to do some research, and meet the man in charge of The Home Office for the entire area. Curious to understand what the Government in Exile does for its people, I inquire about this.

He shares an extensive flowchart of agencies, along with a brief explanation. The Home Office is responsible for all rehabilitation efforts for Tibetan exiles, generating employment and promoting self-reliance among the populace. The organization monitors twenty-one agricultural settlements, eight agro-industries and four carpet-weaving co-operatives in this country, and twenty settlements and handicraft societies in Nepal and Bhutan.

Conversation Group Sans Tibetans

The weather is holding and it's warm and sunny outside; we leave for THC around four o'clock. A new volunteer, a young professional filmmaker from England, walked into the Center last week, offering to make a video. In only a few days, he's done an excellent job of Kusang's documentary targeting young Tibetans, showing how one person can make a difference. The project is exciting and the video will be added to THC's website and Facebook page, to get the word out to potential donors and volunteers.

As I work the video is being shown in the courtyard; the audio can be heard through the window and even without the visuals the impact is powerful. We plan to put excerpts on my website to promote the refugee story project back in Canada. Several months later, when I ask Kusang for the filmmaker's contact information, I am shocked to hear that he died in Bangalore shortly after leaving McLeod Ganj.

Don's conversation group tonight has no Tibetan members in it, a peculiar situation. Three attendees are from a tiny Russian state near Mongolia; the fourth is from Mongolia itself, now a separate country. Two of the Russians, a mother and son duo, have just arrived in town to study English and Buddhism. The mother shares that she brought her 23-year-old son to India to get him away from his entrenched habits of no exercise, overeating and playing video games all day.

Today is the birthday of a group member; singing and laughter float in through the office window as I work on an engrossing story that chronicles the escape of a young man, an old guide, two nuns and an 11-year-old girl from Tibet. Their ordeal impacts me deeply; I visualize them climbing the Himalayas, the nuns so old they must be pulled to the top of each peak, while the young girl had to be carried.

The idea of parents placing their small children in the hands of strangers, trusting that they'll have safe passage on the dangerous journey, disturbs me. In their quest for a better future for their loved ones, desperate people will do anything they possibly can, frequently splitting families up for many years. Sometimes relatives are never reunified, permanently separated by geographic divides.

After the bonfire we meet our friends at Shangri-La Restaurant. Deb and Jolene are already deep in conversation; Hero and Keira join us within minutes, Hero wearing a wonderful, custom-made grey wool vest with wine-coloured satin lining. The six of us enjoy a lively dinner, with plenty of good food and lots of laughter. It's a wonderful gift, coming together like this, in short, powerful bursts of connection. These friendships are like time out of time. At the end of the meal, we reluctantly say goodbye to our Australian friends again, we know it's truly adieu now, as they leave for Jaisalmer tomorrow morning on a camel trek. We hope to reconnect in Canada.

Cleanup at the Old Folks Home

Jampaling Elders Home Doorway
(Photo: Don Smith)

It's Saturday, November 21 and the Hope Center's annual cleanup at the Seniors' home. I enjoy morning coffee on the deck of the café at the bottom of the lane; the weather is cool but nice, it's good to feel like part of the bustling community. The temple gate is congested with cabs dropping people off, and then turning around in the narrow road to wait for their next fare.

I attempt to reach Dekyi to see when we can have a "girls' day out"; her phone's turned off, she must be at work. This idea appears to strike

Dekyi as humorous; she seems intrigued though. In her group oriented community, lives revolve around family, work and temple. Married women don't take time by themselves or to be with friends.

Climbing back up the hill, I notice a crew of men and women have begun the labour intensive task of building a retaining wall near Kirti Monastery's front door, where the lane becomes a walking path. Cargo donkeys carry loads of gravel and dirt to the construction site. It takes a couple of weeks to complete the four foot wall using this painstaking building technique.

By mid-morning 70 volunteers have turned out at the Center, a record number. The group walks together down the main road, then along a pleasant, treed pathway carved into the side of a hill, to the Jampaling Elders' Home, located behind the Dalai Lama's Temple. There are few people on the path, but we do encounter several cows. One will not budge, and almost knocks a woman down the steep hill. Finally somebody encourages Bessie along with a stick. As we approach the home, we see myriad strings of Tibetan flags blowing in the breeze.

Jampaling houses 150 elders, and consists of several substantial looking brick buildings, including dormitories, a kitchen and a garage for the vans used on temple outings. A mixture of lay people and retired monks and nuns live here.

My initial reaction on viewing the inside is one of shock; I am measuring it through my personal filter and it does not match up to the comfort level expected for old folks. The corridors of the dormitory are narrow and dark, rough and cold from both a physical and esthetic perspective. My mother's care homes, although simple, were palatial in comparison.

Floors and walls are made of cement; each room has two narrow beds piled with heaps of soiled-looking bedding and a couple of small shelves for personal items. Every surface is covered with built up dust.

In room twelve, our assigned room, an old gentleman sits on his bed; a staff member gently convinces him it's necessary to leave, so the room can be cleaned. Reluctantly shuffling out, he indicates that we should not touch his things, but we must, because lying on the shelf is a bag full of food crumbs and garbage, a red flag for rodents.

Standing at the kitchen door, I request a plastic bag to separate good food from garbage, but there are none. Plastic sacks are banned in India and storekeepers fashion bags from stapled newspapers. A staff member tells me to throw all the food out except the butter, the one costly but perishable item. The butter is quite the conversation piece as I roam around looking for a way to contain it.

Back in the room, three volunteers have stripped the place, removing all the bedding and mattresses. Scarves wrapped tightly around heads and faces, they're dusting the walls and ceiling with brooms and rags. Dust floats everywhere; clearly it has not been thoroughly cleaned for some time. Staying in the room is not an option without a covering, so I go outside to find another task.

Inside Hallway, Jampaling Elders Home
(Photo: Don Smith)

A group of monks is sweeping the walkways; locating a large grass broom, I team up with them. We work in the courtyard for what seems like a long time. In the washroom area, I'm pleased to discover modern toilets, a necessity not a luxury for the old ones. Finally I join the volunteers washing the filthy bedroom windows with cold water and no soap; they look a bit better afterwards. My work has made a small contribution, though I chastise myself for not cleaning the bedrooms, (still taking myself wherever I go...).

One of Don's jobs is picking up litter; he tells me later that after it was collected, everything was thrown down the hill; ironic, since garbage on the streets and in canyons is a major problem, and once a year a mammoth removal campaign takes place, sponsored by several NGOs.

Despite the physical conditions of the home, the staff are obviously caring and compassionate. The facility is not overcrowded, a luxury in this country. Still, seeing these beautiful Tibetan elders living so roughly disturbs my sensibilities.

The noon dinner gong rings and residents form a line outside the large kitchen, each with their plastic bowl, plate and cutlery. Many pass me by as I sweep the stairs, on their way to their nourishing meal of hot soup and curd. Each bows in a traditional manner as they pass; I return the greeting, the encounters give me a warm feeling.

Since there's no dining room, the residents take their meal back to their room. Afterwards I notice a man rinsing his dishes under a cold water tap in the courtyard, without soap. Sanitation is a special concern for the aging population, who may have weakened immune systems.

Through one of the friendly English speaking staff, I'm able to briefly interview one of the men. This gentleman is 75 years old and has been living at Jampaling for five years; he's very happy here, he tells me, because he's near the Dalai Lama, the staff treats him well and he has friends in the home.

The age range of the residents is mid-60s to 94, with a 30-year-old blind man the exception, as there is no specific facility available for him.

The cleanup over, we're served Tibetan milk tea, cookies and potato chips, and relax in the sun with some of the residents. Two women dance together for a few moments, then one continues alone, moving gracefully and unselfconsciously in a traditional Tibetan number. It's lovely to watch her and we all clap after each song. When I try taking her picture, as some other volunteers have done, I'm rebuffed by a middle-aged man, possibly the facility manager. No explanation is given for this action.

Leaving the elders' home, we travel uphill along a circular route to one side of the temple, in a clockwise direction, as is the Buddhist and Hindu custom. A group of Indian visitors pass us walking in the opposite direction. On the road we encounter a Tibetan woman a few years older than us. To say that this woman is a character would be an understatement; teasing us in that playful, childlike way characteristic of her culture, she first bumps into Don, then pretends to jog past us, since I've slowed to a crawl on the uphill climb. A rest would be nice about now, but if she can do it I can too!

A bit farther along she's perched on a bench taking a well-earned break; we sit down and begin a conversation. The woman is shorter than my five feet, two inches and a little bent over; only one tooth is visible on the bottom. Her English is fluent enough to engage us in a lively discourse, and it transpires that she perambulates the temple daily, both for exercise and spiritual upliftment.

Our hilarious companion goes to great lengths to teach me how to pronounce her name, demonstrating the correct way to place the tongue, but I just can't get it. Bidding us goodbye at the top of the hill, our new friend stops to buy pulses and rice from a street vendor.

The busy day continues as we head up Temple Road to the travel agency, where the younger of the two Indian brothers is on duty. Ravi is also a reporter for a local paper. He works diligently to secure plane tickets for our trip from Goa to Delhi in mid January, for the return flight to Canada; manning two cell phones, a land line and using the internet, he locates seats on a direct flight for the day requested.

This process takes an hour, but time passes quickly as we visit with the people who pass through the miniature office. A young British woman inquires about a guided hike on the same popular trail Don trekked. Then a student from Bombay comes in, saying he flew here on the spur of the moment to celebrate his twentieth birthday in the snow in Manali, 250 kilometres away. His cell phone went missing enroute, and he's unable to invite his friends to the party. The trip was not mentioned to his father, who holds the purse strings, he tells us. A student in mass media, his goal is to direct indie films; he's an excellent example of the juxtaposition of the rich and poor classes in India.

Winding Down

I'm beginning to savour each moment, every encounter, collecting memories to cherish at a later date. Don is looking forward to getting on the road again. I too am looking ahead towards the next step, yet at the same time am not anxious to leave the community that has embraced us. The next phase of the trip feels like a holiday within a holiday to both of us.

Sunday rolls around and the morning begins with oatmeal and fruit in the apartment. Our deck is hot today, quite pleasant. Teenage monks are playing badminton on their courtyard below us. We've not tired of absorbing and delighting in the atmosphere on the grounds of Kirti Monastery.

Later at Moonpeak we drink an Americano with Denise, from Canada, and one of her students, then step into the internet café next door. All is well at home; Mom is doing fine, her weekly visitor writes. I send a long, newsy e-mail to Bronwen while Don researches hotels for the next chapter of our trip.

Little Monk Playing on Our Lane (Photo: Don Smith)

Back on the lane, a diminutive monk is playing with a battery-operated car. We ask if we can take his picture but he does not understand. His adult companion speaks to him in Tibetan and points to the car and the boy accommodates us, holding his toy up. It's reassuring to see that these orphans or children of poor parents enjoy themselves despite living a monastery life. The monks appear to take excellent care of their younger charges, the men guide the youth and the teens treat the boys like little brothers.

On the Chonor House deck it feels almost like the seasons are beginning to reverse, moving away from the rain of earlier November back to the sunny warmth of early fall. We enjoy our soup and Tibetan bread, followed by chocolate coffee and a shared shortbread. Some staff make excellent chocolate coffee, while others dish out vile tasting stuff that cannot be properly termed either coffee or chocolate.

Today I feel an urgency to discover more about NGO agencies that serve Tibetan women, so I plan a quick reconnaissance of the town. I walk to the Tibetan Women's Association, (TWA), on the third floor of an old building on Bhagsu Road. A large NGO, it's one of a select few recognized by the Tibetan Government in Exile.

At TWA I meet with the Board Secretary, Tsering. An attractive, well spoken woman around forty, Tsering tells me their service helps women deal with the issues that arise when adjusting to a new culture. Having little idea what to expect on arrival, the grief of leaving their family and old life is massive and many are traumatized from their escape. To make a challenging situation worse, there is very little work available for refugees in McLeod Ganj.

With the help of volunteer counsellors, a new program has been designed to assist women in violent relationships. It's offered on a one-to-one basis as the stigma against revealing private concerns is great in Tibetan culture. Tsering goes on to explain how she has been able to assist one woman and her baby, neglected due to the mother's depression; they have joined a family member in South India.

My visit to TWA is a positive experience; I am pleased to have found this dedicated and skilled woman to talk to and we promise to keep in touch.

After meeting those new, service minded people and soaking up the energy of McLeod Ganj, I'm keen to keep the momentum going. Next, onto the Rogpa Charity and the Reception Centre for new arrivals, both near the Jogiwara and Temple Road junction.

Something about Rogpa intrigues me. The organization's base is a café, where I once purchased a jacket for the beggar on our lane. The mostly female staff of volunteers make the operation run smoothly, accomplishing so much in a tiny space. Rogpa's café and used clothing store raise money for the baby day care that is free for Tibetan mothers who sell their products on the street.

The manager, a young woman from Rishikesh, about 500 kilometres to the southeast, is in the store today. Her family, though Tibetan, were all born in that part of India and speak only a little of the mother tongue. A strong, articulate feminist with well-formed views on women's empowerment, she has been managing the NGO for eight months as the only paid staff member.

At the nearby Tibetan Reception Centre I'm directed upstairs. The director is away, so I'm sent to a woman referred to by the honorific "Madam", whose name I don't catch as it's an unfamiliar one. She gives me a brochure about the Reception Centre, but cannot answer any questions without a letter of authorization from the Central Office, a confidentiality issue. I realize the government must be cautious, not wanting to reveal how many are arriving from Tibet at any one time. The woman does tell me that the Centre is quite full.

The Dharamsala Centre opened in 1990 in response to high demand. After crossing into Nepal, most refugees make their way by bus to Upper Dharamsala via Delhi. At times dozens of refugees arrive each day, and are given medical care, food and lodging. After a few weeks they are sent on to a settlement housing people from their area of Tibet, often in South India, where the largest ones are located. Some remain in McLeod Ganj. The Centre also helps new refugees enroll in school, search for employment, join monasteries or obtain training and financial assistance to start small businesses.

As I pass through the downstairs entry hall I notice a large, mixed gender dormitory with rows of cots. People of all ages mill around inside the sleeping room and on the front porch of the building. The atmosphere feels upbeat. I go on my way, not wanting to intrude. This is one of the places where I'd like to tutor in the future; there's always a need here since there is no official teaching program.

It's been a packed morning, yet I don't wish to return to the apartment, wanting to stretch out my adventure. At Moonpeak, as I pause for carrot ginger soup and a visit with Denise, my craftswoman friend, Kelo comes down the street. The café is quiet at the moment, so I ask a staff member if he will translate for us if Kelo is willing, and they both readily agree. We talk for about five minutes; I don't want to take up too much of their time.

Kelo is two years older than me and has been in McLeod Ganj for three or four years, after escaping from Tibet with her husband and four children. Their heartfelt desire was to see His Holiness, the Dalai Lama, however, earning a decent living here has not been possible. During our conversation I learn that Kelo's plan to return to her country has been abandoned, as the trip back is costly and dangerous. Obtaining an official passport is difficult and Kelo believes she could be imprisoned on her return.

Thanking both of them for the interview, I give her 200 rupees and select a red bracelet for Jolene, to match her new red coat, purchased as a hedge against the creeping cold. My offer of tea and food is refused; they don't like the Western food served at Moonpeak, the waiter tells me.

Dinner at Passang's

Sunday evening we're invited to the home of a student. We meet her husband, a tall, attractive man named Chogyal in the square at five o'clock; Passang has described us well and we have no trouble connecting. We walk together up a crumbling roadway to their home in an apartment building on a side street.

The large bedsit is cozy, with a three-quarter bed at one end of the living area, doubling as seating, and a coffee table, couch and chairs on the sidewall. At the far end, curtained off from the main room, is the kitchen, beside that the bathroom; both with hot and cold running water.

Our hosts' friend joins us for dinner, an interesting, well-informed Indian man from Sidhpur, the lawyer for the Hope Center. As we relax before dinner, he talks about Indian culture and the growing middle class.

Chogyal makes momos and Passang has cooked up a storm; we're also served tomato egg drop soup, a salad of tomatoes and spicy bok choy, flavourful and deceptively mild tasting, but soon lip burning.

Bright and enterprising, Chogyal and Passang publish a fledgling sponsored political magazine, and Chogyal's skills and political interests have resulted in work that helps raise awareness about Tibet's political situation.

We hope the couple are able to endure the considerable pressures of life as refugees in exile. When it's time to leave, we walk together down to the square, the Indian guest to retrieve his car and Chogyal and Passang to get some exercise.

Russian Sponsored Teachings

For these, our second round of teachings on this visit, we would like to be closer to the Dalai Lama, seated on his throne inside the temple, but I'm unable to obtain my security pass until the first afternoon. Don and Jolene attended the first morning session at the temple, receiving gift bags imprinted with round Russian Buddhist logos from the sponsors; inside were prayer beads, a notebook and books, mostly in Russian. His Holiness spoke English at that session only.

The scene on the temple grounds does not have the intense impact as in October, but the power and significance of the event is still apparent. In those first days here I was in a very open, impressionable state, more consciously awake in each moment.

This afternoon we're seated in the walkway where the Dalai Lama enters and leaves; security staff allow us to sit here with the promise to move when instructed to do so. The teachings are short and not memorable; perhaps they're too technical for me.

When the signal is given we arise and move around behind the temple, sitting in an area of Tibetans and Russian devotees. When His Holiness comes out everyone stands up. Being short, I'm trying to position myself to see him, when a group of tall young Tibetan males rush to the front of the crowd, shoving everyone aside in their urgency to be close to His Holiness - not a pretty sight.

The morning energy in the temple is mellow, making the beginning of the day a nice time to attend the Dalai Lama's teachings. On the second day Don and I sit cross-legged in the courtyard, soaking in the placid energy, as monks of all ages pass through the crowd, giving out rounds of Tibetan bread from large stainless steel pails and pouring milk tea. No one goes hungry here. Another monk walks around giving money to elders, poor people and monks. The crisp new bills appear to be 100 rupee notes, worth about $1.85 Canadian.

Tibetan Security and Himachal Pradesh State Police are out in full force on the upper temple deck. Most obvious are the Indian police; uniformed officers hold rifles while plainclothes ones carry submachine guns. Tibetan plainclothes security carry no obvious weapons. Each officer scans the crowd constantly with his watchful cop's eyes, searching for signs that something is amiss.

Press photographers from all over the world are in attendance. A variety of folks make up the crowd, from bent and wrinkled Tibetan Buddhists, to monks from Korea, Russia and Tibet, Western devotees and lay people from many countries. Monkeys join in the celebration, walking around on the high ledges.

The peaceful spirit of the audience and the presence of His Holiness combine to create a moving experience. Simply being in the healing presence of the Dalai Lama is powerful. After being exposed to basic concepts of Tibetan Buddhism by Changling Rinpoche from Shechen Monastery, Nepal, in our home community, then by the Dalai Lama, we begin to absorb some ideas.

The following is my recollection of parts of this morning's address. (It's difficult to concentrate fully for long periods of time, as much of the material is complex and unfamiliar.)

A main goal of Buddhism is to become empty and without ego. To understand emptiness, we must have *bodhicitta*, defined simply by His Holiness as; "The desire to help others and to become self-realized. When the veil of illusions and delusions lifts, the obstacles to emptiness go", he goes on to say.

After many years of what I previously referred to as "excavating old issues", I am slowly developing the ability to step back and look at the bigger picture, to gain inklings…tiny glimpses that this world and this lifetime we're living, taken so seriously by most of us, are illusion. They are not the essence of who and what we truly are.

"We must understand our own suffering before that of others", the Dalai Lama says. "This does not mean focusing on ourselves always, but we must look after ourselves and be kind to ourselves, then we'll be able to help another". Interestingly, we were taught in group therapy many years ago to care for ourselves at a deep level, then to serve family and community from that place of completeness.

Antidotes need to be applied to our *samsara*, or suffering, because it is false delusion, the Dalai Lama says; by analysis we must figure out what the suffering is about. During a private consult with Changling Rinpoche during his 2009 visit to Canada, when I felt discouraged about my work, he thoughtfully applied this principle of analysis, telling me that my discouragement occurred because I expected to get something back from what I was doing.

His Holiness then goes into an interesting discourse about various religions, saying that they hold a common belief; "We get our body from our parents and our soul from God". Traditionally Christian faith espouses the idea of one life, while the Hindu credo states that Brahma creates the soul, and according to His Holiness, their teachings imply the ending of the soul. Tibetan Buddhists, on the other hand, are of the opinion that there is no beginning or end to anything.

My eclectic approach to spirituality embraces Jesus as an *Ascended Master*, an individual once embodied on earth, who transcended human limitations. I believe we return again and again over many lifetimes.

Buddhist scholars always thought the mind is made up of neurons, but are now wondering if consciousness may be separate from the mind, the Dalai Lama tells us, because certain brain activity can be detected after death. He mentions several lamas whose bodies stayed fresh for days, even up to a month after their physical death.

Scientists have ascertained a brief electrical charge in the brain of a high lama from South India ten days after his death; they hypothesize that this energy is the subtle mind and that this tiny, remaining charge could be the beginning of the next life. The subtle mind has no beginning or end, we are told.

At the end of the morning teachings a group initiation takes place; we take our leave since we are not participating. One idea stands out for me from the Dalai Lama's lessons: "Consider others as more important than the self and your own goals will be fulfilled automatically".

Back at the temple at one o'clock, we find the foreigners entrance closed. At the Tibetan entrance, I'm frisked by a professional guard; she presses my body firmly, authoritatively, but is not intrusive, she even checks my tiny purse. Security turns us back at the stairs, saying only Mongolians can go up. All monitors and cameras are gone and we conclude that there will be no more teachings today, just closing ceremonies.

In the lower courtyard it becomes apparent that the Dalai Lama has yet to arrive, so we join a handful of people behind a low railing near the gate of the private residence. Sikh Indian army officers are in attendance this afternoon, also Tibetan security guards. An undercover Tibetan, wearing a scarf and shoulder bag, stands near us, his policeman stance and roving eyes give him away immediately. I notice a mixture of feelings within me; peace and joy from the healing atmosphere is mixed with nervousness due to the intrusive presence of the security men.

After a while some Russian Buddhists straggle through the gate from the private residence, each with a khata around their neck, they've had an audience with His Holiness. The temple postman, the one who delivers mail to Kirti Monastery, strolls casually up to the Reception Office by the residence gate.

Watching the Russians leaving after their interview, I remember that Dekyi applied for an audience for us in October but it was declined. Meeting the Dalai Lama in person would be a joy, but we know he sees fewer people now due to his demanding schedule and health issues. (Even in 2007, a posted note on the residence gate indicated this.)

Finally we're instructed by security to sit or kneel. The gates open and the Dalai Lama walks out in the centre of a group of senior Russian monks, one carrying a pot of burning incense. It's lovely to see this group of elderly; eminent Buddhists from different parts of the world come together in celebration. The experience feels complete now, and once the group enters the temple we leave. Descending the steps on the far side of the courtyard, I ask a security guard how many people attended the sessions. There were 2000 registered upstairs, he tells me, including inside and outside the temple, plus the unrecorded group in the lower courtyard.

Kale Shoo* to the Hope Center

The Tibetans at THC are grateful for the work we've done, though we don't feel our contribution has been that great. By our final evening at the Center I've reached my goal of completing the first edit and input of the refugee stories.

We both participate in the conversation group for the last time. It's enjoyable in a bittersweet way. Later at the bonfire, Kusang gives us a colourful Tibetan flag and khatas for our journey, then asks us to say something. Not feeling much like talking, I ask Don to say a few words. He speaks eloquently about the pleasure it's been to work there and all the positives we've gained:

---

*   Tibetan for "farewell"

"Each and every student is highly motivated and appreciative of everything we do. We've learned so much about the strong, courageous, resilient and humorous character of these young Tibetans."

I concur with his words and add that it was an honour to be a part of the Hope Center. The Israeli volunteer, previously commended for her seven weeks of service, said she received far more than she gave, and that's exactly we both feel.

Finale – Final Weekend in Town

Saturday is a free day, though it feels like we should attend the Center for some reason. Slowness is a luxury after our busy schedules of the past weeks.

The Tibetan shop on Temple Road, with its beautifully crafted gifts calls to me. There I purchase the purple silk thangka hanging I've been coveting, a mandala of the Tibetan Wheel of Life painted on orange parchment. Monks carried these tapestries, literally meaning "than", or flat and "ka", for painting, from one monastery to another rolled up like scrolls.

Ellen with Friends Dolma & Pema (Photo: Don Smith)

In the afternoon Pema comes to the apartment and gives each of us the traditional parting gift of khatas, then we walk to Moonpeak Café to meet Dolma; there I'm given more khatas. This is the last time the three of us will be together, so we ask another traveller to take pictures.

Afterwards I rest at home, reading, while Don gets a haircut and straight razor shave in one of the tiny barbershops nestled between Temple and Jogiwara Roads. It's a ritual he enjoyed thirty years ago in India and still takes pleasure in.

As the weather cools and additional electricity is needed, power cuts are common around town. This afternoon's outage continues for an hour and a half, so eventually we go nextdoor to Chonor House, one of the few places with an emergency generator. There we find candles burning invitingly at each table, while food is being prepared with the use of the emergency power.

Sunday morning, while Don enjoys his at home breakfast ritual before losing his tiny kitchen, I go out for a quiet coffee and banana bread at the bottom of the lane. The café is busy and a monk asks if he can sit with me; we eat together companionably and he shares his story. He's 40 years old and has spent twenty years in a South Indian monastery. Yesterday he had an audience with the Dalai Lama, he tells me, as he is thinking of going back to Tibet for a family visit. Tomorrow he departs for Delhi to visit the Chinese embassy, seeking a visa. My impression is that he may go illegally if he cannot get one, a worrisome thought.

Many Tibetan refugees, both monks and lay people, wish to visit their aging relatives, some of whom express a desire to see their children once more. Acquiring a Chinese visa is a relatively uncommon occurrence, but not impossible. A monk friend recently received one to visit his family back home after several refusals.

This morning we shop for ingredients for vegetable soup, for dinner at Dekyi and Khenrab's home this evening. Initially I wanted to invite the family to our place, but with three active children and Sonam's inability to climb the stairs out of their compound and down to our apartment, Don suggests that we go to them instead.

Rinzen has invited us to his home for homemade momos. Getting there is like taking a magical mystery tour! With the language problem, we misunderstand each other, thinking Rinzen is picking us up at one o'clock. Around noon, we're just beginning to prepare the soup, when we receive a call telling us the momos are ready.

We say we'll meet him shortly at the Green Hotel on Bhagsu Road. Rinzen phones repeatedly while we're walking in that direction, but his phone cuts out. At the hotel he's nowhere to be seen; the desk clerk says there's only one Tibetan staying there, not a monk, and shows us the register. Thanking her, we call Rinzen, who gives us the name of another guesthouse; perhaps this is his place, we think. The desk clerk recognizes the name and points us back towards the square. As we begin walking in that direction Rinzen suddenly appears beside us.

To our surprise, he says his home is in Bhagsu. We walk together along the dusty road almost to the next town. At the bottom of a curved dirt driveway is the Indian home where he shares a room with another monk.

On arrival, Rinzen discovers he's inadvertently left the one-burner stove on and the momos have almost boiled dry; fortunately both the house and momos survive unscathed. He's cooked so much food it will last several days after our meal together. Made with potatoes, pepper and ginger, the momos are excellent and I thoroughly enjoy four of them. Rinzen offers me more, thinking I don't like them; his generous hospitality reminds me of Dekyi. I convince him that they are delicious, but I'm full.

By now there is a time crunch, tonight's soup is not ready; we explain that the visit will not be a long one. Post meal conversation is slow-paced, with the Tibetan-English dictionary consulted as needed. Rinzen shows us his typed biography, most refugees have them, whether monks or lay people. Before our departure he gives us white satin khatas with Tibetan symbols printed in red, blue and green and a gift of tiny Tibetan flags. A member of the landlord's family takes our picture before we begin the trek back to McLeod Ganj.

Back home with just enough time to complete the soup, we cook the previously chopped veges and add masala spicing, also Knorr tomato soup near the end, as suggested by the shopkeeper. When finished the soup has a rich, tasty flavour.

Carrying our precious cargo carefully down the lane, we climb into a waiting taxicab, asking that the driver go slowly so the pot of soup won't spill, luckily for us he acquiesces.

On arrival at the family home, Khenrab is cooking. I get the distinct impression he finds it strange that we're bring food to his house. Explaining why the Kirti apartment is not suitable for hosting the family, we explain the Canadian custom of potluck dinners, and hope he is not offended.

During the past week, Dekyi has pulled herself away from the demands of family and work, and our girl's day out has been accomplished. It begins with me giving her a short Trager Bodywork session, then a leisurely lunch in the sun on the Chonor House deck, indulging ourselves with their high quality Tibetan food. Although she then feels compelled to return to work, the uninterrupted hours together have been lovely.

Khenrab sits down for a few moments, then disappears to play a board game with Karpe and we're left to our own devices for awhile. Sonam, wrinkled face wreathed in smiles, joins us in the living room; her eight-year-old grandson plays an Indian game on an enormous plywood board, and the four-year-old girl clowns around.

Now Khenrab brings the food in, saying, "You eat my food, then we'll eat yours". The meal is vegetarian this time; they now know that meat isn't big in our diet. Together we enjoy the various dishes, then the family gives us presents for ourselves and our family; Indian wool blankets, Tibetan scarves and, of course, khatas. Pictures are taken and we take our leave, knowing there will be one more meeting before departure.

Despite countless hours dedicated to audiotaping our McLeod Ganj sojourn, once home I discover that there's no record of either our final Hope Center group or the last family dinner at Dekyi's home. Putting words to tape would have made the parting more real, and I suspect they've been unconsciously omitted. The details of these endings remain very much alive in my memory though, and are recreated effortlessly later.

Packing and errands are the main goals for today, as we depart early tomorrow for Delhi. Our first stop is tea and cookies at the home of a Tibetan couple we've chatted with on the pathway for several weeks. Their youngest daughter lives in Vancouver, and will be contacted by us once home.

They show us many family photos, including their daughter's wedding; the two look very much in love. We're asked to stay for a lunch of rice and dhal, but regretfully decline due to our many errands. With typical Tibetan generosity the couple give us presents; a box of incense, massage oil, (risky to carry, so I pass it on to Dekyi), and a set of tiny multicoloured Tibetan prayer flags blessed by the Dalai Lama. We're sent off with khatas around our necks.

Next is a fruitless attempt to phone Bronwen in Vancouver and to send e-mails; all services are out. Someone has cut and removed two to three feet of copper wire from the main hook-up, leaving the entire town without internet and telephone lines. This has happened before, thieves get a good price for the wire; it even happens in Canada on construction sites. The owners of the internet café are patient men; the lines were cut late Saturday and it's now Monday.

We call the Prince Polonia Hotel in Delhi, to reserve a room for the next two nights, asking the desk clerk to note that we'll be arriving late. The cost of international calls by cell is only 10 rupees per minute, but it's now too late to phone British Columbia.

Down the street, the brother and sister begging duo are having a serious fight. Tears stream down the girl's face as she wails loudly. Immediately two Indian shopkeepers are beside them asking what's wrong. These young kids, who spend most of their time on the street, are not as alone as one might think, they're watched over by community members.

Free education is available to all children in India, but street children do not like the confinement of school and receive little encouragement from their parents; their attendance is sporadic, if at all. There is one other pair of beggar children here, brothers in traditional Indian clothes, who sing for tips. These children are safer from harm here than in big cities.

The Men-Tsee-Khang College
(Photo: Don Smith)

This afternoon is our final medical consult. Arriving early at Men-Tsee-Khang Clinic, we enjoy a stroll around the beautiful all inclusive community. Dekyi can leave her work in mid afternoon and help out with the art class at her daughter's creche, returning to the Clinic afterwards.

It's such a small place we encounter Khenrab; on his way to McLeod Ganj to refund his bus ticket to Delhi as tomorrow he will travel with us. At the gathering place above the staff residence Don takes some pictures.

As if by plan Dekyi and her daughter appear at the top of the stairs, back from lunch.

The clinic is still closed, so after dropping the little girl at the creche, Dekyi takes Don to the internet café, where everything is in working order. Now it's our appointment, and Dekyi spends considerable time with each of us, assessing our current state of health, then writes out prescriptions for a three-month supply of medicines.

The astrological branch of Men-Tsee-Khang is also important in the philosophy of health. Don considers having a short horoscope prepared, quite a departure, he is motivated by a poster in the clinic that says this year is the second occurrence of the earth mouse since his birth. Khenrab says they're very busy at the astrological centre, but if Don mails his birth information, Khenrab will have it analyzed. Somehow this never happens.

Back home I'm able to pack quickly, and manage to fit all the presents into my lightweight suitcase, along with the clothes. Donating some items to the Reception Centre has helped.

Don makes a successful attempt to flog his used books on Bhagsu Road, then we go next door to Chonor House for some nourishing, safe food before our travels tomorrow.

"It Takes Forty Days to Know Someone"

Tuesday, the first of December. Our next destination is Rajasthan, and we must return to Delhi to access the route to that state. The separation from McLeod Ganj does not feel like a great wrench in the moment, but five or six days later, after we've reached Rajasthan, it hits hard. Part of me remains in McLeod Ganj, and it takes some time to come to terms with leaving.

Don does not hear his watch alarm beep, so we oversleep and find ourselves rushing to be ready on time. Kunchok, the monastery manager, arrives at the door just after eight, to carry our bags down to Temple Road, where the travel agency driver is waiting.

My planned sit-down breakfast goes by the way and I settle for takeout coffee and thin cheese and tomato sandwiches on white bread from the café at the bottom of the lane. As we're climbing into the taxi, Rinzen arrives for a final goodbye. I give him a magazine on Tibetan politics, written in both Tibetan and Chinese, published by our friends. Khenrab is waiting at the Men-Tsee-Khang compound. There will be no luggage, he's said, so we're surprised to see a small suitcase on wheels, (his), and an enormous duffel bag, (a friend's), sitting on the road. The small car will not hold four adults and all the bags; I suggest we strap the duffel to the roof, but Khenrab nixes the idea and it's left behind.

Saying goodbye to Dekyi, her small daughter and Karpe again, more khatas are placed around our necks, then it's on the road for us. Dekyi's Tibetan stoicism and ingrained acceptance of the impermanence of things supports me.

The title of this chapter is a quote from an old Arab proverb; coincidentally our stay in McLeod Ganj lasted forty-one days. The time here has been a journey into another world for both of us, with the opportunity to come to know many people of all ages and make lifelong friends. Each person has a powerful story to tell and through our day-to-day contact with them we've learned about their lives, their culture and their country.

Indomitable strength, courage and pride, combined with humbleness and an enormous capacity for joy characterize the people of this culture. The Buddhist influence is strong and individuals focus on living in the moment. Our friends live simple, straightforward lives.

McLeod Ganj has impacted both of us, having its most profound effect on me because my past lives here are significant ones. Living in this place of spirit has allowed me to let go, to move into a deeper part of myself, closer to my true essence.

Over time we may grow to understand this society better. Perhaps the reason we'll never fully fathom Tibetan culture is because we have no reference point for what it is like to be unable to return to one's own country or to live there freely. Karen Connelly expresses this well when she says: "Being free, I did not understand much about freedom."

But for this short time we have been part of something greater than ourselves. By the simple act of coming here with open hearts, curious minds and a willingness to help, we've been welcomed and befriended beyond any expectations.

On the Road Again

Having Khenrab with us on the daylong trip from McLeod Ganj to Delhi is a comfort; it feels more like a group of friends on a road trip together. Our driver, booked through the travel agency in McLeod Ganj, is very competent, but the journey is long. The early part, through the mountainous area of Himachal Pradesh, is the most time consuming.

There's little conversation; up front Khenrab and the driver converse in Hindi from time to time. We pause twice for meals at restaurants that are part of the tourist driving circuit.

Khenrab is ill and the driver must stop several times for him to be sick. Later during a phone conversation he reminisces about what a good trip it was, (compared with the bus I imagine); I remind him about the vomiting and we have a good laugh.

No accidents occur during daylight hours, but a terrible one is averted only by our driver's quick response, when a small boy suddenly darts in front of the car. The mother has already crossed the highway, perhaps the boy is meant to stay where he is. I avert my eyes during the incident, fearing the worst.

It's dark now and we're nearing the north end of Delhi. Khenrab has just remarked that the trip has been accident-free, when we come upon a recent disaster. It appears that a motorcycle carrying one passenger has cut in front of a car too closely in the lane next to ours. Both riders lie prone and still on the pavement. Men are working to separate the bike from the bumper of the car, where the two have jammed together.

Drivers ride the roads with a zeal that borders on anarchy in India; this behaviour combined with traffic volume and unsafe vehicles makes accidents more of a risk. In Delhi billboards instruct drivers to "Be sane, stay in your lane", but the reality is quite different, as vehicles of varying sizes ride abreast on the roads, squeezing through narrow openings whenever an opportunity arises.

Eventually we reach Majnu-ka-Tilla in northeast Delhi, where we stayed two years ago. Khenrab will visit with his friends here. At the gate of the compound he and the driver decide that since the driver does not know his way around Delhi, a man should be hired to direct him to Paharganj. The bargaining doesn't go well, though, and our driver makes a decision to go it alone. This is when the trouble begins. "No problem", he tells us; after hearing these words many times we now treat them as a red flag.

We reach the heart of the city; by now we've been on the road for a tiring twelve hours. As the driver circles the Old Delhi roundabout several times in heavy traffic, I worry that he'll have an accident in the congestion of the Old City after driving for so long.

After an hour of stops to ask directions (I lose count at six), and fruitless attempts by us to phone the hotel without the correct area code, Don finally identifies the landmark Imperial Cinema just around the corner from the Prince Polonia Hotel; it's lights are out, making it hard to spot.

Finally we reach the door of the Prince Polonia and send our tenacious driver off with a decent tip for all his aggravation. The doorman helps us with our bags and we wearily climb the stairs to the reception desk, only to find that our room has been given away. Someone has neglected to note our planned late arrival, and reading the registry upside down, I see our names with a line drawn through them.

The apologetic staff take us around the corner and down a long, dark lane of mixed residential and commercial buildings to the Sun Village

Hotel. The road is strewn with household garbage by night time; triggered by tiredness, I find the street scene revolting.

On first glance it appears that there are sidewalk sleepers outside most buildings, later we realize that the street is an overflow room for the downstairs apartments, and residents sleep or sit on string cots abutting the walls of the building. These beds, or *charpoys*, are rectangular structures strung tightly with coir rope to form a strong, comfortable bed or chair.

By the next morning the street has been cleaned up; people from the Dalit caste, formerly called the Untouchables, collect the garbage. The past weeks in McLeod Ganj have accustomed me to a quiet, small town atmosphere, but this bustling lane is what life in urban India is all about, with middle class or even rich people often living cheek by jowl with the lower classes.

Ceremonial canopies, ready for a wedding, are pitched in the road this morning, later the drumming begins. Still tired and a bit disgruntled about being stuck in this hotel on the dark, chaotic lane, I wonder judgmentally if the music will go on all night. Then I ask myself, Why would you want to go on a *slum tour* (a visit to an impoverished community), when you find this street so unappealing? Perhaps I prefer to separate my living quarters from my voyeuristic tourist activities. (In retrospect, I was too hard on myself again; the trip to Delhi was gruelling, change is a challenge for me, and although not yet in touch with it, I'm missing McLeod Ganj.)

Several weddings take place in Paharganj today, and we watch as a bride and groom leave the bride's house near the hotel, symbolically walking under a canopy. The wedding party then parades through the street accompanied by drumming; shortly afterwards the canopy is removed.

Astrology is widely used here to predict couple compatibility and suitable wedding dates. The Times of India reports that hundreds of thousands of couples are being married in the month of December all over the country; about one hundred thousand of the marriages are taking place in Delhi. Now is an ideal time, as the first six months of 2010 will be inauspicious.

The Prince Polonia desk clerks invite us back to their hotel, but we paid for two nights at Sun Village on arrival and don't want the trouble of settling into a new room and a different bed. Sun Village is a mid range Paharganj Indian hotel, not a tourist inn; the feel is different, it's plainer in decor and more formal. The staff are not as knowledgeable about the preferences of foreign travellers; they tend to either hover or hang around at loose ends in the rather empty hotel.

While the room is fine, food service is another story. On the first morning, we inquire about the location of the dining room and a staff member takes us up to the deserted outside deck, where two dirty tables sit. "No thank you", we say, and go round the corner to the Prince Polonia's rooftop restaurant, where their usual high quality breakfast is being served by friendly people who know us. In early December it's still comfortable on the roof, but by mid-January it's a different situation, and everyone has room service.

There is only one day to rest and enjoy Delhi before moving on to Rajasthan. Robert, the in-house travel agent, tells us that a slum tour is impossible, as that involves travelling many miles through heavy traffic to the outskirts of Delhi.

A short outing by metro feels right, so we take the subway to Connaught Circle again; really not our style, but easy to reach. After walking for over an hour, we stop for tea in a café. There we're approached by a friendly man with a different, more sophisticated angle than the garden variety street tout. Asking if he can share the table in the crowded café, he chats with us for a while, saying he's in town for a wedding. Then he mentions in passing that he has *pashminas*, (shawls), made by his family members. As we're leaving, he asks if we'll meet him again the next day; "We'll be gone by then", we reply.

In the afternoon we select some of the gifts given to us or purchased in McLeod Ganj, and walk to the nearby post office a few blocks from the hotel. The shopkeeper next door packs everything in a cardboard box, and then hand sews a white cloth bag around it, in the old fashioned way. While waiting for him we have an interesting talk with an older Israeli man, who's also sending a package home.

A short while later this man and his partner are in the post office upstairs. They've been waiting more than half an hour for service and are worried that they'll miss their plane to Europe. Once the staff have finished their lunch break they're back at work again, and it takes only moments for both of our packages to be processed. The price of the shipping is equivalent to 50 dollars, it's worth it, and for once I can easily find what I want in my suitcase.

On the second floor deck of the post office there's a bird's eye view of life on the street. A funeral procession passes by, with several men carrying a body, laid out on a board, high above their heads. The deceased is wrapped in orange cloth, signifying an older female. Behind the pallbearers walk other men, then the women come last.

At the Burning Ghat in Varanasi on our first trip, a volunteer taught us that women are not allowed to attend the funeral itself, as it's feared that they might throw themselves on the funeral pyre; it's also thought to be too emotionally upsetting for them and Hindus believe that the soul is held back by the weeping.

In some of the poorer, traditional northern states, especially Rajasthan, there's been a revival of *sati* since Indian independence in 1947, the custom whereby women are expected to die with their husbands on the funeral pyre.

Our business completed, we locate a third floor restaurant overlooking Paharganj's main square. From here the market activities below can be clearly seen, it's an excellent position for picture taking. I particularly enjoy watching the white water buffalos pull their carts, and the bicycle rickshaws; they express the character of the neighbourhood.

We notice six or eight young female teens in school uniform piled into a bicycle rickshaw; the load is so heavy the driver cannot ride his bicycle, so he drags the rickshaw along. To me it smacks of exploitation of the poor by entitled young people, but Don, with his more seasoned, analytical travel perspective, points out that it provides safety for the girls and work for the man.

This evening, our last on this visit to Delhi, we have invited Denise, our Canadian friend from McLeod Ganj, to dine with us at Prince Polonia, where she's staying on our recommendation. Our note to her, left at the front desk this morning, has been efficiently delivered and she's waiting in the rooftop dining room at seven. Denise is flying home at midnight, and rather than trying to rest, usually a lost cause, she prefers to be up and about, drinking Indian soda to keep alert. During her last days in Delhi, she's been sightseeing, shown around by an Indian book publisher who splits his time between Canada and Delhi, where his family lives.

We share memories of our time in McLeod Ganj, covering lots of ground over the course of the meal. Denise, a lone traveller who keeps her eyes and ears open and engages easily with others, has come to know the beggars of the town quite well. She discovered that the young sister-brother team live in Bhagsu with their two-year-old sister and widower father, a serious alcoholic who drinks away their money.

Denise also found out somehow that the small beggar woman, the one I gave the heavy sweater to, does not really have an injured or leprosied hand, the handwrap is a prop to encourage better donations on the street. To me she's a sweet woman, simply doing what's necessary to survive, in a relationship with a physically handicapped man, another acquaintance. It's easy to picture these two gentle people together.

A humorous story, told by Denise, underscores how begging is a job, like other forms of employment. Whenever the younger woman saw

Denise, she would approach and request something, money or food; the only time no appeal was forthcoming was during her lunch break with her partner; then she was off the clock and would not give her the time of day.

Early in the morning of December 3 we check out of the Sun Village Hotel, to begin the trip to Jaipur. The desk manager presents Don with a bill for 800 rupees, car tax for the car and driver we ordered, not from them, but from the Prince Polonia Hotel. This attempt at extortion is "Old India" style behaviour, common thirty years ago when Don visited the country. He naturally refuses to pay this outrageous baksheesh, and takes the matter up with the Prince Polonia owner in mid-January. Brij is unimpressed with what he hears. He tells Don he's awaiting repayment of a small investment loan to Sun Village Hotel, that's why his staff placed us there.

As this book goes to print the situation in Tibet has worsened considerably. The number of self-immolations (setting oneself on fire as a political protest), by monks, nuns and lay people continues to rise, peaking in November 2012. Free Tibet writes: "These protests are aimed at sending the next generation of China's regime a clear signal that Tibetans will continue to fight for their freedom despite China's efforts to suppress and intimidate them."

PART TWO
Rajasthan: Land of Contradictions

Jaipur

We leave Paharganj early Thursday, December 4 to get a jump on the traffic. Our driver for the Jaipur trip seems like a sweet guy, he drives frenziedly though, tailgating beyond even Indian standards and honking as a matter of course.

After we leave the city state of Delhi and travel west into Rajasthan, we're surprised to see camels pulling carts of produce, an exotic feature to us. Women in bright, ankle length skirts and short tops, called *lehengas*, toil in the fields, their heads covered with a piece of cloth for protection from the heat and for modesty. Female garments are brighter here than in other parts of India, sharp primary colours adorned with tiny mirrors and embroidery.

Breakfast is at a modern tourist restaurant that doubles as a women's clothing store and there are no other customers. While we eat our eggs, the chauffeur sits in the driver's room at the back of the building, drinking tea. Even with the stop, our arrival in Jaipur is much earlier than planned.

Neither of us is impressed with the first sighting of this chaotic place, called the Pink City; it actually looks orange. I'm not much of an urban person, although born in Toronto; I gravitate towards smaller centres wherever I am in the world.

The state's largest city, Jaipur is the capital of Rajasthan and a busy business centre. With a population of 2.5 million, it's small by Indian standards. Predominantly Hindu, Rajasthan is India's largest state, with over 50 million people, bordering Pakistan to the west and the Punjab to the north. Although it covers 10 percent of the country, half of Rajasthan's land is taken up by the Thar Desert, so the state has only one percent of India's water resources.

This area of the country is culturally rich, with unique and colourful art, classical music, folk music and dance. Tie and dye prints, Zari embroidery, wooden furniture, handicrafts, carpets, and blue pottery are exported. Its flamboyance and myriad historical places make the state one of India's most popular tourist stops.

Rajasthan is one of India's most backward states, however, both economically and socially, with the vast majority of its village women illiterate. The good news is that literacy rates improved significantly between the 1991 and 2001 census taking, and the gap between males and females is narrowing. Standards of measurement are low in India, however, so it's difficult to tell how inflated the figures are.

Rajasthan

148

Our driver takes us to the wrong hotel, one with a similar name to ours. When advised of this, he calls ahead twice to clarify the location, dropping us off at Hotel Madhuban just after the noon hour.

This hotel, suggested by Don as a treat, is palatial by any standards, a heritage home, owned by the head of the Tanwar Rajputs, a high Rajasthani caste. Although located in the heart of the city, the large property is entirely enclosed by tall, lush hedges, trees and flowering bushes, creating an isolated, quiet oasis. The exterior resembles a small palace and the additions have been done so expertly one cannot tell they were not part of the old building.

The dining room is traditional Rajasthani Rajput design, with high wooden beams; each brightly accented archway has panel insets of local motifs, while the walls display murals and artwork. All the furniture in the hotel is heavy faux antique.

Madhuban is quite a contrast to Kirti Monastery, in comfort, price and ambiance. Our ground floor room, with shared flagstone patio, is large, and the bed excellent quality, with an open-topped canopy, all very comfy. My blowup mattress is relegated to the bottom of the suitcase, completely unnecessary here. The bathroom, with both tub and shower, is quite a luxury for us. After living simply for two months, we appreciate the small luxuries.

Advertised as a home away from home, this hotel indeed has a restful feeling. The 50 dollar per night equivalent for our deluxe room is well worth the money, if you don't mind the formality of the staff and their odd looking, (to my eye), traditional Rajasthani costumes.

We eat lunch on the lawn, seated at a heavy marble table; it's well past meal time so we're the only guests. The garden, where most people take their meals during daylight hours, is large, the tables spread out, resulting in little interaction between guests.

This first day we take a short walk around the neighbourhood, leaving the heart of the city for another time. Don calls Dr. Dekyi, who tells him that she has added money to our telephone, this can only be done in McLeod Ganj, the point of purchase for the phone.

Later we enjoy a dinner of curry and rice in the busy dining room, it's mild but tasty. Afterwards I sleep for ten hours in the peaceful, darkened room, still tired after the two road trips. The tranquil atmosphere at Madhuban allows me to rest deeply.

Market Day

Breakfast at Madhuban
(Photo: Don Smith)

Many guests are up and about in the garden when we step outside. Breakfast is a tasty Western buffet, all laid out on long tables, except for the made-to-order eggs. Fresh drip coffee is served, a much appreciated luxury.

The staff are courteous and helpful, but don't engage much with guests. Brief conversations reveal that most are unsophisticated boys from the villages around Jaipur. As the days pass, I observe that the servers and houseboys are kept on a short leash, constantly watched by the hotel management.

Their uniform consists of *angarakhas*, long red and white tunics reaching below the knees, with a white cotton *dhoti*, or pajama, underneath, folded and tied at the waist. Short-style red and yellow turbans, called *pagri* sit atop their heads. They make a whimsical display placed in a row along the wall of the staff dining area, when the workers are off duty.

The difference between travellers and tourists has often been debated and one thought is that tourists come to see *places* and travellers to *absorb culture*. For me, one of the most interesting parts of travelling is meeting individuals from every walk of life and learning about their lives, and after the friendliness of McLeod Ganj, the lack of connection in this tourist hotel is a bit disconcerting.

A young German woman travelling alone, based in New York City, initiates a conversation with us; other guests respond in a friendly manner if I introduce a topic in the buffet line. During our time here we meet another German woman, in India with a co-worker to train IT workers in Puna and Bangalore, as her company outsources their work. Each day she wears a different salwar kameez suit, custom made in Puna.

Spice Man in Market
(Photo: Don Smith)

It's Friday now; since it's our only full day in Jaipur, we decide to check out the Old Jaipur market downtown and buy some books for the next leg of the trip. Our driver, one of the regulars who hang about outside Madhuban waiting for fares, is an anomaly...a good driver, he's friendly too. Today I wear a surgical mask, purchased in Paharganj for city travel, it helps with the dust problem.

The driver knows the downtown core and locates the English language bookstore easily. The tiny store has an excellent variety of both fiction and non-fiction reading. After purchasing a couple of books, we begin walking to the main market, forgetting once again the difficulty posed by long walks in the heat and the tumult. Those who can afford transportation for relatively short distances, either by auto rickshaw or in their own vehicle, know what they're doing, they're not being lazy.

It takes a while to locate the market entrance and it's getting warmer by the moment. We're on the wide, noisy main street of the bazaar when I realize I've forgotten my ear plugs, an aid that can make a significant difference to one's level of relaxation. We try to purchase some at one of the medical kiosks along the street, but are told no one uses them here.

The Jaipur market is enormous and has some interesting stalls, but it seems less organized than others we visit. Some areas are designated for particular products, but for the most part goods are jumbled together, with bicycles and tricycles alongside fabrics and saris.

A young man approaches as we inquire about earplugs, asking in perfect English if he can be of help, and we stop and chat with him for a while. He's a college student, studying Spanish so he can work in his family's gem company; this industry is big business in Spain and Italy.

As we stand on the street corner, I happen to glance down the lane and notice a number of men urinating against the wall of the building, into a cement trough running alongside and out to the street. I avert my eyes; I can get by without seeing this sight. What is it about all this male public urination? It's not as if there are no toilets (though I suppose this is considered a toilet). In her hilarious book, *Holy Cow*, Sarah MacDonald jokes that many men have weak bladders and urinary problems in India!

We bid the student good day and locate a quieter side street, where we explore for a while. My word for Jaipur is erratic; the city has its own unique brand of chaos; it's hotter and noisier here than in Paharganj and vehicles go much faster, even in the market. Motorcycles and cars speed by pedestrians as they move into the roadway to avoid broken, garbage- strewn, kiosk-filled sidewalks.

By the time my body says "enough" we're deep in the market, and the temperature is thirty-two degrees. I love to walk, but don't tolerate the heat and noise well. It's no fun for Don either when I crash, or declare "I'm not doing this anymore, let's go back to the hotel", as happens on rare occasion. At that point he usually comes up with a workable plan.

As we leave the bazaar, I get a flash from the past, suddenly understanding how I walked out of the Grand Bazaar in Istanbul, Turkey in 1975, hot, hungry, on automatic pilot, and made the mistake of eating chicken from a street rotisserie, making myself extremely ill.

After several failed attempts to secure an auto rickshaw, we walk the rest of the way, finally spying the restaurant we want on the far side of the road. All bets are off when crossing busy roads in India; traffic patterns are different from those in the west and rules not enforced. Drivers are not trying to hit you, although it sometimes seems that way. The best plan for reaching the other side without mishap is to cross when the Indians walk, staying as close to them as possible.

The restaurant Don has chosen from the guidebook is famous with both tourists and middle class Indians. Neros was founded in 1949 and serves good Indian, Continental and Chinese food. We enjoy pasta, drink some coffee and relax in air conditioned comfort.

The place is full and we notice several groups of tourists sitting with their guides. Tours can work well; we occasionally take short car or walking tours to get a general impression of an area when time is limited, or to reach out of town sites.

By the time we start back to the hotel the traffic is even heavier, and it takes a while to cover the 2.5 kilometre distance. We have an opportunity to people watch as our auto rickshaw crawls slowly along the street. A motorcycle rider makes a phone call at a traffic light, shoving the phone under his helmet, something we never see at home! Two teens, a boy and girl, run along the road, each carrying a crutch that serves as a begging prop, reminding me of our acquaintance in McLeod Ganj with the bandaged, but uninjured hand.

There are fewer beggars in Jaipur than we expected in a big city, but the ubiquitous "mothers" with babies are present. We see a few child beggars and I notice an entire family of sidewalk dwellers, with an apparently able-bodied man sitting with them.

In large cities beggars are usually organized by mafia bosses and must give the greater part of their earnings over to these men. All the NGOs say "Don't give them anything, it's a scam, the money donated goes to liquor and drugs for the pimp bosses." Additionally the beggars are often supported by charities.

Today, when our vehicle stops at a red light, a beggar approaches, appearing suddenly from her position on the centre island of the roadway, holding her "rental baby". As the woman nears our auto rickshaw, I pull the canvas blind over the open back window, forcing her to remain at the front. This aggressive beggar stands with her hand out, staring at me, for what feels like several long minutes, trying to wear me down. She leaves only when the driver tells her in Hindi to go; he's said nothing up to this point, perhaps waiting to see how things will unfold.

My modus operandi is to not make eye contact with her. I do look at the baby, and notice that the child is almost as white as my own daughter's fair British skin. In my mind I travel back to the ashram nursery full of abandoned baby girls, some light skinned, in the Paharganj temple, where Brij took us two years ago. Mixed race babies are even more undesirable in India than girl babies.

To modulate the effects of Jaipur's confusion, I use a protective exercise taught to me by a healer friend, Judith, circling my body symbolically in a clockwise spiral motion; after a few moments this has a positive effect. Judith said I absorbed too much on our first trip to India. The world is made up of energy, our bodies themselves energy fields, therefore it affects us whether we realize it or not. My sensitivity stems from being an empath, someone who intuitively picks up impressions from people and the environment around me, an ability developed over time. We complete our day with a tasty dinner in the Madhuban dining room and enjoy a relaxing evening. Jaipur has been a stopping point enroute to Shekhawati, an historically interesting area 200 kilometres to the northeast; we leave for that destination tomorrow morning.

Shekhawati

A Voice from the Past

During the night I'm awakened by an all-over body buzz from the powerful heart medicine. Near the end of our time in McLeod Ganj, when Dr. Dekyi was called away to Delhi, the meds ran out, and my body is now re-adjusting to them. By morning I feel a fresh charge of energy and vitality that's new to me.

We eat a last breakfast on the hotel lawn, seated at a white, wrought iron table amidst the other guests. This morning we depart Jaipur for the Shekhawati region, billed by Lonely Planet as "magical, like going back in time".

Yesterday we discussed the difficulties of getting from point A to point B in India with the German woman who works in Puna. She described it as "painful"; well put, I thought, so glad it's not just me. Thanks to a conscientious driver booked though the hotel, today's trip will prove to be one of the better ones, and we arrive at our destination in a few short hours.

Camel Cavalcade Protest Enroute to Jaipur
(Photo: Don Smith)

We pass a coterie of camel carts on their way to Jaipur, 150 in total, our driver tells us. Along the way they'll be joined by other demonstrators, in a highly organized venture protesting the lack of water and electricity in the Bikaner region of western Rajasthan. It will take several days for them to reach Jaipur moving at their leisurely camel pace, but they'll be comfortable, as vans carrying tents accompany the cavalcade.

Our driver, a Jaipur resident, is a gentle, well-spoken man; he's forty-eight but appears a few years older. At age thirteen he married an eight-year-old girl, a successful marriage, he tells us, and their three children are well educated. We are aware of this historical custom, but are shocked to find that it still took place in our generation.

Many organizations, including The Universal Declaration of Human Rights and the Convention on the Rights of the Child, forbid the degradation and mistreatment of girls inherent in child marriage. Commonly these marriages take place for economic reasons, sometimes to secure guardianship for female children; they result in the child's separation from her family, lack of interaction with peers, few opportunities for education and exposure to health risks.

The driver hastens to assure us people do not marry at that age now in Rajasthan. Early marriage in India is still a contentious issue, however, more common in this traditional, poor state than in other parts of the country. A recent University of Chicago article notes that roughly 80 percent of Rajasthani females marry before the age of fifteen, whereas in the country as a whole only half are married by age eighteen.

The Shekhawati region of northeast Rajasthan is a scattered group of desert towns built around the forts on the old China to India Silk Road. Often called the Open Air Art Gallery, it's the most artistic region of India and home to Hindi, Marwari and Rajasthani art, the three cultures and languages of the region. The dry desert air preserves the walls of buildings, and paintings and frescoes dating from the 17th to early 20th century can be found both within and outside them.

Historically the area was tribal, its inhabitants brave, sacrificing and hard working. In fact Shekhawati still contributes more personnel to the Indian Army than any other region. First settled by Muslims in mid 15th century, the Rajput Shekhawa clan took it over in the early 18th century. They were often at odds with the Marwaris, who built *havelis*, or private mansions, and many Marwaris moved on to Calcutta and Bombay, becoming merchants and abandoning their havelis to ruin.

The climate is harsh and extreme in this land of deserts, inundated with sea water millions of years ago and later transformed into desert by earth quakes. We arrive in winter, when daytime temperatures reach 30 degrees Celsius, (about 86 Fahrenheit); it's warm but comfortable because the humidity is so low. Evenings are cool and temperatures go down as low as 10 degrees Celsius. Summer temperatures heat up to over 40 degrees Celsius (more than 100 Fahrenheit).

Shekhawati receives 450 millimetres of rain annually on average, (eighteen inches), between July and mid September; every third year is dry and every eighth a famine. Rainwater is therefore an important part of the water supply and while we're at the eco resort we learn about water conservation.

Apani Dhani: Juxtaposition of Old and New

Don in courtyard of Apani Dani Eco Resort

157

We're driven through the outskirts of Nawalgarh, near the resort. The community appears plain and arid looking, a working desert town, not gentrified in any way for the tourists.

On arrival at Apani Dhani Eco Lodge we're greeted by Ramesh, the owner. The resort is beautiful; it consists of one-story terracotta huts built in a U-shape around a central courtyard. Flourishing bougainvillea bushes in a variety of colours creep up to the roof of the central pavilion where guests gather to read, chat, or listen to harmonium concerts. At the end of the courtyard is a building that houses the dining room and kitchen.

A slim, attractive sixty-something man wearing simple white cotton pants and shirt, Ramesh wears traditional Rajasthani white stud earrings in both earlobes. His bearing is aristocratic.

Ramesh is a devout Hindu and a member of the Rajput caste, the second highest in the state; he's multilingual in English, French and German, as well as Indian dialects, having lived in Europe for several years. There he became interested in the environment and Swedish and German ecology, he explains. Our host still spends a third of each year in Europe and half of Apani Dhani's clientele is French. Ramesh's altruistic values, common among higher caste Indians, are reflected in the fact that 5 percent of the resort's gross earnings are contributed to a school for handicapped children.

I initially find Ramesh's manner somewhat superior and off putting; while clearly used to being in charge, he does prove to be a congenial host. Later I experience something similar with our Goa hotel owner. This may be reverse snobbery on my part, having little to do with Indian culture and more bearing on my own class background and politics.

Ramesh purchased the land for Apani Dhani, meaning "our home", in early 1990, building the family residence on the property. Over the next few years he fulfilled his dream of expanding and hosting guests. Now the eco resort is developed as finances allow; in 2002 solar panels were installed. All huts and bungalows are traditional Rajasthani design, using local supplies for the clay brick walls and straw thatched roofs.

The resort has eight rooms, plus three high-end overflow tents beside the garden, at the back of the property. Each guest quarter is roomy and attractively furnished, with tiled floors and private washroom with sink, odourless composting toilet and shower. As our reservation was made late, the room assigned to us has a squatter toilet, a bit of a challenge for me with an old knee injury.

On arrival all guests are told that they are expected to respect this traditional Rajasthani home where the family rises early and is in bed by ten at night. The place has a cloistered feel, reinforced by fences around the main compound area and heavy front and back gates that are locked each night.

Two women cook most of our meals in the kitchen adjoining the communal dining room; one is Ramesh's daughter-in-law, the only female family member we get a glimpse of, the other an employee. The food is served family style in large bowls, brought in by either a male staff member, Ramesh or his son. When the cooks occasionally enter the dining room, they quickly pull the end of their *pallu*, the sari over-layer, across their face in the manner of modest rural Hindu women. When they encounter me alone they leave their faces uncovered. Once during a brief meeting, we manage almost wordlessly to exchange information about our children, a universal topic for mothers.

Each day we notice two male children arriving home after school, our impression is that one is a family member and the other the child of an employee who lives in the compound. We see no female children during our stay at Apani Dhani, but Ramesh tells us he has a granddaughter, the daughter of his second son who runs a nearby guesthouse. His well-educated eldest son lives and works at Apani Dhani and his daughter resides with her in-laws in a distant region, following Indian custom.

The cosmopolitan Ramesh reverts to tradition when at home, and each room of the lodge has a binder with an exhaustive list of traditional Hindu customs and guidelines that clearly demonstrate this.

Both males and females are advised to cover most of their body: "No sleeveless t-shirts or shorts, transparent or revealing clothing, no braless look; wear a long sleeve t-shirt or shirt covering the buttocks for women", (the last is traditional in most of India, even in the more progressive South).

Some of the French tourists, perhaps unable to read the English-only guidelines, bare their legs and arms. Always attempting to dress modestly in India, respecting the cultural norms, I feel controlled by "the book of rules", and by the atmosphere in this ultra conservative setting. There's a sensation of being watched and I likely would have opted not to come here had we known more about the place beforehand.

Alcohol is strictly prohibited: "Don't bring it to your room out of respect; it is against our way of living and you would deeply offend us", I read in the book, hearing Ramesh's voice in my head. The Prince Polonia Hotel in Delhi is run by devout Hindus; however the atmosphere there feels calm, not constrained in any way.

Wells must be dug deep in Shekhawati and Apani Dhani's is 80 metres in depth. Each year the water table goes down by one metre, a serious matter. Residents have of necessity adopted specialized ecological practices to deal with the water shortage, washing themselves, their clothes and preparing food with very little water.

In addition to regular electricity, each room has solar powered lights and water. We're encouraged to use the solar lights as much as possible, considerably dimmer but adequate. While each room has a shower, there's also the option of using the Indian *mandi* method to wash; it requires 15 litres of water instead of 30 to 45 and is done by wetting oneself with a mug of water scooped from a pail, soaping, then rinsing with the mug. Leftover water is used to irrigate the flowers or for some other greywater function.

While we're here Don chooses to wash himself the Indian way, as on his first trip to this country as a young man, while I take brief showers as needed. Mid afternoon is the best time for showering, when the solar heated water has reached peak temperature, we're told, however, our New

Zealand neighbours, who shower frequently, say there's plenty of warm water in the morning.

Apani Dhani is a sustainable resort, growing its own wheat, barley, maize, vegetables, some fruit and keeping animals that provide milk and methane gas for cooking. Rajasthanis do not grow or eat rice, as in other parts of India, rice growing requires vast amounts of water, Ramesh tells us. They do serve it to their "honoured guests", however.

Lunch and dinner are delicious vegetarian fare from a fixed menu, as most high caste Hindus are vegetarian. Breakfast is modified continental, perhaps in deference to the European patrons, consisting of excellent coffee, Indian bread and fruit.

Touring the Town

Old Haveli
(Photo: Don Smith)

It's Sunday, our second day at the eco resort, and we take a walking tour of nearby Nawalgarh with our New Zealand neighbours, led by a knowledgeable professional guide. Billed as a two-hour tour, it's actually twice as long, not uncommon. Neither of us are history buffs, and while the first half interests me, I tire of it.

We visit many havelis, each with colourful frescoes of Hindu myths covering the walls and ceilings. The buildings are made of brick and local stone overlaid with plaster, and the murals painted on either dry or moist plaster surfaces, using natural pigments from indigo, ochre, lead, copper, lapis lazuli, lime and even gold.

Still privately owned, many of these ancestral homes have been refurbished and turned into museums; others remain in their natural state. Vivid scenes of Hindu life are visible everywhere; in one haveli a marriage procession of elephants and well-wishers parades across an exterior wall; inside, through a finely carved wooden gate, the courtyard walls are decorated with scenes from the Sanskrit love tale Ramayana. Hindu gods and goddesses, historic events, daily life and images of the seemingly curious ways of the British occupiers are favourite subjects for the frescoes.

The fresco painters smoked a lot of *ganja*, (cannabis), and drank copious amounts of alcohol, according to our guide, to make their minds freer. They were permitted to paint whatever moved them and we're surprised to see a beautiful painting of Jesus in one haveli.

A large, very dark haveli interests me. Standing in it I sense the ancient atmosphere of the place and receive an impression of activity around me, that of the people who once lived in this busy household. As was the custom, the home is built around two courtyards, a general one and an internal compound where the women of the family lived in *purdah*, isolated from the outside community, except on special festival days. Only family could enter the inner sanctum of the house.

Rooms rise three stories above the courtyard, with walkways where the women could stand to overlook the activity below. Hindu custom dictated that the females of the home prepare the food, even among the wealthy, while servants performed all other household tasks, going out into the community to take care of business.

The outer courtyard was the place where the men of the household did business with the traders who passed through Nawalgarh on the Silk Road. Travellers would be seen in the business area until eight in the evening, we're told, while later arrivals slept in a special area of the courtyard.

The tour over, we decide to have lunch in the market and our guide locates a decent restaurant on the upstairs deck of a hotel. During the meal the young man tells us he takes pride in being a Brahmin, the highest of Rajasthan's twenty-three castes. Officially abolished in 1949, the caste system is alive and well in the rural areas of northern India. We're told that visiting a lower caste home and drinking tea with the family is acceptable now, however, as a dutiful son, his bride must be a Brahmin woman of his family's choice.

Our guide knows we'll never meet again, he also probably assumes that, as westerners, we're broad minded, and he reveals a more surprising detail about himself during our shared meal. In addition to his tour guide business, unbeknownst to his family, he is also a sports bookie with a busy operation that requires three cell phones.

The dusty, sandy town of Nawalgarh appears quite small, but has a good-sized population of seventy-five thousand. After lunch we walk through the large market, window shopping as we go. Life is more rustic and less sophisticated in rural areas of Rajasthan, and tradeswomen stare openly at us as they sit outside their kiosks, faces uncovered.

Nawalgarh Market
(Photo: Don Smith)

163

On the mile long walk back to Apani Dhani I become separated from the rest of our party, and on the edge of town encounter a group of Muslim teenage girls, out of school for the day. They speak some English and ask my name. In traditional fashion, their bodies are covered from head to toe in black *burqas*, with a veil, called a *niqab*, covering their faces below the eyes. Being stylish young girls, their head covers are sprinkled with rhinestones, adding a bit of pizazz to the plain garments.

I ask the most outgoing group member about her veil; she surprises me by whipping the niqab off her face, as if in the privacy of her own home. She's brash as she knows there are no males nearby; her behaviour is really not much different from a typical, cocky teenager anywhere in the world, I think to myself. We wave goodbye and the girls turn down a side road that runs at a forty-five degree angle to the freshly paved two lane main road.

A Day in the Life

When we return a bangle-making workshop is in progress in the courtyard, given by a married couple. The woman's face is covered during the entire class, except when she introduces herself to her New Zealand students, I'm later told. I purchase several bangles, for myself and as gifts.

The guest population this week is comprised mostly of a French group. They're sociable at meals and many speak English, so I don't have much opportunity to practice my French; their sheer numbers intimidate me also. One member of the party, a gregarious commercial banker, whose job it is to lend money to airlines, speaks excellent English and enjoys interacting with us, cracking numerous jokes.

The French folks are travelling in a luxurious van with a driver, on a business-pleasure trip, seeking to partner with resorts that will offer their spa treatments and products.

Later in our visit we meet a younger Dutch couple whose company we enjoy. During a chat in the courtyard, they describe their bus trip from Dharamsala to Amritsar. Early in the journey their vehicle slammed into a tree and every window on that side of the bus broke, spraying glass chards over the passengers. The woman, seated in that area of the bus, automatically ducked down, she tells us, a smart move on her part. Fortunately no one was hurt. Everyone brushed the glass off themselves and the driver nonchalantly drove on. We shake our heads, not really surprised, it's all in a day's travel in India!

Despite its restrictions, Apani Dhani is indeed a beautiful resort, and our little room with its thatched roof, mud brick walls and window seat is becoming more familiar. The guests' gathering place in the bougainvillea-laden courtyard offers a variety of current European magazines, arranged on wicker coffee tables, and dusty novels in both English and French, on a small bookshelf. In this charming setting one can almost forget we're in the midst of semi-desert, but the dryness is noticeable in that no amount of cleaning by the hardworking staff can ever remove all the dust and sand that permeate the air and settle on everything.

Tomorrow we're planning a tour of some villages and will also research transportation to our next location. Jaipur, like Delhi, is a central hub, and it appears we must travel back there in order to move on to either Udaipur, Rajasthan or to the state of Gujarat, farther south. We've heard that Lake Pichola, Udaipur's focal point, is dried up due to lack of fruitful monsoons over several years, so the city may not be an attractive place to visit. Wondering if it's best to skip this stop and fly straight to Gujarat, I make a phone call to a random hotel in Udaipur and am informed that the lake is half full. Encouraged by this, we firm up our plan to go to there, pre-booking a hotel that resonates with us.

Had we made a different choice, we would not have met the Udaipur travel agents who were to become our friends, but we don't know this yet. Many people believe there are no accidents in life, perhaps this is an example of that.

The Villages

Today is Monday, December 7, our third day here; this afternoon Ramesh's younger son, Babu, takes us on a tour of the villages. A convivial young man, he's less formal, more relaxed than his older brother. Babu knows the area well and suggests that we visit only two towns instead of the three originally planned, since they're quite far apart.

Both Dundlod and Parasrampura are unique, very different from Nawalgarh. Dundlod, just seven kilometres away, is built on a squared-off grid. A clean, barren looking town, it has only a sprinkling of mid-sized desert trees and almost no flowers due to the scarcity of water. The odd cow roams the streets. From our vantage point on a rooftop the structures of the town appear to stretch over a wide area of land. The settlement feels spacious, larger than its population of two thousand would imply.

We visit a haveli that's been transformed into a museum, my favourite of all we've seen so far. Because the home has been staged, one can easily imagine what it was like when a family and their servants lived in the building. In addition to the beautiful wall frescoes and other decorations, the haveli exhibits dishes, statues, furniture, even mannequins symbolizing the people who dwelled here. The household feels almost alive.

Our next visit is to Parasrampura, 20 kilometres southeast of Nawalgarh and a long drive from Dundlod. We travel down a busy highway for a time before turning onto a secondary roadway, then the paved road narrows and becomes a dirt trail with sand dunes on either side, resembling a beach road back home.

Parasrampura is a small, quiet town of 1,000 people, a contrast to Dundlod's expansiveness. Its surviving art is amongst the oldest in the Shekawati region, and there's a timeless atmosphere in the tranquil streets of this tiny, remote village. Very few people are out and about while we're here and the ones we do see on the street are male.

The main feature of the settlement is its centrally located cremation ground, where Maharajas and their immediate families are still cremated when they pass away. The gate is locked when we arrive but Babu quickly locates someone with the key to allow us entry. The burial grounds cover an area about the size of two urban Canadian lots put back to back; at the front is a large domed monument much like an old style Western bandshell in appearance. The funeral pyres of the Maharajas are built on the stone platform of the monument, while smaller, lower cremation platforms for other family members are located at the back. We crane our necks as Babu describes in detail the story behind each intricately drawn picture of gods and goddesses on the dished ceiling of the main platform.

After our tour we return to Apani Dhani for a snack of tasty pakoras, to replace the lunch we've missed. Tomorrow Ramesh's driver will take us to Jaipur; the fee for the trip is reasonable, lower than city prices, and we know the driver will be reliable. We'll go back to the Hotel Madhuban for one night, it's peaceful there; hopefully the front desk manager can book us tickets on the busy tourist train to Udaipur.

Shekhawati in Retrospect

My descriptive word for Shekhawati is disturbing. Travelling to this area of Rajasthan *is* like visiting the past, but not in a good way, and without the magic. The Lonely Planet writer who said Shekhawati is magical either exaggerated or had a different sensitivity to atmosphere, I muse to myself.

Unprepared for this ancient rural desert and its traditional practices, I find that the energy here makes me uneasy. I pick up on both the events that took place in the past and the current energy of repression of women, girls and marginalized lower castes.

When Alma does a reading on Shekhawati at a later date, I tell her I felt unbalanced by the very foreign energy there. "We never saw any women in the resort, except the cooks, who covered their faces", I remark. Alma agrees that the energy of the current restrictions is present, plus that of ancient battles.

She adds that Shekhawati is very earthy and does not suit me. "It's the opposite of Dharamsala, more of a *base chakra* vibration" (chakras are body centres that express our life force; the lower, base chakra connects us to the physical world). "It would irritate you, in the way that certain music can", Alma says.

She understands why the guidebook says visiting Shekawati is magical; "It *was* repressive, but it's magical too, but more the *phenomenology* of magic than spirituality though, as you would expect to find". Then Alma gives two simple examples to clarify what she means; a levitating table and a snake being charmed out of a basket. The guides are now saying, through Alma, "Shekhawati is not for your path, it's for the path of sensuality, it's a path of diversion, not a path to enlightenment". "When people need to stay on the earth longer and they don't want to, they're given lives like that", Alma tells me. "They get juiced through the energy of earth, sex, food. Or when people get too rarified, spending all their time in temples, perhaps, they may need a reintroduction to the pleasures of the flesh. But it does not have a lot to do with you."

I'm glad our visit is over. When the place you're in doesn't resonate, all your activities have a pall over them. Despite this and the restrictions of the household, the stay at Apani Dhani has been made as pleasant for us as possible; we've enjoyed delicious meals, made with care and attention, learned new ways to preserve the environment and met some engaging people.

This area of Rajasthan remains with me, despite, or perhaps because of its negative appeal. We've had a unique opportunity to visit this unusual region before it becomes transformed into a busy tourist destination. Old havelis are already being purchased and transformed into boutique hotels. It will be interesting to see the effect these changes have on the lifestyle of the area residents, particularly that of the younger people.

Jaipur Replay

Canopy Bed at Madhuban
(Photo: Don Smith)

It's December 9 and we're back at the Madhuban Hotel in Jaipur; the trip with Ramesh's driver was comfortable. Once again on arrival in Jaipur we're taken to the wrong hotel, one with a similar sounding name; I think the driver misunderstood his instructions. He self-corrected quickly though, after showing our Madhuban Hotel card to a staff member at the first hotel.

The camel cavalcade has now arrived in town, complete with myriad camel driven carts and buses full of male protesters, flags flying from their windows. Leading the parade are several men on camels. It's a well-organized, peaceful protest, with a police presence, and takes up only two lanes of the highway into town.

An online article reports that in addition to the water and electricity protests, the procession is rallying to demand that a new state called Maru Pradesh be carved from the western portion of Rajasthan, with Bikaner as its capital. Neglected by the Jaipur government, this region of 300,000 people has less industrial development, more unemployment and only one third as many roads as the rest of Rajasthan.

Now two months into our three-month voyage, we've passed the length of time we're normally away. Almost two weeks since leaving McLeod Ganj, nearly half our time has been spent on the move; down from the Himalayan foothills to Delhi, then in and out of Jaipur. The journey has been hard, the towns dusty and dirty and there's a sameness to many places. The many changes and uncertainty are clearly affecting me, my skin's starting to itch a bit, a sign of stress. Part three of the journey, Goa, will be calmer; it's the vacation portion.

Our travel awareness grows over time; after visiting many parts of India over the course of two trips, we would now like to begin strategically targeting destinations, to both preserve energy and maximize our experience, volunteering in McLeod Ganj again and perhaps returning to the state of Kerala in South India.

The next goal is securing a seat on the overnight train to Udaipur in South Rajasthan, but it proves an elusive one. This city, famous for its beautiful Lake Pichola, is billed as the most romantic in Rajasthan, but I no longer trust the guidebook since the Shekhawati experience.

Afterwards we'll go on to the state of Gujarat before Christmas in Mumbai, then our final destination of Goa in the south.

If you're anything like me, some of your very favourite things are probably the inexpensive ones; the boiled wool black vest, purchased for one dollar at the Women and Violence Thrift Store in North Vancouver is a case in point. It came along to India in 2007, to Southeast Asia in 2009 and is with me again. (Before leaving Udaipur I give it away to someone who needs it more than I do.)

A small event pleases me today; my lovely red scarf, the one bought from a street merchant in Paharganj for 25 rupees, (about 50 cents), has disappeared. Back at Madhuban a young staff member says: "I have something of yours, I was keeping it until you came back". "But it could be years before my return", is my reply, and he simply repeats, "I was keeping it for you until you came back", and hands me my scarf.

Later we venture out into the hubbub of Jaipur, returning to Nero's Restaurant for comfort food, not all that different from what we prepare at home; breaded fish and veggies, with a few french fries thrown in and our usual shared beer.

Unfortunately there's no chance of procuring seats on the train in the busy tourist car, so we're scheduled to depart for Udaipur on the overnight bus tomorrow evening. At the thought of yet more travelling, particularly by bus, a part of me would like to turn around and go back home, still there's an intuitive sense that Udaipur will be both enticing and relaxing.

Once we reach that city, we'll have to fly and hang the price; I've had enough and want no more extended trips by bus, train or car.

Falling in Love with Udaipur

Looking Across Lake Pichola at the Old City
(Photo: Don Smith)

171

The Trials & Tribulations of Overnight Travel

The night before the bus trip to Udaipur I lie awake in the big canopy bed at Madhuban Hotel, worrying about what's to come. Tired of my insomnia, I simply ask the Universe for help, and drift off to sleep. Things begin to go fairly smoothly from then on, though it's more accurate to say that *my reaction* to the events that transpire is different; I'm relatively calm and unflustered. This positive attitude enables me to get through the seven-hour bus trip to Udaipur mostly unscathed.

Our hotel manager has apparently taken a liking to us on this, our second visit to his hostelry, and we're delivered to the bus station in a brand new Chevy van, compliments of Madhuban, safer than an auto rickshaw after dark. The juxtaposition of high-end transport and bus travel is interesting. He advises us to remain in the Udaipur bus station on arrival at 5:30 a.m., drink tea, then travel into the city when it gets light, in about half an hour.

The Jaipur station is farther than the promised one-kilometre trip, so we're doubly glad to be in the van. Sadly things go downhill from this auspicious beginning. There are some positives to be thankful for; our luggage is efficiently marked with chalk by the driver, the bus looks fine and does not break down during the voyage.

The only Westerner passengers on a bus crowded with Indians, it's reminiscent of the voyage from Delhi to McLeod Ganj in '07, with Indians taking the place of Tibetans. This trip takes half the time though, and the vehicle is in better repair. I experience no claustrophobia, as on the dark, closed-in Bangkok to Laos bus.

The road from Jaipur to Udaipur is considered a good main road, but it's bumpy for most of the trip, despite the driver's skill. We're assigned two reclining seats with accompanying overhead berth. The bunk, with its sliding plexiglass door, reminds me of a closet and I decide at the outset to remain in my chair below.

The bus pulls away from the station just before 7:30, thirty minutes late, and travels until 10 o'clock, when suddenly it comes to a halt. Sometimes passengers are given no information at all during layovers, alternatively, staff shout in Hindi and I begin querying other passengers, "What? What did they say?" until someone gives me an answer.

"How long?" we ask, and the driver replies "five minutes"; we rush towards a doorway that has the word "toilet" written on it in big letters. Inside there's a squatter, an excellent prospect right now.

There are no women in this typical rural bus station and the men gape at us, particularly at me. They look rough, like they've been working hard with their bodies, and when you stare back at them they don't look away, as is often the manner of lower caste, uneducated men who speak no English and have had little contact with foreigners.

The bus makes three more stops before its arrival in Udaipur. The first is for a meal break at a proper rest stop; we remain on the bus as the hour is too late for eating. By now Don is upstairs resting; I lie down across the seats, covering myself with my coat and resting my head on my cushioned travel pillow. The bouncy bus, travelling through the dark night, feels safe and relatively comfortable and I'm just beginning to doze off when it stops again, spoiling my lovely nap.

At 2 o'clock there's another stop. We both disembark and the driver says: "No toilet, go around the back". With the help of two friendly workers I locate a room with stalls; it looks like a washroom, but there are no toilets of any kind in the walled cubicles. Who knows when we'll stop again, so I go into a room with a muddy floor, (hopefully it's mud), and manage to urinate.

While Don is still behind the building, the bus begins to move; I call out but it's not really leaving, just pulling up to wait for us. Although the transportation system appears random and chaotic, in actuality the staff are aware of and taking responsibility for each person travelling on their bus. They know everyone's destination, and sometimes wake people up at their stop by rapping on the door of the berth or shaking them awake if necessary.

After tearing along the roadways for a couple more hours, the bus stops yet again and we're astonished to hear that we have arrived at the Udaipur bus station. It's four-thirty in the morning and pitch dark!

Stranded in the middle of nowhere, on the outskirts of the city, we're not sure what to do. Two auto rickshaw drivers offer us a ride. The men wait patiently while we call the hotel we've booked into, but there's no reply as everyone is asleep. Their non-aggressive behaviour is refreshing after other places we've visited.

I'm not keen on travelling several kilometres in a flimsy vehicle in the dark but there are no taxicabs. The driver we choose assures me that there is no highway, and in response to my next query, placidly responds that he has headlights (one can never be sure), and that yes, he will use them!

The asking price is 600 rupees (about $12), a premium charge for night work in this popular tourist destination, no doubt. Don completes his negotiations with the driver (he's taught me you seldom pay what's initially asked in India). As I sit wearily on a station bench, a bird poops on my head, yuck. Don and the kindly driver gently wipe me off; I roll my eyes and laugh, what else can I do at this point?

We reach the heart of Udaipur and drive through winding laneways crowded with tall houses; this city of half a million people really does sleep, a rarity in India. The town has a soft, peaceful, almost medieval feel to it.

On arrival at Dream Heaven Guest House, our driver suggests I wait on the street with the baggage while he and Don go into the hotel to rouse the doorman. In my exhausted state I go along with this plan, and the men climb the stone steps of the lane leading to the hotel and disappear. About fifteen minutes goes by as I stand alone on the deserted street in this strange Indian town, becoming increasingly uneasy. Cars and motorcycles begin to pass by as workers start their early day, and I begin to feel unsafe out here alone.

Finally saying to myself: "To hell with the luggage, I'm not staying here one minute longer," I walk up to the hotel. When I arrive at the door, anxious and overtired, I have a brief meltdown, angrily berating Don for leaving me down below by myself, where anything could happen.

The housemen, awake now, take us upstairs to the rooftop restaurant where they offer us a resting place, as our room will not be ready until 10 a.m. On the deck are two beautifully decorated Rajasthani-style pavilions, each adorned with brightly covered throws, cushions and mattresses. We're given a space the size of a queen sized bed and blankets to pull over ourselves. It's noticeably damp here above the lake, but we sleep comfortably for a couple of hours, awakening to the spectacular sight of the sun breaking through and the mist rising off Lake Pichola.

Dream Heaven Guesthouse

Dream Heaven Guesthouse, Deck Restaurant
(Photo: Don Smith)

Fortunately our room is ready by 9 o'clock, so after breakfast it's time for a nap. I feel a bit ravaged from lack of sleep and a headache that began on the vibrating bus.

175

We chose this guesthouse intuitively from Lonely Planet guidebook, their low to mid price recommendations are usually excellent. Located on the far side of the lake at Hanuman Ghat, away from the main retail area, Dream Heaven is perfect for us.

The owner, Dilip Singh, opened the hotel 11 years ago, to fulfil his father's dream of offering a relaxing accommodation where visitors would feel safe and comfortable. It had only two rooms and four restaurant tables originally but by 2005 it was billed as a seven-room budget hotel and it now has eighteen rooms.

This latest addition was well done, the building looks like a big house, with a warren of hallways and winding stairways, confusing at first. The family lives on the main floor; the matriarch sits silently at a small sales kiosk by the front door each afternoon, selling candy and toilet paper to guests, keeping her finger on the pulse of the place despite the language barrier.

We're offered an upgrade to a larger space with a view of Lake Pichola for 700 rupees, instead of the original 500, an excellent price. The medium-sized room is simply appointed, it has a double foam bed, couch and two miniature shelves for clothing. The decor is Rajasthani-style, with a hand-painted mural on one wall, flowers flanking both the doorways and the mirror and ceiling lights made of coloured glass. On the small deck a pigeon sits on her two eggs, she's there the entire two weeks we live in the room. We don't use the deck, keeping the red embroidered Indian cotton curtains drawn across the door out of respect for her and her fledgling family.

The bathroom, our least favourite part of the suite, needs an upgrade, but is adequate. There are several problems here; the paint has peeled off the walls, the tap drips steadily and the toilet must be hand-flushed with pails of water, due to low water pressure. Despite these minor nuisances, the view of the Old Town's architecture and the length of the four-kilometre lake is spectacular, so we decide to remain in this room.

Dilip manages the hotel with his brother-in-law, assisted by a group of young men and boys, who prepare food, carry bags and clean the rooms. We never see the daughter of the family, typical in traditional households. In conversation with Dilip shortly before our departure, we discover that this sophisticated man, whose home base is Udaipur, also has a Canadian wife and small child living in Montreal, he visits them a couple of times each year.

The rooftop restaurant serves excellent food, prepared in a miniscule kitchen off the eating area, accessed by a winding staircase just outside our room. The café doubles as a lounge and residents are free to sit here anytime, sipping tea, enjoying the view, reading or talking with other travellers.

Don is reliving his youth vicariously through two young guys from Vancouver, who are touring the disorganized roadways of the country on Royal Enfields, classic Indian motorcycles. He keeps disappearing downstairs to the front walkway of the hotel where the bikes are parked to talk to the men, but mostly to gaze longingly at the vehicles. One of the bikers had never been on a motorcycle before he began riding in Udaipur. All I can think is, "His poor mother." We laughingly joke about how Don would like to go off with them on their road trip.

View of Lake Pichola from Dream Heaven Deck
(Photo: Don Smith)

The Old Town is built around Lake Pichola, and even with the lake only half full it's a feast for the eyes. From our window and the restaurant deck

177

we take in the beauty of the ancient, pale-toned buildings, interspersed with lake palaces and temples.

Our first day is a quiet one; we rest again in the afternoon and remain on our side of the lake, after dinner retiring early and sleeping for an extended period of time. In the morning we eat breakfast on the deck, as we do most days during our stay here.

If I was asked to coin a phrase to describe Udaipur, it would be uncomplicated. We've fallen for Udaipur at first sight; its beauty and soothing ambiance make us want to linger, and we feel very comfortable at Dream Heaven Guesthouse. Udaipur does not have the discordant energy of other places, and before we even cross the footbridge to the business side of Lake Pichola we decide to remain for two full weeks, skipping the state of Gujarat and going straight on to Mumbai from here.

Udaipur is one of the areas I inquire about in my reading with Alma. "It's quite soothing, like nice elevator music," Alma tells me, "My guides say it has a civilized vibration, not exactly like the West, more like Europe. It's a place for you to simply rest; it feels really, really good, not as intensely Indian as other places in the country." She wonders if many expats live in the city, affecting its atmosphere; "I didn't see many," I reply.

Udaipur still has prostitution and other vices, Alma senses, but the sins are more hidden than in other parts of Rajasthan. Her guides coin a metaphor for the city, showing her a picture of "a beautiful woman who is a good hostess, but she has a secret life."

A Kindred Spirit

We consult Dilip about changing our flights and he sends us to Shree-ji Tours 'n Travels across the lake, where he knows the owner. This random decision to change our itinerary means we will meet some wonderful new friends.

Today after breakfast, we cross the long footbridge over the lake, a two-minute walk from our hotel, to reach the travel agency in Old Udaipur. The main street is extremely narrow and winding, with tall buildings built on angles. Not designed for the multiple vehicles that are often too large for the old lanes, it's congested most of the time. Where the storefronts jut into the road one must wait for a break in the traffic before continuing on.

The travel agent, Deepti, is welcoming, and we trust her immediately. We're cancelling the plane tickets purchased in McLeod Ganj for the trip from Gujarat to Mumbai. Deepti explains that she can do this for us, then once we've given our approval by telephone, the McLeod Ganj agent will refund the money into Shree-ji's business account. Deepti will then issue a cash refund and sell us new tickets for the flight from Udaipur to Mumbai. This is explained clearly and concisely, and there is no question as to the veracity of the plan.

As it's a busy time of year she has reserved seats to Mumbai on December 23, our preferred flying day. The price is reasonable, since Udaipur is a hub for travellers going south; however, she plans to keep shopping for a lower one.

In India service is always high level, Deepti goes way beyond the usual level of good service, however, and we've taken an immediate liking to each other. No request is deemed too troublesome or inappropriate; when Don wants his stained teeth cleaned, Deepti finds him a dentist, saying, "This is the best one, it's only five minutes away, call and make an appointment".

During our stay we see each other often, first for the ticket arrangements, later to use the internet services as the hotel's facilities are intermittent, then simply to spend time with her and her business partner, Lal Singh.

Next we enjoy an excellent lunch upstairs in the Hotel Minerwa's fourth floor Mediterranean restaurant. A French resident of our hotel in Udaipur for an extended time on NGO business told us about this place. "Udaipur has lots to see and do, it's an easy place to be", our fellow traveller tells us, "you couldn't get to all its rooftop restaurants unless you stayed in the city for a long, long time." We find his prediction to be true.

Now that we're away from Shekhawati I feel better overall. The audio recordings I made there sound noticeably different; when played back my voice is weaker than the ones made after our return to Jaipur. Shekhawati affected me, perhaps drawing energy from me.

Yesterday, in a delayed reaction, I felt the loss of leaving McLeod Ganj keenly. I did wonder about my tempered response on departure, after the profound impact the town had on me during our six weeks there. The pain of being away from the spiritual oasis where I felt so at home, so "me", has been slowly coming into my conscious awareness, the impact growing over the past ten days of challenging travel. My time in McLeod Ganj was a turning point, and the processing of this transformational experience will continue after my return to Canada.

The City

The City
(Photo: Don Smith)

Udaipur is 450 years old, hard to conceive when one lives in a young country like Canada. Founded in 1559 by a Maharaja, it is also known as The City of Lakes, Venice of the East and, my favourite, The White City. Many places in India are billed as beautiful, but turn out to be less impressive in real life. This is not true for Udaipur, however; the word charming, normally not part of my vocabulary, really does suit this town.

The District of Udaipur now has a population of six million, but the city has not grown as quickly as other parts of Rajasthan. Udaipur's literacy rate in is 83 percent for males and 72 percent for females, slightly above the national average, but this relatively sophisticated, economically comfortable urban centre is not a true measure of the overall state. Women's literacy drops dramatically in the villages just outside of Udaipur. A Vassar University study of 1000 rural Rajasthani women found only 15 percent to be literate, while another study discovered that lower caste women had less than a 5 percent literacy rate.

Almost 90 percent of Udaipur's population is Hindu, with Muslims making up close to 10 percent, and Sikh and Jain residents about 1 percent each. But when the call to prayer takes place five times each day, led by the *muezzin,* one would think the city is full of Muslims. As I record this, chanting filters in through the bedroom window from neighbourhood mosques as the droning from several of them intermingles. In the evening as we eat dinner on the deck, we are transported by the melodic prayers. In one mosque the women chant after the men, in moving harmony.

Today while I wait outside the hotel for Don, six of us, some tourists and some residents, engage in a brief, delightful exchange. The conversation starter is the English-speaking parrot belonging to the family that lives and works on the sloping lane outside our hotel. This bird has entranced a small European girl and the Indian men encourage it to speak, while the girl's Mom and I stand by enjoying the show. Then a German friend comes by and the excited girl grabs her hand, saying: "Come and hear this. The parrot can meow like a cat and say 'cool baby' ". We all derive so much pleasure from this simple, human interaction, a very pleasant moment in our day.

In a residential side street off the Indian market, we meet some warm and friendly Muslim women wearing pastel-coloured dresses with head scarves spilling over their shoulders like round capes. The women were interested in us and keen to engage in the minimal, but special ways available; they made us feel welcome in their neighbourhood through their smiles and gestures.

Udaipur is known for its many artists in residence. Don has enjoyed meeting several carvers and painters on his lone travels and has treated himself to a tiny oil painting.

On Sunday we take some time to window shop and wander the Old Town. I try on a couple of pairs of pants but they're cut for a slighter woman; the brightly coloured fabrics are a pleasure to look at anyway. Then we're back to our default lunch spot at Hotel Minerwa; it's decorated in simple Rajasthani style, with white walls and low couches with coloured cushions, as well as regular dining tables. Spacious open walls give one the feel of being in a treehouse, looking down at the tops of buildings from high up.

Each dish is excellent. Today we eat veggie burgers and Israeli food, hummus and falafel balls. The latter are not served in pita bread, as in the West, but if you ask, the waiter will bring *chapatis,* flat, unleavened wheat bread, to roll them in. The plate comes with Israeli salad, like ours, sans lettuce, safer that way.

Udaipur is an active town both day and evening, with loud music playing most nights. I think of it as "pop music on the move", as the musicians walk along, pause, then sing and drum. Concerts mostly take place on the far side of the lake, but sometimes the men venture over the footbridge to our side.

The residents are big on fireworks and set them off almost daily year-round, with any event being an excuse for a celebration. New Year's Eve is a huge blowout here, too bad we'll miss it. Some fabulous effects explode right over the lake during dinner; it feels like they've been planned for our enjoyment, as we watch from our first-rate seats high up on the deck.

Dhobi Washer Women
(Photo: Don Smith)

The rhythm of the day is measured by the sound of the *dhobi* women slapping laundry on the *ghat* across from our hotel. (The dhobi are the caste that specializes in washing clothes; ghats are wide steps descending to a river or lake.) Crouching on the lowest step, they wet the clothes in the lake, rub them with bar soap, smack the garments with wooden paddles to remove the dirt, then rinse them in the water. It's the same basic process as in Varanasi, where clothes are washed in the Ganges River; there the drying system is better, the clothes are spread on huge cement walls angled at forty-five degrees for that purpose.

There are quite a few touts in Old Udaipur, because it's a relatively popular tourist destination, but their number and level of aggression doesn't come even close to those in Delhi, where visitors to Connaught Circle have at times complained of cow dung being dumped on their shoes when they're not looking, then washed off by an associate, for a fee, naturally.

Touts here are more reputable, still it's best to ignore them as much as possible.

A guy badgers me, asking where I'm from, as I walk along the main street near the agency. When I reply, "Canada", he says: "Canadians don't buy". "That's right", I answer, laughing as I walk on. One man pursues Don annoyingly day after day, as he passes by his store near Shree-Ji; it's become either a game or a point of honour with the merchant to sell Don something, we're not sure which.

Our Dreams Renew Us

It's Monday morning in mid-December and I awake from a dream with a single word in my head. Yesterday, at Sunday breakfast, we met a couple from Colorado in Café Eidelweiss, off the main street of the Old Town. These folks chose to deal with the economic downturn in the U.S. in a proactive way, first by renting their house out and living in a suite above their garage, now journeying for six months, expanding themselves and riding out the recession. Their recent, relatable struggles with work, along with our shared interest in living our dreams, lead Donna and I into a discussion about happiness. Out of this conversation the word "blessing" emerges this morning.

In my dream I'm in a small blow-up boat near the shore of an ocean; I've travelled a long way along the shoreline, "all by myself". When I arrive at my destination, I don't know any of the black clad people on the beach; they're not part of my tribe of like-minded people or from my culture. I do not interact with them; instead I go by foot back to my starting point, to see a lawyer about some legal matters.

The dream feels transformational; the overriding sense is that I've come a long, long way. From dream dictionaries I learn that an ocean indicates spiritual refreshment, while sailing across the ocean signifies newfound freedom, independence and great courage. A lawyer in a dream indicates that help is available for the asking. There's also the obvious interpretation of travelling a long distance to India, a place I love, but is not my true home in this lifetime. I belong to another culture and will return to it.

Udaipur's Best Kept Secret

Udaipur Vegetable Market
(Photo: Don Smith)

Today is our first visit to the Indian market. The auto rickshaw driver is young and the vehicle an upscale one, the fanciest we've seen yet, with a sound system that emits upbeat Indian music. It is colourfully decorated, with a tassel inside the front window and an artificial flower on the windshield wiper. Two thirds of the way to the market, we meet another driver on the road; he has just received a phone call for our cabby, and shoves the phone towards him. It's most peculiar, how did anyone know he was coming? We all have a good laugh about it, then move on.

We're dropped off in a large, open, triangular area where several streets converge. This is the vegetable market, the most attractive of all the bazaars, with its colourful goods spread out on blankets and displayed on stacked crates.

The marketplace consists of stalls and storefronts, covering an area of perhaps twenty square blocks. One can buy just about anything imaginable here: spices, vegetables, sweets, dried fruit, pots, pans, dishes of metal and clay, electrical equipment, used televisions, pottery, jewelry, wooden toys, puppets, antiques, the famous miniature paintings, wall hangings, cloth lanterns, handmade paper, painted wooden boxes, greeting cards, brassware and terracotta sculptures, traditional batik and hand printed cloths, scarves and saris… I'm sure I've left something out!

People are friendly and helpful, and the bazaar seethes with life and vitality. A few kids ask for money and chocolate; they don't speak English and don't appear to go to school. Small girls work for their keep, carrying aubergines and cauliflowers around in baskets for sale. It's a case of generational poverty; lives are circumscribed due to their caste and the resulting lack of education.

Surprisingly, tourists do not venture into the market in noticeable numbers, to avail themselves of its amazing wealth of experiences. During our many trips here we see perhaps half a dozen in total. People acknowledge us, no one stares, and the women seem especially interested in me, exchanging nods and smiles.

We carry a map showing the locations of the various markets, but it's difficult to follow, even for Don, a land surveyor, so we ask shopkeepers and others on the street for directions from time to time. Don has fun tracking down and purchasing a small handheld squeegee for our bathroom floor; it has no defined shower area so the whole room gets soaked. He gives the shopkeeper 50 rupees, ($1), for the sponge, but the man calls him back, saying the squeegee costs only 15 rupees! (We've ineffectually requested one from hotel staff; acquiring a bathmat to confine the water to the bathroom is easier once I realize we simply need to request an extra towel.) Don also buys light bulbs, as the ones in our coloured glass ceiling shades are only 15 watt, dull to read by. It's fun to have specific buying projects in mind and well worth the small investments for two weeks in our lovely room.

My goal is to buy a watch; I've been without one for some time and prefer not to support China's economy by purchasing one at home. We locate a watch kiosk and I choose a simple, small Indian watch with a blue band, at a price of less than a $6 equivalent; it matches my blue glasses, also purchased in India two years ago, when my red ones broke. As is the custom, the watch seller offers a high level of service, removing two links from the strap so it fits well, changing the battery and giving me a one-year guarantee on my purchase!

We conclude our shopping at a store that sells scarves and I buy five enormous rayon ones to use as tablecloths, wall hangings and for gifts. The shop owners, a middle-aged man and his son, help me choose them, then give us directions for finding our way out of the heart of the market.

Notes from the Window

The shade angles onto the lake and the side of the building as I sit looking out the window; it's getting late and people are hurrying across the bridge in both directions, returning home at the end of their day's work. Along the pathway comes the blind man accompanied by the young girl, his granddaughter perhaps; they were begging outside Café Eidelweiss.

Inadequate monsoons over several years have depleted the water supply, and the parched lakebed looks like a tidal flat. Cow dung patties are spread out on the sand. The cow and buffalo dung is collected, shaped, then dried and sold as fuel by a Dalit woman.

The young guys enjoy teasing the cows, just because they can; they feed them then play with them. One is chocolate brown and the other, a small one, darker brown with a white belly. Now someone is chasing them off the tiny packed-dirt lawn below our window, and they scamper friskily along the street, if that term can be applied to cows. They're then herded onto the bridge by their owner.

On the far side of the bridge, a langur monkey, its tail more than a metre long, sits on the arched parapet of the gate and dangles its long legs, forced there by a dog. After a while this curious creature descends, then gallops down the centre of the walking bridge like a bat out of hell, so fast it's crossed the footbridge, (about three-hundred-feet in length), and jumped to the top of the building next door to us in only ten seconds. This crazy monkey then takes a seat on the edge of the roof, legs sticking straight out, feet like tiny little hooves, a hilarious sight. Another monkey joins it and they race back into the trees.

187

Walking Bridge to the Old City
(Photo: Don Smith)

As the day draws to an end, I see Chris and Eileen, from the interior of British Columbia, come across the bridge; we met them in Café Edelweiss earlier today and spent an hour together in conversation. Eileen came to Canada from Germany to visit a friend seven years ago, met Chris and decided to stay. She's also a therapist, but does not practice in Canada. Chris has been to India six times since his youth, each time saying he's never coming back; a great example of the draw this complex country has on people.

My internal resources have dwindled after two months in India; frequent moves in the post McLeod Ganj days have contributed to this. To replenish myself, I need to remain settled in one sympathetic place for a while.

In order to become a successful traveller we need psychic and emotional stamina, along with physical strength. One of my favourite counselling instructors talked about "burn-through" as opposed to "burn-out"; riding the stress like a wave, restoring yourself before reaching full burnout.

This concept can be applied to travellers; several times during this trip I've become tired, overwhelmed and fed up, then, after some R&R moved through it, coming out the other side feeling buoyant again.

Chris, currently on his sixth trip in India, says he decides to return after refreshing himself back home because he finds the country enticing. He agrees with my sense that India can be both wonderful and awful at the same time. "It's more of a challenge," he says, "a place where you get pushed and elbowed. I can never relax, it keeps me on my toes. Thailand is different, a very easy place to be." My brother prefers to winter in Thailand, finding India excessive now, and with our own limited experience of Thailand, we certainly notice the difference.

Chauvinism Rears its Head

As a Western feminist raised in an era of gender discrimination, I can spot chauvinism anywhere, if I care to look for it. But dwelling on it diminishes my experience and my enjoyment of the culture; it angers me, triggering residual issues from my past. India is what it is…a traditional culture that is evolving into a more progressive one as time passes.

What's noticeable in Udaipur, as in most parts of India, is the absence of women on the street in significant numbers. For the most part, employees in the service industry are male, as traditional, upper caste Hindu and Muslim women are hidden away at home. Women from less conservative families travel by auto rickshaw to the market, face uncovered, to make their purchases. Some young working women travel about, as Deepti does, riding from home to office on her motor scooter during the day. While having dinner at a deck restaurant in the Old Town, we notice a woman pacing back and forth on her small rooftop below, and fantasize about why she's there; perhaps she's had a fight with her husband, or she's worried because he hasn't come home, or maybe the roof is the only place she's allowed to take her exercise. Deepti later confirms that this woman lives in purdah, confined to her home. "Even here in the city women live this way, so imagine the lives of rural women, where nothing has changed", she says.

Confinement is only one aspect of purdah; covering their bodies, veiling their faces and physically segregating the sexes are others. Purdah symbollizes authority and harmony within the family, according to my reading. The concept disturbs not only Western women, but also educated Indian women like Deepti, because it keeps women illiterate and ignorant, lacking in power and often in basic skills like food sanitation, thus also affecting their children in many ways.

Other experiences during this trip remind me of how males are accustomed to being in command. The first is when a middle-aged post office employee in Paharganj initiates a photo session with us, with Don as cameraman, posing with his head pushed close to mine, arm forcefully around my shoulder, unexpected and controlling behaviour. The second incident occurs at The Garden of Friends when a child, a boy of no more than twelve years old, shouts at me in Hindi and shoves me into position beside his family, again for a photo op. (Indians love having their pictures taken with foreigners.) In the case of the boy, although it's annoying, I understand that he's been brought up to act this way, to take charge as a male member of the family.

The first situation caught me so off guard I didn't say anything, just pulled away as soon as possible. Both events bring home the way some males use physical force to control women. If Don was not present, incidents like this and worse would surely occur more often.

The Dowry Maids

Ellen, Garden of Maids
(Photo: Don Smith)

We decide to enjoy a quiet day, so we travel to the northern part of the city to visit *Sahelion-Ki-Bari,* The Garden of Friends. Designed in the early eighteenth century by a King, for the princess who became his wife, it was rebuilt in the late nineteenth century when a dam broke. The queen and her forty-eight maids, part of her marriage dowry, relaxed and enjoyed themselves there in their life of purdah.

The grounds are lovely, with four decorative pools, beautifully maintained flowerbeds of lotus blossoms, bougainvillea creepers, one hundred varieties of roses and well-kept lawns. Men were never allowed in the garden historically; in keeping with this tradition the present day gardeners are female, their lineage descending from the daughters of the original maids, Deepti explains to me.

A bit rundown, the property is still very attractive. Stone walls, a variety of large shade trees, marble pavilions, carved marble elephants and a lotus pond complete the charming tableau. The fountains in the middle of the pond, added during the rebuild, function by natural water pressure. At one end there's a curious little museum with a collection of old pictures, stuffed cobras and various animals.

Though still part of the city, it's very relaxing in the quiet garden. Once inside, one could be almost anywhere in the world. After strolling the grounds for awhile, we sit on a bench and read before going back into the heart of town; the garden has provided the idyllic rest we needed.

Auto rickshaw travel on Udaipur's narrow roadways is generally slower than in larger cities, and for the most part quite comfortable. It's not unusual to see cows and donkeys around town, even on the highways. In the Old Town, animals move along with the cars, motorcycles, bicycles and walkers. Vehicles slow down when necessary for pedestrians and animals alike, with the exception of the narrow, twisting, road near the travel agency, where the motorcyclists sometimes speed.

The roads in this ancient city are actually too narrow for cars to travel in both directions, only ten feet wide on average. As we arrive back from the Garden, our auto rickshaw driver heads towards the vehicle bridge that leads to our side of the lake. Near the on-ramp we encounter a traffic jam; cars crowd the street waiting to enter the bridge as vehicular traffic streams off in the opposite direction. In the midst of this chaos a woman leads several donkeys along. A late model red car coming off the bridge edges forward, the driver uncaring that the donkeys are being pushed into other cars. I feel sorry for these poor animals, thinking the experience must be traumatic for them, but perhaps it's all in a days work. Finally our tiny auto rickshaw darts around the traffic and onto the bridge. As we pass by, I call out to the woman in the red car, "That's mean"; I hope she hears me.

Homeless in Mumbai

We're back at the travel agency with the aim of finding a new hotel in Mumbai, after our Denver acquaintances mention there have been problems at the Colaba hotel where we've reserved rooms. Two years ago they had bedbugs, plus their staff is extremely antagonistic. When we check their customer reviews we discover it's no secret that the lodging is a hostile place. The two most damning accounts are from a self-described "burly Brit", who strongly advises single women not to go there alone, as even he felt slightly intimidated by the staff; the other is from a female traveller who had a fight with the manager when he tried to force them out in the middle of the night for no apparent reason. We promptly cancel our reservation.

As we research other hotels in downtown Mumbai, we encounter a serious problem; it's too late to get a mid-range room this close to Christmas and the Muslim holiday, Muharram. Deepti, with her indomitable will and energy, takes up the cause, calling hotel after hotel, vowing to find us something in a realistic price range. We begin to think our flight may need to be cancelled and Mumbai skipped, but Don is looking forward to it and I want him to see the city.

Tired and frustrated from our fruitless search, we head off for some fun activities; a tour of the Hindu temple a few blocks away and a visit to a fair trade store I read about in the guidebook.

Dedicated to Lord Vishnu, preserver of the Universe, the Jagdish Temple is the largest in the city, its Indo-Aryan architecture dominating the skyline of Udaipur. The eighty-foot spire of the three-story building is adorned with sculptures of dancers, elephants, horsemen and musicians, and the temple itself has striking, ornately carved marble pillars, decorated ceilings and hand painted walls.

We climb thirty-two marble steps to the main area, passing beggars on the way. From this vantage point we can see four small shrines around the courtyard, each for a different god or goddess. In the centre sits the main shrine of Lord Jagdish, or Vishnu, with a statue of the four-armed god carved out of a single piece of black stone.

Two huge stone elephants guard the entrance of the temple, up another short flight of stairs; both temple and shrines boast exquisitely carved statues of gods and goddesses. The inside of the sanctuary, called the prayer hall, is a beautifully appointed, shallow room; to my eye it resembles a large shrine. In the back the priest of the temple, in orange robes, lights candles. An older couple sit outside the door; they are the keepers of the temple, a position passed down through generations. Anyone can light temple candles, but only the priest and the keepers can go inside.

An artist introduces himself and begins to guide us clockwise around the outer courtyard, as is customary at Hindu and Buddhist temples. He explains the meaning of the intricate carvings of gods, goddesses and small elephants covering the pillars and outside walls.

I'm drawn to the small raised shrines in the courtyard, each on a platform accessed by a several stairs. Everyone is welcome to enter and pray to the Hindu deities represented in them: Lord Ganesha, bestower of good fortune, Surya, the Sun God, Shakti, manifestation of creativity and Lord Shiva, God of mercy and compassion.

Behind the temple is a girls' school, an auspicious setting. To one side is a building where food is given out to the indigent and handicapped daily. When I express a desire to make a donation, I'm told the person in charge will not be back until evening.

We thank our artist guide and depart, stopping to give a few rupees to each of the handicapped beggars outside and to four older women standing on the steps leading down to the street.

Next we search out the Women's Handicraft Co-op. Someone points us towards the Indian Market. On the way we discover a shop displaying woven embroidered hangings, for the top of doorways; I've been looking for them. The shopkeeper's English is excellent, picked up from the tourists, he says. His business opened only four months ago and is not thriving yet with this year's poor economy.

Traditional wall hangings are displayed all round the shop, and the owner explains that they're made from old festival dresses. This handiwork is becoming a lost art, unfortunately, as women are no longer creating traditional crafts.

We purchase a door hanging for the kitchen at home, also one as a gift for our daughter. I request and receive a discount, my instinct telling me not to go too low. Both of us satisfied with the exchange, the owner offers me a gift of a tiny silk shoulder purse.

All the right ingredients are here for a successful business; an honest, well informed shopkeeper, with excellent quality products, and I encourage him, saying he'll do very well in his store. The location is perfect, just a short distance from the centre of the Old Town and the Indian market, on both the tourists' and locals' routes. As the city grows this will be the next tourist street, in fact it's already mentioned in Lonely Planet travel guide.

The Sadhna Womens' Co-op is easy to find in the next block. Beautifully displayed products frame the window and each offering in the store has been carefully and lovingly produced. The place has a wonderful, warm feel of "woman energy".

Sadhna was established in 1988 with fifteen founding members, to provide rural and urban slum women with an alternative means of income. The co-op now has over six hundred members selling their crafts at a fair trade rate. The card attached to each product reads: "We strongly believe in women's empowerment through enhancing their own agency. Every product sold helps take the women further on this journey."

While we're in the store a group of Rajasthani women come in. They admire my red resin bangles from Shekhawati; today I wear four thin ones along with two thicker ones, all decorated with rhinestones and yellow stones. The women express enthusiasm for the jewellery in non-verbal ways, validating my opinion that the bangles are unique and good quality. After they leave I buy a thin, knee length, royal blue cotton top with short, hot pink-edged sleeves; useful in warmer areas.

On my return home, impressed with Sadhna's worthwhile work, I develop a vision of selling their products through my website. Deepti makes several trips to their larger main store on my behalf, purchasing cotton handbags, silk covered notebooks and bangles, shipping them to Canada.

Lunch with Lal Singh

After all this activity - can it only be lunchtime? Deepti suggests we meet her at the restaurant she frequents, instead of eating at Hotel Minerwa, then I can interview her as planned. She asks Lal Singh to take us there, saying she will join us in five minutes. The restaurant is in a small hotel owned by Lal Singh's brother, and he's in the lobby when we arrive. Climbing the stairs to the rooftop dining room, we're seated in the almost empty room.

Since Lal Singh is with us, I'm thinking now might be a good time to interview him about Rajasthan and Rajasthani women, as Deepti has encouraged me to do. (I'm not sure why I'm interviewing a man about women, but discover that he is indeed very interested in the empowerment of Rajasthani women.)

Lal Singh graciously agrees to speak with me and spends twenty or thirty minutes answering my spontaneous questions, while I take copious written notes. During our conversation both his phones erupt repeatedly, like a Western drug dealer's, we joke. One call is from Deepti, who says she can't make lunch as the travel agency has suddenly filled up.

A gentle, patient man, Lal Singh is willing to share many interesting details about his culture with me, and mentions that he would like to take us to his village, 20 miles from town, to meet his family and see the sights, perhaps on Sunday. This would be more interesting than touring with a guide, as originally planned.

Some of what we talk about is duplicated in my comprehensive interview with Deepti later. We speak of the complexities that make up Rajasthan. Religion is one of them; although most Rajasthanis are Hindu, some celebrate Christmas also, and the Muslim population celebrates their Muharram holiday immediately after Christmas.

Marriage is later now, at age twenty-five or twenty-six, Lal Singh tells us, and only about half are arranged. Astrological compatibility is important in all matches, as we learned from an Indian teacher we visited with on a train in South India during our first visit here. Lal Singh says it's more acceptable to marry out of caste these days in Rajasthan.

Few women are forced to stay at home at present, he tells us; this varies somewhat from Deepti's later account. Lal Singh's married sister, previously pressured to remain in her home in the village, has more choice today. His mother still covers her face in the traditional Hindu way, but the whole family supports and encourages her in making changes and they go on outings together.

Many Rajasthani Indians live to eighty or ninety now, Lal Singh says, especially those in villages; there they eat less and get more exercise, caring for animals and walking. His father, who worked at the Lake Palace Hotel, located on an island in the middle of Lake Pichola for many years, has retired back to his village.

Both Lal Singh and Deepti feel strongly about helping the village women who have very hard lives. Widows, some as young as twenty years of age, are not allowed to remarry, even when childless, while widowers can, we're told. Lal Singh, his wife and son plan to volunteer, teaching village women to read and write in Hindi.

Although India's population has doubled since the fifties, its fertility rate has actually declined by 40 percent since the sixties, and the average woman now bears only three children. The urban, educated Hindu middle class has begun to transition to extremely small families; Lal Singh and his wife Roop, with one son, exemplify this. Some families stop at one child now even when the firstborn is a girl, a positive development for females with respect to educational opportunities and other overall socio-economic improvements.

The information Lal Singh provides is interesting and helpful; I'm sensing, however, that it may be the sanitized, PC version of Rajasthani women's rights. In fact Deepti's female, feminist perspective proves to be much harder hitting.

After lunch we return to the travel agency, where Lal Singh arranges an auto rickshaw for Don's dentist appointment. The office is still bustling and I'm surprised to see that three British travellers have taken over Deepti and Lal Singh's front service desk; I joke about the tourists seizing the agency in a coup. The owners have graciously offered them the use of their more efficient computers so the men can search for accommodation and transportation.

The office quiets down again and Lal Singh suggests that Deepti take me back to his brother's hotel for our interview. I beg off, by now tiredness has hit me, plus an odd headache and sinus congestion has been niggling at me all day, perhaps from the dust floating around town.

Resting at the hotel, I gaze out the window once again. There's always something different to see and today three small green parrots sit in the tree adjacent to our window, three boys go by on one bicycle, not an uncommon sight, and several people wheel their bicycles cross the bridge. It's the rule, I believe.

A well-covered teenage girl jogs around the tiny scrap of lawn below our window, round and round she goes. Her run would be a more satisfying one on the sidewalk, but she's not allowed to jog in public. A small girl and boy, hotel family members, walk the powerful white boxer dog belonging to the Mexican guest who is performing Shakespearean plays at a local theatre (who would have expected that?).

The sound of dhobi women smashing wooden paddles on wet clothes floats in through the window from across the lake. Our neighbour on the lane sits outside her home, washing the family's clothes in this way.

The weather is changing; it's quite cloudy this afternoon, normally there's a late day haze over the lake. The hotel manager tells us the clouds are coming down from Kashmir in India's far northwest, when they leave the cold air will come directly south into Udaipur. The temperature has been a comfortable 25 degrees Celsius during the day, (about 75 degrees Fahrenheit), but will be cooler by January. When we leave Udaipur just before Christmas it's still warm. Then the summer heat arrives two months early, in March, with daytime temperatures soaring to 44 degrees Celsius. Deepti is ill periodically for weeks due to this extreme weather.

Sunday at the Palace

City Palace Complex
(Photo: Don Smith)

On the banks of Lake Pichola lies Udaipur's City Palace, the most visited tourist attraction in the city and the largest in Rajasthan. Originally built by Maharana Udai Singh, then added to by his successors, it's actually eleven palaces.

We're not overly impressed with historical sights as a rule, but both thoroughly enjoy our visit, spending several hours roaming the warren-like hallways of the palace, looking at displays and appreciating the architecture. Visually eye catching, City Palace is built of granite and marble, blending medieval, European and Chinese styles. Encircled by fortifications, it consists of assorted towers, domes, arches, courtyards, corridors, rooms and hanging gardens. Visiting here is truly like going back in time; there's even an arena where elephant fights were once staged.

The interior decor is worth seeing; unique paintings, antique furniture, glass mirror tiles and ornamental Chinese and Dutch ones, figurines of crystal and porcelain, and collections of miniature paintings owned by past residents. One palace even has glass mosaic peacocks set into the walls. The re-creations are so effective and the atmosphere of the palace so authentic, one can almost feel the presence of the royals who lived here.

Eventually we move on to find a bite to eat, since we don't realize there are several adjoining hotels, each with a restaurant. On our way out we discover a large courtyard restaurant, being readied for a maharaja's evening birthday party; long tables have been arranged for a buffet feast and round tables are decorated with canopies of streamers and flowers. When we inquire, we're told that it's open to the public, but find that the tickets are an exorbitant price.

Massage on the Lane

Don is off to an early morning appointment with his proud and proper dentist. After breakfast I sit on the deck, reading and taking in the view. Some new guests have arrived from England and we chat for a bit.

Then I cross the lane to inquire about a back and shoulder massage, keeping my request straightforward, there's less chance of being injured that way. Bodywork in a foreign country always carries some risk; my neck was injured in Laos during a reflexology treatment!

The massage therapist, Arti, is the daughter of the dhobi woman. She's 20 years old and studied massage and esthetics in college, marketable skills in this tourist town; she now continues her schooling with a view to becoming a teacher. Arti is very sweet, with gentle, skilful hands; she kneels beside me as I lie comfortably on a blanket spread on the floor. The fee for the massage is extremely low, so I give a substantial tip to help Arti with her schooling. Then it's her turn, and I offer her a brief sample of the Trager bodywork I once practised.

Arti invites me into the small house across the lane where her family lives and works. In the front room family members create and sell their art, the diminutive paintings unique to Udaipur; the back is their private area. The narrow front wall of the house is completely open. At night while the residents rest, a door is slid across.

Today I have the good fortune to meet the entire family, including the parrot enjoyed so much by the small girl the other day. Arti's mother does not speak English, but her father and brother do. After I sit in the store for a few moments talking to the men, Arti brings me a small cup of mild masala tea, tasty, even with the unexpected added sugar. It's an honour to be invited into an Indian home, even briefly.

The Search Continues

Don returns, sections of his mouth white and other parts brown, as his teeth whitening/cleaning regime involves four appointments. We take the ten minute walk across the bridge to Hotel Minerwa's white rooftop restaurant to reinforce ourselves. Then we descend the four flights of stairs to Shree-ji and resume our attempts to locate a Mumbai hotel room. Deepti and Don make phone calls, she from her desk, Don from the pay-per-minute tourist phone in the corner, while I fruitlessly search on-line for vacancies in hotels mentioned in the guidebook. As the hunt continues Don and Deepti find more lodgings that are either full, too expensive or have received bad reviews.

A couple of hours go by in this way, then, feeling tense and a tad desperate, we go to Café Edelweiss to drown our sorrows with coffee and cake. Our peaceful interlude in this interesting city suits me well, but today, in addition to the Mumbai accommodation problem, I'm beginning to feel some general anxiety about moving on.

While we've been indulging at the café, Lal Singh called a colleague in Mumbai. This agent comes back with four or five hotels in his area offering deep discounts to travel agents. The 6000 rupee rooms are 4000 for us, expensive at $90, but at this point we don't have much choice if we're to visit this international city during the holiday season.

We choose a preferred hotel and Deepti books it, sending a travel agent's voucher to secure the room, rather than using a credit card. "This way there will be no nonsense;" she tells us, "the room will be clean, there will be no bait and switch, no violence or rudeness and you'll be in a good location". (Bait and switch is when a hotel draws you in by advertising a low price, then on arrival tells you the cheaper rooms are not available. It's done all over the world; a Google search reveals a nightmare version of this in Alabama, USA, where a woman paid almost $200 for a room originally billed at $29.)

The new hotel is about a forty-minute train ride from downtown, negligible in a city the size of Mumbai. We're both relieved, happier now that we know Mumbai is still on our itinerary. The motto of the story is book ahead in big cities, especially at holiday time, and always thoroughly research hotels!

Back at the hotel, we find the weather has become even cloudier and cooler than last evening. A staff member tells us there's been a hailstorm 100 kilometres away. For a change of pace tonight, we search out a new deck restaurant in a tall, triangular-shaped building in the Old Town, at the corner where three streets meet. Initially we're shown to seats on the busy third floor deck, with a view of endless rooftops. A nearby television blares the 1983 James Bond movie Octopussy; filmed in Udaipur it's one of the city's claims to fame.

After inquiring, we're told there's another restaurant on the next floor, so we climb the stairs and take a seat on a small deck. The enclosed ceiling, abundant plants and Rajasthani decor combine to give the impression of being inside a hidden turret, its walls open to the streets below.

We ask the waiter if we can order beer, against the bylaws of Udaipur. He replies yes, and brings us a large bottle of Indian beer, disguised in a cloth bag with a drawstring top, placing it on the floor beside the table. This reminds me of Kerala, the South Indian state, where we enjoyed our pre-dinner beer in our room; if the alcohol is unobtrusive, chances are the police won't say anything.

The food takes forever to arrive, but we don't mind, as we're captivated by scenes on the street, watching the miniature people and the automobiles attempting to wind their way around each other. As we stand at the railing of the deck, we're excited to see an elephant, adorned with beaded tapestries, lumbering along the street.

Elephants Are Part of the Town
(Photo: Don Smith)

Out and About

It's a day full of small adventures, beginning with my favourite breakfast, Dream Heaven's excellent pancakes with honey and a large bowl of fruit and yoghurt; I need help to finish. Some days we're able to order real coffee, then they run out and it's instant for awhile.

We decide to buy flowers for Deepti and Lal Singh, a thank you for finding us a room in Mumbai. With two travel agencies involved in the booking, I doubt anyone received a commission worth mentioning. We hire an auto rickshaw driver to take us to the flower market, the one on the market map, but in typical Indian fashion he drives us out of the Old City toward The Garden of Friends, to a small flower kiosk on the side of the road; no doubt the proprietor is a friend. The flowers are fresh and inexpensive and the trip there and back low cost, so why make a fuss. I'm surprising even myself with my flexible attitude. We purchase a dozen sweetheart roses with accompanying greenery and tiny yellow flowers, then return to the Old City.

Instead of letting us out at the walking bridge, to cover the last couple of blocks to Shree-ji by foot, our driver travels along a short back lane running parallel to the main street and Lake Pichola. This alleyway is narrower than the street, with an art gallery on one side and a ghat with shrines on the water side. When we pass by the laundry ghat a woman is washing herself today, rather than clothes; she's removed her top and is bent over to hide her body, a surprising sight in this country of female modesty.

Farther along our progress is halted by several cows in the lane. The driver shouts at them repeatedly while inching the auto rickshaw forward and they finally move out of our way. Up ahead he spots a scaffold loaded with men working on the wall of a building, and says he can't go any farther. "Aren't you going to yell, 'hnn, hnn' at them?" I joke and he replies, "They're not cows". We climb out of the auto rickshaw, all three of us laughing uproariously.

Walking to the top of the lane, we double back down the main street the few yards to the travel agency, where Deepti and Lal Singh are surprised and pleased with the gift of roses. They can't find their vase, so after we drink our chai, sent out for on any occasion, at all times of day, I rinse out a mug and put the flowers in water.

Our friends remark that they need some time off and would like to take us to Lal Singh's and some other villages this afternoon, then up to Mount Abu. Don and I had considered going there immediately after McLeod Ganj, but Tibetan friends said it would be too cold there by December. The chance to spend time away with Deepti and Lal Singh, travelling comfortably by car, strikes us as an enjoyable opportunity. As an unmarried Indian woman, Deepti must seek parental permission to make the trip to Mount Abu; she phones her father, the more progressive parent and he agrees.

While we wait for them, I do internet searches, read e-mails and blog. By now it's mid-afternoon, and the office becomes busy once again. At this rate, it will be too dark to see anything by the time we get on the road, Deepti suggests Don re-schedule his Saturday dental appointment so we can leave Saturday morning. He's able to do this, but the dentist is displeased with him on his next visit; he doesn't seem to think Don values his professional services.

Once the agency has quieted down Lal Singh and Deepti, now in holiday mode, invite us out for lunch. Deepti, Don and I take an auto rickshaw, arranged by her, at a special Indian price, no doubt, to an upscale part of town. It's an area of stylish hotels, across the street from the famous Rose Garden and next door to the vintage car museum. Lal Singh arrives on his motorcycle shortly.

Barista is a replica of a cafe one would see in Vancouver or LA, offering good quality paninis and coffee. Our Indian friends seldom eat Western food, being traditional Hindu vegetarians, the Tibetans are the same, but they've been wanting to check out this café since being given complimentary coupons. We enjoy our food and relax together, talking and laughing. Don has his camera with him and is able to show Deepti and Lal Singh pictures of our trip to date and of our home in British Columbia.

Deepti has told us that they can only obtain visitor's visas to countries like Canada with an invitation, a bit of a surprise because they're Indian citizens, unlike the Tibetans. We would very much like to invite them for a visit, we say, also Lal Singh's wife and son; hopefully they will come next summer, before their busy fall tourist season.

On the way back from lunch we become entwined in an enormous traffic jam between the market and the travel agency, on the stretch of road where the lanes are at their very narrowest and curviest. Suddenly a gigantic elephant appears from a side street at the head of a parade, he's coming right towards us. Following him is a man on a white horse; he looks a lot like a bridegroom, but Deepti says no, it's another kind of festivity. Now a large marching band fills the roadway, so noisy I cover my ears as we wait, a captive audience. The band is followed by a multitude of women and girls, each carrying a brass bowl on her head, then at the very end of the parade comes a silver coach with an elderly man seated in it, a woman too I believe, but it's hard to see clearly from inside the low auto rickshaw. Deepti tells us the man in the coach is being celebrated on this, the birthday of one of many thousands of gods.

Heigh-Ho, Heigh-ho, it's off to Mt. Abu We Go

On Saturday we arrive at Shree-ji in mid morning, but the office suddenly fills up again with tourists from all over the world and the four of us don't get away for a couple of hours. The time passes quickly as we visit with other visitors, one from Canada.

Eventually we head out of town, with Lal Singh at the wheel. He's an excellent driver; having ridden a motorcycle for many years, he obtained his license fairly recently, however, none being necessary for bikes. Lal Singh's village is not part of our route to Mount Abu, a disappointment, but we pass through several other small villages.

A short distance from the city, in a village cut through by the highway, we stop to watch a man sharpening instruments at the side of the road in front of his home. Abutting the house is a small lean-to, a shed for the animals. The worker's method is crude and labour intensive; using heat from an open fire, he shapes and applies new handles to the tools.

The villages close to Udaipur are quite well off, but as we drive farther out, the poverty is more obvious. Large numbers of rural poor struggle with endemic poverty in this parched region, an area where deforestation and lack of knowledge about land management make it even harder to eke out a subsistence living. The state is poor on the whole, but Udaipur is kept solvent by its tourist and marble industries. Some families are now very wealthy from the marble business, Lal Singh explains.

The town of Mount Abu, less than two hundred kilometres west of Udaipur, is the only hill station in the entire state, and can be accessed by car, bus or train. Today we're taking secondary roads in order to see the sights, mostly dry farmland, so it takes several hours to get there.

Part of the Aravalli Range, one of the world's oldest precipices, Mount Abu has an elevation of 1,200 metres. For centuries, it's been a popular retreat from the dusty, dry heat for Rajasthanis and their neighbours from Gujarat. Indian royalty and British army families summered here after the British established the hill station in the 1800's about the same time as McLeod Ganj was built.

The last part of our trip is the slowest as we climb winding switchbacks, heavy with traffic. Deepti, in the back seat with me, becomes a tad carsick from the winding roads and the change in elevation. Mount Abu is lower than the McLeod Ganj area and I have no issues with elevation sickness this time.

When we arrive it takes a while to find a hotel that suits Deepti's taste; her criteria is nice rooms and ideally a restaurant. The first lodging is run down, the second an improvement. Indian hotels are normally quite plain, with little or no art; these particular ones both have dark hallways.

Our rooms are a good size, each with ensuite bathrooms. For the first time we're asked by staff if we want toilet paper, as Indians traditionally clean themselves using their left hand and warm water, believing this to be more hygienic and natural.

Once settled, we stroll around the small town. Mount Abu is quite crowded this weekend, with Indian, not foreign tourists. It's a bit cool for Western visitors now that December has arrived, although not cold by our standards. Daytime temperatures reach a comfortable 20 degrees Celsius now, at night dropping to around ten; just a month ago it was 30 degrees during the day.

The atmosphere here is carnival-like, complete with candy floss and Rajasthani-costumed folks for hire, to pose for tourist pictures. Most visitors are from Gujarat; Ahmadebad, its administrative centre and former capital, is only two hundred kilometres away. Gujaratis enjoy coming here to relax and have a few drinks, as their state is dry.

Around seven we go out for a meal, Indian vegetarian food, at a restaurant selected by our friends. As is frequently the case in India, the plates have been placed on the restaurant table ahead of time, an invitation to patrons. We notice that our friends automatically wipe them with paper napkins to remove any dust that may have accumulated; we never thought to do this before, but will now.

After the tasty meal we stroll around for a while, window shopping, checking out some clothes, then return to the hotel where we share some beer and a snack ordered up to the room by Lal Singh. While the men drink their beer, I give Deepti a sample of Trager bodywork to help her relax.

The travel agents are still working even though they're on holiday. Deepti has a network card for her laptop computer to check flights, while Lal Singh is on the phone in the middle of the night, as he is most nights, assuring that everything is on schedule for the next day. I'm sure this extremely personalized service will change over the next few years and customers will begin checking their own flights by computer or telephone as in the west.

Next morning we eat breakfast at an Indian restaurant a few blocks from the hotel. Don and our friends have a full Indian breakfast of rice, chapatis and breakfast curry; I prefer a simple Western breakfast, my choice is fruit with yoghurt and a little taste of curry with some type of fried bread.

After the meal we begin the return trip to Udaipur; it takes considerably less time on the new highway. It's been a long time since Deepti and Lal Singh had a break; they feel refreshed from this short holiday and we've enjoyed being away with them. As I write this, I relive the bittersweet feeling of that weekend spent together, just a few short days before our departure from Rajasthan. The time with Deepti and Lal Singh was precious, as our next meeting date is an unknown.

They do apply for Canadian visas, submitting invitation letters from us, but approval is declined for both, to our collective surprise and disappointment. Our federal MP's office suggests that the Delhi agent hired to submit the applications may have made an error or the financial data was somehow incomplete.

Deepti's preference was to visit us by herself, but it would be a struggle for her to obtain parental permission to visit non-family members abroad. In the end she and Lal Singh each apply for individual visas at the same time. Don develops a theory to explain why the visas were declined, this idea is validated by a Punjabi immigrant here at home: the Canadian government perceived them as a flight risk, believing the two were running away to Canada together!

The new highway from Mount Abu to Udaipur opened a year ago, but parts are still incomplete; at times there are two lanes in each direction, then suddenly there's only one. As we motor along at high speed, a row of small rocks appears in front of us, blocking our lane; they indicate that we should divert to the other side of the road. The stones are hard to see, from a distance I thought they were birds sitting on the road. Just past this barrier men are working on a bridge in a painstaking, labour-intensive way.

Observing the traffic patterns of the various vehicles on the mountain highway, I joke that in Canada the white lines on the road are meant to be obeyed, it's the law, while in India they're only a suggestion. My remark is taken in the humorous spirit it's meant in.

There's a surprisingly high level of pedestrian traffic on the side of the road, perhaps these people have not adjusted to living beside a high speed roadway.

Although it's a common sight in India to see people sitting or lying on the median as cars drive by, vehicles normally travel at a slower speed. Three women and a man carry goods on their heads, and we pass the odd goat, a cow and a camel being led along. A group of women in multi- coloured saris climb out of a truck and children wave bags of produce in the air, but no one can brake to buy anything at this speed. Our friends tell us it's very dangerous to stop for any reason at night, as the people are so poor they will rob you.

A visit to Deepti's parents was planned for this weekend, but because our trip day was changed, they're entertaining friends when we return to Udaipur, and Deepti is needed at home. After spending a quiet afternoon at the hotel, as the light begins to fade, we take a walk in the historical residential section, behind the main street of the Old Town.

The residences in the back streets are mainly two and three-story row houses, built on narrow lanes not more than five feet wide, with the occasional single family dwelling visible. Picture taking feels intrusive; we simply enjoy looking around this interesting neighbourhood. Residents of the lanes are surprised to see us, several assume we're lost and ask if they can help. A few inquire as to why we're there in a curious, but not unfriendly way; one shows us a large, decrepit haveli, set back from the lane in a crumbling courtyard. Our long walk takes us in a circular route, ending back at the main street between the Indian market and the temple, as darkness begins to fall.

Capturing the Memories

It's now December 21 and there are only two days left in our Udaipur sojourn. We'll miss this friendly, aesthetically pleasing city and its people. Don departs for his final dental appointment, after this session his teeth will all match!

At breakfast I meet a young professional couple, the man is from Seattle and his partner from Ohio. They're on holiday from their community development work in Kabul, Afghanistan, taking in the sights and planning to hike in the Udaipur area.

The man, D, is with an Afghani government organization and his partner, L, with a private one. His government job is low tech and low on funding, D tells me. "The situation feels hopeless, after only three months there." L appears to be feeling more positive; her NGO has more resources, including a large security budget to keep workers safe on the streets of Kabul. His job takes him out of the city frequently; it's a very dangerous situation, with bombs going off around them in the field. That even happened once in Kabul, they tell me. Shifting gears (sometimes it's hard not to slip into counsellor mode), I ask how they deal with their trauma, and they reply that they feel okay about it all. That's not my impression after just skimming the surface with them; he has a heavy cold and appears to be experiencing at least some level of burnout. I wish them well as they leave for a day hike.

Laneway, Indian Market
(Photo: Don Smith)

After doing some hand laundry in the room (we combine do-it-yourself with sending clothes out), I cross the footpath to meet Don at the travel agency. On my way, I pass three women carrying heavy goods; one has large, wok-like bowls piled on her head, while the others each balance two large bags of grain on theirs, one also carries a baby over her arm.

Don arrives in an auto rickshaw and I climb in for the short ride to the Indian market. It's our final visit, and we want one last glimpse of this vibrant place. No purchases are made today, our time is spent wandering around in familiar areas and locating some markets not yet visited.

We notice tiny clay chai cups, the kind used exclusively in India for tea thirty years ago, when Don first visited the country. Indians from all walks of life drink chai at intervals during the day, but plastic cups are most commonly used now. There's still a market for clay cups in certain sectors, and we find that some of them are manufactured in Dharavi, Mumbai, the slum community we later visit.

The fabrics are brilliant, and the vegetable and spice markets particularly eye catching. We fill up on the rich variety of colours that surround us. The purposeful energy of the place makes it exciting to be here. A woman passes us on the street, carrying an enormous bowl of vegetables on her head; she puts out her hand to indicate a right turn before crossing to the other side; the way vehicle drivers signal turns manually.

This morning we visit the houseware, hardware, fabric and basket making areas, and walk through the dry goods market, past burlap sacks overflowing with pasta and various grains and pulses. We notice big chunks of sweets, what we called *burfi*, or Indian fudge at my old yoga centre in Toronto; we pass them by as they have flies all over them, like the dates we saw on a previous visit.

Finally we stop at the small watch shop, where a neighbour shopkeeper says the proprietor will be back in five minutes. When he returns, regarding me warily, I tell him his watch is a good one, thanking him, and am rewarded with a smile. (In fact the watch still runs well two years later.)

Udaipur's Indian market captivates me; I can't get enough of the place, but this must suffice until we return on our next trip.

An Interview Worth the Wait

I'm in the Hotel Minerwa café waiting for Deepti to join me for our long awaited talk. Ten Indian women and one small girl enter the restaurant, each wearing a bright Rajasthani sari. They look around inquisitively, as if the surroundings are quite foreign to them. Each woman dips her head briefly and greets me with, "Hello, Namaste" as she passes by and I reply in kind.

Like other women we've encountered, they do not speak English, but by their warm and friendly manner, express their interest in me. The waiter enters the room and immediately ten scarves are tossed, in a chorus, over ten faces. The women perch for a moment at a table with a view, then troop upstairs to the open rooftop deck.

212

Two gentlemen pass through the restaurant and also climb to the upper deck; one is an elderly man, the father-in-law of the hotel owner, according to the waiter. The group has come to the hotel as 14 days ago there was a death in the family, he goes on to say. In the Hindu religion there is a formal protocol for grieving, and one day this week the women of the family sat together in a small room off the downstairs hallway keening; Deepti and Lal Singh closed the office door to give them privacy.

After two weeks of visits to the restaurant, the waiter and I are well acquainted, and while I'm waiting for Deepti I have an opportunity to speak with him. The topic on my mind is the prolonged staring I've been exposed to in rural bus stations. "This is not sexual in nature", he says, "it's a different mind, a different way of thinking. They're rural men and they're curious about European and other Western women", he continues. "I look at women when I go out, that's what women and men do." We agree that this is okay, but staring isn't. The conversation is helpful.

In this, the poorest of states, women live more traditionally than in many other parts of India, following the established ways, including covering their body. Deepti also does this, at the office she alternates salwar kameez suits with blue jeans and sweaters. Traditional women also cover their heads with the end of their sari or with a *dupatta,* a long scarf.

Rajasthani women are expected to associate with kin or approved companions; Lal Singh fulfills the latter for Deepti. They must remain sexually chaste. Traditionally women travel for family-sanctioned purposes only. Although Deepti can afford to go almost anywhere, her parents will not allow that, thinking it's unsafe as well as improper. In the time I've known her she has occasionally gone away by herself, always for a specific reason; a business trip, a visit to her father at his new police posting in Jaipur, the occasional visit to a Delhi friend.

Deepti straddles both the traditional and the new India, struggling to blend the two worlds. Although from Rajasthan, her formative years were spent in relative freedom in Delhi, giving her a unique take on life and a lifestyle that's different from other Rajasthani women her age.

Our conversation reveals the complexity of the social situation here and demonstrates the complexities of her life. She is a university educated, 27-year-old Brahmin woman. Outwardly lovely, Deepti also has an inner charisma and beauty, and is well informed about women's issues. She relates on an equal footing to people of both genders.

"Deepti's not Indian…well she is, but she isn't…she's very modern", Alma says when she tunes into her energy. "A lot of women like Deepti were men in a past life; they will not be the old fashioned woman."

When she was nine years old, her father was posted to Delhi for his police work; Deepti and her two brothers accompanied him, to take advantage of the superior schooling there, while the matriarch of the family remained in Udaipur, teaching in a government school. Those nine formative years in the progressive city of Delhi have made her who she is today.

After returning to Udaipur to study accounting at college, Deepti was unable to get a job in her field. She came to her career of travel agent almost by accident, when her cousin invited her to Mumbai to take a six-month tourism course with her. Deepti's welcoming, helpful personality and high skill level make her well suited for the business and her financial background is an asset to the company. Formerly colleagues at another agency, she and Lal Singh now own Shree-ji Tours 'n Travels jointly.

Our discussion focuses on women's lives in Rajasthan, and we begin with Deepti describing the life of an average woman. "Even five years ago all women were housewives," she says. "Now more study and work, but a certain part of society will not allow women and girls to go outside their home. Most village women and girls are illiterate. It's changing, changing, changing, but still not in all parts of Rajasthan."

The lives of rural and city women differ dramatically. "City girls are encouraged to get educations and jobs," Deepti tells me. "More than half are educated and work outside the home; this is what the husband and his family want at the time of marriage. In the villages they follow the traditional patriarchal ways."

Some well-educated married ladies do stay at home when the family can afford it, she tells me, "One of my sisters, (her sister-cousin in Ahmedebad), is well educated and is now a housewife," Deepti says. "Her husband thought it was better for her to stay at home because she was offered only 5000-7000 rupees a month for employment, ($100-150). Men don't think too much about the expansion of the woman or their thoughts," Deepti adds.

Deepti believes if you're educated, "You know what is good and what is bad and can make up your own identity and ideas, then people will respect what you think more." She is an example of this; her intelligent, confident manner commands respect.

I'm curious about how other aspects of big city life compare with less sophisticated parts of India. "Is it stricter in Rajasthan than in places like Bombay and Delhi?" "Delhi's like out of India," Deepti replies. "Every day it becomes more western, western, western. Nobody's going to ask you what you're doing, with whom you're living, where you're going. Mumbai and Delhi are like foreign countries now, but other cities are the same as they always were," she tells me.

There is a new generation of young urban people who want to enjoy all the modern social opportunities, Deepti says, the ones considered bad by the older generation, so they "push back, push back, push back," with the result that sometimes the young people hide what they're doing. I tell Deepti it's the same in Vancouver, where unmarried South Asia career women frequently live double lives, with sisters, friends and even brothers covering for them when they party at nightclubs.

We go on to discuss the influence of caste on women's lives. At this point the restaurant cleaner hovers near our table, he seems interested in our conversation; we wait until he leaves before continuing.

Lower caste women receive only primary education (5 years), Deepti tells me. Many are illiterate even in their own language, and consequently work at the lower jobs. Deepti and other educated people I speak with believe it's not in the best interests of the politicians to "equalize them", as she terms it; "Then who will do the work?"

Deepti's mother, an educated, traditional-minded woman, and her own mother, also a teacher, are very much against inter-caste marriage, while her father does not mind. When I ask Deepti what might happen if she met a man who is not Brahmin, she replies; "It depends upon the situation; I think after a period of time it would be okay if I got a good boy, a standardized boy, someone equal to me."

When a couple marries in Rajasthan, the bride still brings a dowry with her, although they don't call it that now. "It's whatever is agreed upon by the two families", Deepti says. "In poor families, though, with no father or other responsible male relatives, there is no money for the dowry, so no family wants to take the girl on."

My understanding of who lives together is hazy, so I ask for an explanation. "The girl usually goes to the house of the boy when they marry, but if he has a job elsewhere, if he can afford to, he takes his wife with him. Alternatively she stays with his family and he visits every month or few months," she replies.

"What happens when the husband is away, if the couple owns their own home, (as mentioned by Lal Singh), must the woman live with her new parents?" I ask. "She must live with *someone's* parents," is the reply, "*Nobody is allowed to leave the woman alone.*" This turn of phrase catches my interest. "Fathers and other male family members are duty bound to protect the family," Deepti explains. This chauvinistic belief that women need protection results in drastic limitations to women's freedom.

As a westerner it's difficult for me to accept that a woman is compelled to stay with in-laws she does not know when she has her own family, but in this culture women effectively change their family alliance when they marry.

"When a woman becomes part of her husband's family, the mother-in-law often forces her to do many things," Deepti tells me. I remark that the mother-in-law would not have the same love for the young woman as her own mother and Deepti replies "That's exactly right; in a poorer family they want someone to do household chores and care for children; they don't have the respect or the love for her."

Deepti has a personal conundrum; she does not like living in Rajasthan. I ask how her life would be different if she and her family were still in Delhi. "I was different there, going places and hanging out with my friends," she replies. "Nowadays my thinking has changed; your thinking will be like whatever you see and whatever you feel," this wise young woman says.

"I don't like the people's thinking here," she continues, "because I've been there (Delhi and Mumbai), and they had broad thinking and a free environment. Here in Rajasthan, even in Udaipur, your neighbours, the whole community, know you and what you're doing. The people keep saying to me, 'Oh this is not good', 'You should not do that' all the time." As I write this, I think about the pressured life Deepti has; it's like living in a fishbowl.

Although Deepti's family gives her freedom within Udaipur, some of her friends do not have the same choices, she says. "They compromise because they don't understand what goes on in Delhi and Bombay. Most are compliant," she tells me, "very quiet…but I'm different. I get so frustrated and sometimes very angry; I fight with my parents to leave Udaipur. But they want me here with the family and they see I'm happy with my job; the job also keeps me stuck here."

When I meet Deepti's mother shortly before we leave town, she puts up a wall; although polite, she doesn't seem interested in engaging with me in the ways women usually do, despite language barriers.

I ask Deepti if she thinks she'll have to stay here, and she replies that sometimes she thinks that if it was not for her travel agency, she'd go to Delhi or Bombay. "But that is not easy," Deepti tells me, "I must fight (my parents) because they won't let me go by myself." She remains torn, saying, "It's okay because I have my good job, but sometimes it's stressful when I think about wanting to leave."

With respect to her arranged marriage, I wonder aloud if Deepti's parents are seeking city men for her. She explains that where the man lives hardly matters to them, but because they love her and know that leaving will make her happy, their preference is for men outside Udaipur. "After that I could go anywhere, even to a foreign country; if I get married they won't have any problem if I leave." As I re-read this statement, I feel somewhat more hopeful about my dear young friend's future.

The final topic of the interview is gender selection; it's a hot topic in India and I'm not sure how Deepti will feel about discussing it openly. This is not a problem for her, and Deepti's strong feminist views come through even more powerfully here.

In India's male dominated society, boy babies are desired to carry on the family name, support the parents in old age and to avoid costly dowries. Technology now makes gender selection prior to birth a reality, and not just in India. It's big business in many countries, including the United States. Canada, parts of Europe and Australia have banned the procedure and most American clinics perform it on a restricted basis.

Both female infanticide and gender selection, the latter termed sex-selective abortion, are shockingly high in Rajasthan when compared with the rest of the country. In India as a whole there are 927 girls for every 1000 boys, while in Rajasthan the number of girls drops to 750 per 1000 boys: in other words (also assuming deaths from natural causes or spontaneous abortions), up to 25 percent of females conceived are eliminated by gender selection.

"We can openly say that here girls are not a priority," Deepti tells me; if the family is rich or poor, their first priority is the boy. The poorer families don't like girls at all; in high society, (it's somewhat more acceptable), they say 'Oh we got a girl.' Sometimes it's okay to have a girl once they get a boy in the high or mid level society, but if they don't have a boy they then try again or they abort the female fetus."

"Rich families often hide the abortion so it doesn't go public." She then asks if I remember the lake we passed yesterday outside Udaipur, and says that on several occasions the newspaper reported multiple aborted fetuses discovered there and the police were called to remove them. I read that gender selective abortions became public in a rural Rajasthani town when fetuses were discovered in stopped up drains behind a doctor's office. "It's happening." Deepti says.

When I ask why gender selection is more common in Rajasthan, I'm told the main reason is that most people are uneducated. "When the women are illiterate they follow the men, that's why all these things happen".

I wonder aloud how Deepti feels about being a young woman in Rajasthan, where females aren't wanted. "I don't feel good about it" she tells me. "I feel the pain of the mother, she can't do anything about it. I don't think a mother would ever want to abort her child, but they're forced to do this.

"Do you feel angry?" I ask. "I feel very angry, very angry." Deepti says. "I'm also a girl. I feel so bad, so bad, that people around me think they should not have a girl child, that a boy is special. I just want to change their minds. Then at times I feel helpless, very helpless. I'm a girl and I'm proud to be a girl."

Deepti insists the most important thing is that women improve their standard of living and self-respect, then others will respect them. But change comes slowly; when women are mistreated, for example, forced by their mother-in-law to do work, people say, "It's always happened (this way), it's okay. Why is it okay?" Deepti asks rhetorically. "They shouldn't accept bad things their mother-in-law or father-in-law or their husband says."

"We need to start…I need to start…for the sake of my child so it can continue into the next generation. Motherhood is very high work," she believes; "the woman having and raising a child is doing something for the country, preparing the new generation, not only doing something very personal."

Deepti goes on to say that "Indian culture is not for the sake of you, the individual, women live their lives for their grandmother or grandfather or parent, but they need not accept this anymore."

When Alma examines the energy system of Indian society, she finds it's entirely different from our Western system: "As part of a group soul, you can't step out of your role, or you mess up the whole order, it's like rowing a boat," she says. "Therefore discommunication is the worst thing that can be done to a member of the society."

I ask Deepti for her final thoughts. "Over there," (in the West), she says, "and over here, women are the same. I've found so many similarities between them. A woman has something a man doesn't have, the love for others; women do things for the sake of others." She believes that women have "the soft corner" and at the same time "the hard corner. We can do the hardest things."

"Always be proud to be a woman", Deepti finishes. "Only women can help women…help them stand on their own two feet." "Spoken like a true feminist," I reply.

Several months later, Deepti begins her Women's Welfare Society, using her own money for start up funding. She learns that sanitation issues, particularly food sanitation, are the most important themes among the three women she works with, taking precedence over education right now. Another focus is producing craft products to raise money for the Society and the women. Deepti hopes to have both national and international memberships for her association.

A recent Vancouver Sun article stated that more children under age five die in India than in any other country in the world; many of these deaths relate to diarreal diseases and infections that can be prevented with improved sanitation.

India is speeding ahead, in many ways beyond expectations, its technology and young, highly skilled workforce moving the country into the 21st century. Some experts, such as Nandan Nilekani, author of Imagining India, believe the country is now more linked through the idea of "Indianness" rather than by caste, region or religion, as ordinary people begin to take charge in many ways, cleaning up garbage, demanding more local representation, power and government transparency.

A generational divide separates the India of old and India today, author Jay Panda says; half the country's population is underage today, but in just a few years, by 2020, fifty million more workers will enter the workforce and begin voting, hugely impacting the society.

"Women hold the promise of a better tomorrow for families living in poverty," says the United Nations Development Program. As women take on leadership roles at the local level, working on serious concerns such as domestic violence, child marriage and improved educational opportunities, the results are promising.

It is hard to say how many generations of enlightened females it will take to change hundreds of years of ingrained traditions and doctrines; the actions and words of young women like Deepti with their social awareness and education are just the beginning.

A One Day Marathon

It must be time to move on; the hotel restaurant has run out of espresso again, provoking me to utter the 'f word', (for Don's ears only). It certainly doesn't feel like Christmas is coming, here in the warmth of India. Unfortunately I've succumbed to a cold, my second this trip; at home I seldom experience them. After getting some instant coffee and breakfast into me I feel better.

We make one of our last treks across the bridge to the travel agency, where we're meeting Deepti for a visit to her Mom's school. When we reach the office she hasn't arrived, so I write some e-mails, to Bronwen in Vancouver and Dekyi in McLeod Ganj. From here on our day becomes so busy it's a challenge to recall all the activities.

After a time Deepti arrives on her motor scooter, accompanied by a 3-year-old boy, scarf wrapped tightly around her head and mouth; she has a cold too. This child's family lives in another apartment in the police residence, where Deepti's family is located, but spends a lot of time in Deepti's home. She's good with the boy, a natural. He's really bad, she says, going so far as to call him a beast. I'm shocked at this negative description of such a young child, unexpected coming from her, but later in the day I begin to get an inkling of what she means when he acts out, even trying to bite Deepti. There's something wrong with this picture, a serious problem, I think, and develop a couple of working theories to explain his out-of-control behaviour that involve various types of family abuse and neglect.

We can't go to Deepti's mother's school until noon, then the students will be finished writing their exams. On hearing this Don changes his dental appointment yet again, from four o'clock to six; it's the second re-scheduled session, I imagine this is why the dentist is displeased with him.

On the way to the middle school, Deepti warns me that her mother is self-conscious about her poor English. When we arrive, the two of us chat a little, I keep my English simple. Hoping to make a mother to mother connection with her, I show her a picture of our daughter Bronwen. My goal is to demonstrate that we are a responsible couple, suitable to host Deepti next summer in our home.

We visit several classrooms and meet the principal and teachers; everyone is friendly and courteous. The principal, new to the school, is more formal than the teachers, as befitting his position as headmaster.

The male English teacher and female science teacher are both comfortable speaking English and spend some time with us. They confirm the widely known fact that government schools have a lower standard of education.

Aggressive state government action has resulted in Rajasthan having the largest increase in literacy of any state between 1991 and 2001, from 40 to 60 percent; called spectacular by some observers. Every village now has a primary school. This is good news, but much more is needed for girls and women; by 2001 only 44 percent of them were literate, compared with 75 percent of the males.

It will take many years to raise the standards to meet those in more progressive areas. Illiterate parents of rural students do not see the need for education; many jobs do not require it, and often poor children quit school to begin working before they complete their education.

The curriculum in government schools is of a low standard; material covered in fourth grade in other states is taught in 7th grade in Rajasthan. It is difficult, especially in the case of rural areas, to attract well-qualified teachers, as the wages are low.

Deepti requests that we speak to a class of middle school boys. Their English is limited, but we ask them a few questions, while Deepti helps interpret. Later, outside the school, Don speaks with some of them, while I'm soon encircled by a large group of girls. They're much shyer than the boys, but a couple of the bolder ones speak up.

We leave the little boy with Deepti's Mom, bid her and everyone else goodbye, and climb into our waiting auto rickshaw. It's on to the next phase of the surprise day our friends have planned for us.

Lal Singh and Deepti attempted to buy us gifts of clothing yesterday, then decided it's best that we choose for ourselves. Today I'm asked if I prefer a Western or Indian-style dress and request an Indian outfit, naturally. We drive to a women's clothing store not far from the Market.

Upstairs, the clerks invite us to take a seat and show us so many salwar kameez suits that I quickly become overwhelmed. All are high quality, custom made garments; they're cut out but not yet sized. At my request, Deepti selects several for me, she has good taste. The first suit pulled down from the shelf is the one I fall in love with, even though the men show me many others.

The tunic is teal blue embossed cotton interspersed with three-inch gold and rust designs. At the bottom there's a band of rust fabric, imprinted with gold and teal sparkly circles. Brown cotton pants with tiny blue polka dots, and a rust dupatta scarf dotted with teal and gold and trimmed in gold ribbon complete the outfit.

At close to 2000 rupees, the outfit is pricey, but Deepti says, "This is my gift to you", so I say no more, not wishing to offend her. As professional tailors, the men are allowed to touch women, and they carefully take my measurements. The outfit will be ready in four hours; there will be no need to try it on, Deepti says, they'll send an office boy to pick it up.

Our next project is the hard part; Deepti wants to buy a long top to wear with jeans for Bronwen, her "unseen friend", as she calls her. It's not easy choosing clothes for someone, and this project takes the three of us close to an hour to accomplish.

With our women's purchases complete, we motor on to an upscale men's shop, where Lal Singh awaits us. The attentive staff show Don a selection of elaborate tunics, called *kurtas*. He chooses a wine-coloured, crinkled silk one with a nehru collar; the neckline and the centre of the tunic are embroidered with silver, gold and green. The extra large size comes to mid-calf on Don, who's over six feet tall. White cotton pants complete the outfit.

Being showered with gifts has been loving and nurturing, very special. We appreciate the time our friends have taken from their busy schedule to honour us in this way. We're friends for life now, that's the way it works here. Next summer when they visit us, we'll return the hospitality, wining and dining them in our home community.

Ellen & Don in Their New Clothes, with Lal Singh

The purchase of clothes complete, Lal Singh drives off, and the three of us return to the travel agency, where we deposit Deepti, then travel on to Savage Restaurant for a late lunch. Deepti and Lal Singh beg off, as Tuesday, the day of the Sun Goddess, is the day they fast until sunset.

We discovered Savage, the excellent, slightly pricey Mediterranean restaurant just beyond the walking bridge, through their promotional brochure. For our last meal here, we enjoy delicious falafel, eggplant, pesto pasta with yummy cheese, cucumber salad and bruschetta, followed by an espresso.

After lunch we're back at our travel agency base, partaking of each other's company on this last afternoon. As usual, the traffic in the office ebbs and flows, with the internet café pulling in as many travellers as the travel agency area.

My cold is intensifying. I take an aspirin, then we walk to the nearby used bookstore to trade in old books. Books are like gold to travellers and used ones are nearly as expensive as new. I bargain with the shopkeeper and purchase my choices for under 200 rupees, plus the trade.

By now I am not well enough to go to Lal Singh's house for dinner this evening; in fact I need an immediate rest. We renew our invitation for everyone to dine as our guests on the rooftop restaurant, and Lal Singh and his family agree to come over at eight o'clock. Unfortunately, unbeknownst to us, his wife, Roop has spent the day cooking up an Indian feast. I feel badly, but an evening out after such a busy day is really not an option; we have a flight to catch tomorrow. Deepti, depleted from her own cold and the fasting, passes on dinner.

Before leaving the office we ask her to pose for a picture on her motor scooter, parked on the street, but she adamantly refuses, saying she's ashamed, (perhaps embarrassed), for people on the street to see her. We must satisfy ourselves with a picture of the scooter.

Don is off to his final dentist appointment and I'm resting before our dinner guests arrive, exhausted but happy. These folks sure accomplish a lot in a day.

At dinner time, Dilip instructs his staff to set up a table for us in the corner of the deck, where the view is most outstanding. There we enjoy a light meal of dhal and curry together. Indians dine late but eat sparingly. Roop is elegant in her colourful Indian outfit and their son, 15-years-old, is courteous and gentle, like his father, with perfect English.

Since Roop speaks little English, we don't interact as much as I'd hoped; she understands it quite well though, Lal Singh assures us. (Many women we meet in our travels and immigrants at home are self-conscious about trying out their English, unlike the men).

Before they leave, we again invite the family to visit us in Canada. The boy is going to Europe on a school trip, Lal Singh says, and we're not sure if Roop would feel comfortable in Canada with the language barrier.

Our dreams reflect the small details of ongoing life in interesting ways, while also working at deeper levels. After our dinner, I dream we're in another restaurant, the location is not clear, but it's not India. With me are Don, Bronwen and my Mom, then a man, a stranger, comes to sit with us. After a time we change tables; then I notice that Mom is no longer with us. "Where's Mom?" I ask, and Don replies "Her ashes are at home." It's odd, short but powerful, neither restful nor disturbing.

A stranger in a dream may represent different aspects of ones self, while the someone disappearing indicates concerns about those close to you vanishing. As I continue my unconscious preparations for Mom's death, this is foreshadowing of the future: as I write this, Mom's ashes, in a handmade wooden box, sit in a place of honour on our living room mantle, to be taken to Toronto to rest with our Dad at some future time.

Goodbye Udaipur

Deepti & Ellen Outside Shree-ji Travel Agency
(Photo: Don Smith)

It's Wednesday, December 23; we eat breakfast, pack, then cross the foot bridge to the Old Town to say goodbye to our friends. Both of us are wearing our Indian outfits; Deepti has not seen me in mine yet.

She is upset about our departure; I'm her ear, a trustworthy mentor, Deepti can confide in me and we discuss feminist issues at length. Perhaps talking to me is a way of processing as well as getting support, helping her feel more hopeful about creating the kind of life she wants. Deepti and I have formed a strong bond; our relationship has some older-younger woman aspects to it, but mostly it's two women, in a trusting alliance sharing what is important to them.

We take a few pictures inside and outside the travel agency, then return to the hotel to say goodbye to the staff and others we've met at Dream Heaven, and ready ourselves for the trip.

The two weeks spent in the city of Udaipur have been an absolute pleasure. It's a unique place: relaxing, comfortable, interesting to explore… uncomplicated. Our friendship with Deepti and Lal Singh and their families has enriched our experience tremendously and given us some sense of the lifestyle of upper middle class Indians in this Rajasthani city.

PART THREE
MUMBAI & POINTS SOUTH

Mumbai & Points South

Old Bombay

We've almost reached Udaipur's domestic airport when a cow ambles remarkably quickly onto the highway, mere feet in front of our taxi. The driver brakes hard, swerves to the left in front of a bus, then veers back into his own lane, somehow negotiating around both cow and bus; this all takes place in a matter of seconds. Hitting a cow has to be very bad karma for

Hindus because they're considered holy, but it does happen from time to time, resulting in a fine and several months of jail for the driver.

At the airport we have a two-plus-hour wait due to flight delays, but it's a comfortable place to hang out, bright, modern and, even more surprisingly, uncrowded.

The Mumbai leg of the trip has been designed so we can settle in before Christmas. Eventually the plane takes off, and the trip is only one hour. Upon arrival a driver meets us at the airport holding a sign, and in only fifteen minutes the Ledger Hotel comes into view. Located in a busy suburban neighbourhood in North Mumbai, the hotel is not far from the Santa Cruz railway station.

Our hotel is fine, but I'd be happier downtown in the Colaba district. This area is perfect for Don though; here he has the opportunity to ride the rails like in Calcutta thirty years ago, one of the reasons he came to Mumbai, I think.

The room is large and clean, with bare walls, and an abundance of side tables plus a desk, luxurious after the two tiny shelves at Dream Heaven. I thought there'd be a great selection of TV shows to watch by satellite in cosmopolitan Mumbai, but the reception is blurry.

Dharavi Slum Tour

Thursday morning we go downstairs for the buffet breakfast, as it's part of our room package and there are no other eateries nearby. We're the only foreigners in the dining room; the other guests are male businessmen, with a sprinkling of vacationing families. Indian breakfasts are heavy on carbohydrates and on offer today are: *paratha breads,* (flatbread stuffed with vegetables), juice, yoghurt, fruit, tiny omelettes, (good but always cold when we arrive), instant coffee and tea.

By noon, with the aid of Tylenol and homeopathic sinus remedy, I've rallied from my cold, determined to go on the slum tour booked for this afternoon. Don kindly locates an air-conditioned taxi to take us through the city to the central train station where the tour begins.

The first to arrive, we chat with the guide for a while, then others trickle in, until the assembly has swelled to twenty-five people. Small groups are formed, each with its own guide; we're fortunate to be assigned to the last one, with the tour organizer as our guide, along with a British couple, newly arrived in town. They're jetlagged, dressed inappropriately by modesty standards and are wearing flip flops instead of enclosed shoes, as advised. They hang in for the whole tour, but ask no questions and utter barely a word, quite different from Don and I, who are full of curiosity about everything.

Slum from Train Window
(Photo: Don Smith)

India's slum population has risen 20 percent since 2001 as more people migrate to the city to find work. At over 20 million residents, Mumbai is India's largest city, with close to 2,000 slums. Nearly two thirds of Mumbai's population - 12 million people - live in these communities, euphemistically referred to as "informal" housing, in one of India's richest states, Maharashtra. Only 36 are legal, owned and run by the government; some of these are better organized and have sewers and electricity.

Slums are defined as "Poorly built, congested tenements with inadequate infrastructure, lacking in proper sanitary and drinking water facilities". There is lack of safety, and, in the illegal settlements, the constant stress of eviction and confiscation of goods by officials. Young children are at high risk of undernourishment through poverty and/or dysentery.

On our train and taxi travels we see slums of every shape and size around the city, from one-family cardboard lean-tos to gigantic settlements like the mosquito-infested one alongside the airport; sometimes they're even built beside upscale retail areas. The Indian government only includes settlements of at least 60 to 70 families in its slum count, however, despite giving lip service to a recent senate committee report recommending that the number be reduced to 20 households.

We enter Dharavi via a walking bridge over a busy roadway, after a five minute walk from the train station. Many taxi drivers refuse to take people into the community, but during our daytime visit it appears safe and welcoming. The co-operative spirit our guide speaks of is evident in the busy streets and laneways and the smiling faces that greet us. In a city where house rents are among the highest in the world, Dharavi provides an affordable, convenient option for many.

The settlement has long been incorrectly described as Asia's largest slum; Mexico City's Neza-Chalco-Itza barrio is four times its size and now Mumbai itself has four larger slums in the suburbs. Dharavi is one of the city's government-sanctioned slums, housing up to one million people at times on under 500 acres in central Mumbai, an area half the size of New York's Central Park. Hindus, mostly Dalits, Muslims and Christians live there side by side, peacefully for the most part, at roughly ten times the population density of the rest of Mumbai.

The film *Slum Dog Millionaire* highlighted only the negative aspects of the community, depicting it as "a feral wasteland" lacking both order and compassion. Dharavi, like the country as a whole, experiences corruption in many forms as a way of life. When the majority of the population is forced of necessity to live in slums such as this, criminal activity, child labour and dishonesty are a way of life for some people.

The inhabitants have made efforts to nurture strong collaborative networks, often across lines of caste and religion. Resident co-ops help compensate for the inadequate government services by partnering with grassroots organizations to provide basic services such as healthcare, schooling and waste disposal, even addressing issues like child abuse and violence against women.

> "Most of our (Indian) movies highlight the hardworking adults and children studying and helping their families, and tend to push the stark poverty into the background. The foreign films tend to do just the opposite. The truth lies somewhere in between."
>
> Nita J. Kulkarni, Journalist

It would be easy to get lost walking through this city within a city, a seemingly unending stretch of narrow lanes, dense mazes of alleyways, open sewers and cramped huts. Roads and laneways and are made of dirt and sand for the most part, few are paved. The ground is dusty and at times grungy, but no more so than some other places. Buildings are no longer made of plastic and cardboard, most are now cement with a few metal structures here and there.

Dharavi is a recycling community: computers, cardboard, oil drums, paint cans, plastic, it all ends up here to be recycled. Small and medium sized industries export an astonishing 650 million U.S. dollars' worth of recycled plastic, leather, pottery, fabric, clothing and aluminum blocks each year by truck and railway, to be sold in domestic and international markets.

There's a theory every household in American has at least one object that originated in Dharavi, from recycled plastic pellets sold to China, to leather, eventually sent to companies like Gucci and Armani. The working poor of Dharavi see precious little of this money, however, often exploited by rich factory owners who live off site, they receive minimal remuneration.

Many residents, like our guide, are second or even third generation inhabitants. Fahim is proud of his slum, he was born in Dharavi and plans to be here always. "Why leave, you have everything you need?" he says. Currently a university student, he plans to get a Masters degree in business and eventually start his own company, either inside or outside Dharavi. As we pass through various parts of the settlement, we stop frequently while Fahim exchanges greetings with friends.

There are 10,000 small factories in Dharavi according to estimates, most illegal and unregulated. We watch a family hand-making chapatis outside their home, to be sold to restaurants, and I read about the recycled footwear business, where women clean piles of used shoes in the heat of a windowless room.

Residential homes are not part of the tour, but to reach the plastic recycling business, our guide leads us through narrow warrens of alleys two to four feet wide, past ground level row houses. Each column of houses backs onto another, leaving the homes with small windows on one side only. No sunlight reaches the area.

A typical house is 10 by 10 feet, some with a sleeping loft. An average of 4.5 people live in each home, Fahim tells us, from villages all over the country; when they retire they return to their rural home.

We pass the open door of a home shining with bright yellow floor and wall tiles, its single room bare of furniture, rugs, gas stove and cooking pots at the moment. Even the smallest homes have continuous electricity and many have cable television and sometimes a video player, according to my research. Pictures are not allowed during any part of the tour at the stipulation of the residents.

Rents in the community are as low as 200 rupees, (about $4), per month, higher in the slightly larger homes and highrise apartment buildings. Residents can purchase their own home for one and one half lac, (about $3500), an enormous amount to a poor Indian; most cannot afford to do so.

The best way to get a sense of the enormity of the community is to climb up the ladder to the roof of the recycling building, from that vantage point there's a complete overview of Dharavi.

The bulk of our time is spent touring aspects of the plastic recycling business, the largest industry; it involves many complex procedures, with tiny, dyed-to-order plastic beads as the end product.

A sideline of the business is the manufacture of equipment to grind the plastic. We're walked through the hot, dark building where migrant workers fabricate the machines in archaic conditions, using little or no protection against flames and toxic chemicals.

At the leather factory, the smell of animals permeates the air from piles of hides strewn everywhere. Just about anything imaginable is made here, from belts to hassocks to leather coats, most for export.

The pottery studio produces tiny *chai* (tea) cups; although plastic cups are popular now, pottery ones are still in use. We do not visit the fabric shop, an interest of mine, as Fahim takes us on a predefined route. From the rooftop the plastic factory we're able to see huge piles of multicoloured garments and fabrics lashed together on the roof of the fabric shop, ready for shipment.

We're shown only what the tour company is authorized to present, and the information given puts a positive spin on the Dharavi situation. While it is true that Dharavi is a vital, connected and economically viable community, the settlement has a variety of major problems, as expected in a slum of this size.

Severe public health problems abound due to a colossal scarcity of toilet facilities – one for every 1400 people, according to a 2006 report. Instead the nearby river is used by locals, leading to the spread of contagious diseases such as dysentery and malaria. Tuberculosis is a problem, and the government is studying its incidence in slums. The area also suffers from inadequate water supply and there is no comprehensive garbage pickup service.

Child labour and exploitation remain great problems in the industries of Dharavi. There are hundreds of child labour factories according to Reva Sharma; in an embroidery factory the owner turns a blind eye as boys under 18 years of age toil, the BBC's Tinku writes.

Housing conditions are crowded everywhere, and migrant labourers sleep six to eight men packed into tiny shacks called *pongal houses*.

Although Dharavi is a belt of urban poverty, its location next to a high-end commercial district makes it an area with major real estate value. The state government plans to "rehabilitate" the slum by privately redeveloping it into a modern township, with better housing, shopping complexes, hospitals and schools.

The plan is to level much of the neighbourhood in a slum clearance program, then to build a mixture of small units for slum dwellers, slotting them into multi-story housing blocks beside luxury apartments that will be sold on the open market.

This scheme would be a disaster for the poor, says a resident advocate; they cannot afford the massive amounts of electricity needed to pump water to high floors or the maintenance of elevators, cleaning and so on, involved in the upkeep of the free apartments. Consequently many residents would sell and move back to the street.

Development has not yet begun because the people of Dharavi have stonewalled the redevelopment project ever since it was announced, and in early 2011 the plan was sent back for revision. There is a fear that the only people who will profit are builders and corrupt politicians.

Residents have not been consulted about the redevelopment, although resident groups have successfully partnered with governments in the past. The federation of slum dwellers living along the Mumbai railway tracks was involved in all aspects of the project when 20,000 households voluntarily moved to allow improvements on the railway line. When the city threatened to demolish huts in Mumbai, women sidewalk dwellers formed an association called Mahila Milan, (Women Together) and drafted their own vision for the buildings, using the length of their saris to measure the designs. They lobbied for and received another floor in each tiny apartment so two and three generations of families could remain together.

Redevelopment of Dharavi is slated to begin soon, however, amidst the competing demands of different interest groups and the political candidates vying for votes.

In order to obtain lucrative building contracts and to remain a mainstream force in Mumbai, the radical rightwing Shiv Sena party, originators of the Dharavi redevelopment plan in the late 1990s, has come up with a clever strategy. To win the Dharavi votes, Sena is pledging to block the plan, unless residents are guaranteed homes 400 square feet in size, twice that of the original designs.

"We are seeking justice for the poor of Dharavi", says Baburao Mane, a former Sena member of local parliament. But the residents of Dharavi, a third of whom are Muslims and another third migrants from the poorer north, have difficulty swallowing this, since both groups have been targets of Shiv Sena for decades in their mission to fight for the rights of people born and bred locally in Mumbai.

Slum tours, also called *Poverty Tourism* are not new; for many years tour operators have been escorting foreign visitors through Rio de Janeiro's shanty towns, called *favelas*, and through the townships outside Cape Town and Johannesburg, South Africa, where tourists meet and mix with locals in *shebeens*, (illicit beer halls).

The concept is a controversial one and the Dharavi tours have been called "an exercise in voyeurism and a sleazy bid to cash in on the 'poor-India' image". This viewpoint sees slum tourism as dehumanizing to the citizens.

That is not the intent of Christopher Way and Khrishna Poojari, who run the tours to showcase the settlement's economic underpinnings and to challenge stereotypes about the poor. All revenues go to the Community Centre and Kindergarten in Dharavi.

Middle-class Mumbaikars tend to avoid this hotly contested area in the heart of the city. Whether visitors to Dharavi are foreigners or Indian citizens from more privileged economic and cultural groups, I feel certain that touring this community will educate and help open people's eyes to how a significant part of the world lives in a way no amount of reading or oral presentations ever could. The tour was a powerful experience, a demonstration of the spirit of survival of the residents of this vibrant, active community with its problems and its considerable successes.

"You could learn a lot from the people in the slums," says Sam Cameron. "They have a sense of community that is way stronger than what we 'civillized' people have."

Colaba

Leopold Café, Setting for *Shantaram*
(Photo: Don Smith)

The walking tour is much longer than planned; after three plus hours I'm fading and we tell Fahim it's time for us to leave. It's been a case of mind over matter today; my high level of motivation and the engaging excursion helped me last this long.

We emphasize that the day has been a valuable experience for us, and Fahim kindly locates a cabby for us on the main street to drive us to Colaba. Now rush hour, it takes almost an hour to travel the short distance. A new Mumbai by-law stipulates that drivers may no longer honk, but ours ignores it.

A tourist hangout, Colaba is still a bit funky from its hippie days, not upscale, as expected. Leopold Café and Bar, a key setting for Gregory David Roberts' *Shantaram* epic, is a must see. The café is crowded and noisy, packed with tourists and middle class Indians because of the book. We're fortunate to get the last table. The place is a bit worn, but interesting, significantly smaller than the book description implied.

Open squared off archways serve as the front doors of the restaurant. During the Islamic terrorist attacks of November '08, mostly confined to South Mumbai, Leopold was one of more than ten targets. Guerrilla soldiers walked in through the open doors and shot eight people. I notice what could be a bullet hole in the thick wooden pillar beside me.

At the next table we meet an interesting couple from Iran, and in a 'small world' kind of way, discover that the man received his masters' degree at the University of British Columbia. They are in India for a few weeks' vacation and will also visit Goa later.

Leopold's other claim to fame is beer served by the yard or half yard, in three foot high square plastic dispensers. Being light drinkers, we share a bottle of Kingfisher beer, our favourite local beer, along with some pasta. Our waiter tells us a movie is being made of the book *Shantaram*, with Johnny Depp playing the lead. He himself has met Roberts during his visits to Mumbai.

Exhaustion slams into me as we wander along the street, so Don locates a cabby in a black and white government taxi. The driver refuses to drive all the way to Santa Cruz on the grounds that the trip would take three hours in

Mumbai's extended rush hour, (it continues until 9 o'clock), too expensive for us and an unpleasant experience for him, he tells us. Insisting that the train is the only sensible plan, the kind man drives us to the station a few blocks away, advising, "Don't take first class; why waste your money, ride in a second class car and your wife in the second class women's car." Before driving off we're given instructions about what side of the tracks to wait on.

First class tickets are purchased for a bargain price of less than eight rupees each, (about $1.50), and we board the train. The ride takes 40 minutes, a much better prospect than the three-hour car trip.

Outside the train station we attempt to flag down an auto rickshaw for the last leg of the journey, but they're all engaged. By now I'm getting irritable; after the long day's touring, we've climbed several steep flights of stairs and walked across train station overpasses on the return journey. Finally we give up and walk, it's a much shorter distance than anticipated, less than 10 minutes along side streets in a pleasant neighbourhood of homes and small stores.

Christmas in Mumbai

It feels odd to be in Bombay on Christmas morning instead of at home. We rested well after our busy day, but now Don's health is taking a turn for the worse, while I'm on the upswing. After a breakfast of excellent curd and fruit, a cold omelette and unbelievably terrible coffee, (who knew instant coffee could taste so bad), we reach Bronwen at her friend's co-op house; it's Christmas Eve in Vancouver and they're having a good time. Mumbai doesn't appeal to me much, I say, except for the fascinating Dharavi tour, but she'll hear a different story from Don, I tell her. She's amazed to hear the population of the city is over 20 million people.

Since we're spending Christmas abroad this year, I've requested a traditional Christmas dinner to set the tone of the day, and reservations have been made at an upscale hotel on the Mumbai harbour, called The Intercontinental. Don thinks the trip will take too long by cab, even today, so the privacy of a taxi is denied me yet again. He prefers the train, and now over the worst of my cold, it seems I'm destined to travel that way. So we walk over to the train station just after noon.

Quite a few Christians live in Mumbai, so today is an official holiday and the train ride is quite pleasant. After we exit the station, a taxi takes us the short distance to the hotel. The Intercontinental is on Marine Drive, a chic part of Mumbai. One of my fellow coaches grew up in the city and suggested this area as a base; we much prefer colourful locales to five-star hotels, however.

Marine Drive is a C-shaped, six-lane road in South Mumbai, built on reclaimed land that runs three kilometres along the coastline, beside an expansive natural bay that's part of the Arabian Sea. The focal point of the drive is the palm tree lined promenade along the waterfront, where citizens get their exercise and watch the sunset at the end of the day. No one can live along the seawall and vendors are not allowed either.

Real estate prices along the esplanade are the fourth highest in the world, (more than 2000 U.S. dollars per square foot, according to Wikipedia). Some of the buildings were built by wealthy Parsis (members of the *Zoroastrian* religion; a tiny minority group, they have contributed much to India). These structures have art deco designs, popular in the twenties and thirties, similar to those in Miami, Florida.

To be admitted to the Intercontinental Hotel everyone must go through an electronic body scan, manned by professional, but friendly hotel personnel. The main floor of the building is elegantly appointed, with festive Christmas decorations in silver and gold. The décor in the upstairs restaurant is quite plain and the room almost empty, but the windows running along its width offer a spectacular view of the harbour and the sparkling water. We're seated at a window table, laid with a white tablecloth.

The turkey dinner is delicious; Indian turkeys are smaller and chewier, with a slightly different flavour, very appetizing all the same. We enjoy the tasty, well-prepared vegetables and tiny garlic and butter potatoes, but there's not quite enough of them. We would like a glass of wine with our meal, but the 700 rupee price tag for each glass of imported wine (almost $16) is off putting, so we resort to Perrier as an alternative. Dessert is delicious mud pie served in a little dish shaped like a flared ice cream cone. At the conclusion of the meal Santa comes into the room, saying "ho-ho-ho" and shaking hands with everyone, giving us all candy.

At a nearby table we notice a family of sophisticated, beautiful people; they look Indian but sound American, Don thinks they're from California. They leave before I get a chance to say hello, but the manager says "Yes, they're from here but they now live in the U.S."

He chats with us for a while, then offers to take us up to the rooftop. It's another world up there, with almost a 360 degree view of Mumbai; the entire bay, the homes of the rich on Malabar Point, and even the suburbs can be seen from here. He points out the Taj Mahal Hotel behind us.

The final place on the tour is a large dining room, elaborately decorated in red Indian motif, plus Christmas décor; it's closed at the moment. Taking the elevator downstairs with us, the manager says goodbye after offering a hotel brochure.

The irony of having Christmas dinner at a five-star hotel immediately after our visit to Dharavi is not lost: the bizarre juxtaposition of the two worlds, physically close but light years apart, enhances the impact of the slum tour. The two will be forever inseparable in my mind, fused together; Don feels somewhat the same way.

After the meal we walk around the neighbourhood, but don't travel far as I find the hot, humid weather uncomfortable. Winter begins in November with temperatures dropping to a humid 30 degrees Celcius during the day, (mid 80s Fahrenheit). Summer arrives in March with daytime temperatures up to 40 degrees. Monsoons are variable, often arriving in June.

The previous summer was particularly hot because the monsoons didn't arrive, I was told by a Mumbai woman named Mystry in McLeod Ganj. So hot in fact, that her cousin's eyes began to bleed and she had to flee to her aunt's air conditioned home.

Mumbai has a relaxed atmosphere; it's more liberal than other cities, also safer. Many women wear Western dress and – almost shocking after two months in India – a few couples touch in the street. Last evening on the train, a woman had her arm around her partner; another couple held hands walking up the stairs of the station. Mumbai is unlike any other part of India we've visited.

The Trains

Women's Car (Photo: Don Smith)

Most of the trains look old. The cars, with their hard wooden benches, some with plastic overlays, are in need of new paint. Floor to ceiling grates have been installed between first and second class sections of cars. There are a few newer, bright yellow trains on the route. We always make sure to board a train that stops at the Santa Cruz station, two thirds of the way along the route, as we don't know the difference between express and local trains.

This morning on the train a small boy on hands and knees, sweeps the floor of the car; at every station he brushes the garbage, onto the tracks, then he pulls on men's pantlegs, hoping for a tip. None of the Indian men offer him anything; finally Don gives him a bit of money. "The poor little boy," I say; later Don tells me he felt bad watching the boy demean himself crawling around at people's feet. This is his lot in life as a child of the Dalit waste-picker class.

Having heard about overcrowded train cars in India, I had no desire to put myself in the position of being groped. First class is fine, however, uncongested, the passengers are mostly older businessmen. In second class cars the passengers really do hang out the doors, as depicted in documentaries. It's in these jam-packed cars that the poking and pinching of women has gone on, perpetuated by younger, less educated males, hence the introduction of "women only" first and second class cars.

Nevertheless, while sitting on the train today, while Don stands in the open doorway, I feel more comfortable with my red shawl camouflaging my chest. Why would I feel the need for protection here, when the thought would never cross my mind at home? Perhaps I've absorbed the atmosphere and have reverted back to my modest upbringing.

Sarah Macdonald, author of Holy Cow, chose to cover her body more and more during the time she lived in India, never showing her legs and always draping a dupatta shawl across her breasts. She resented feeling the need to do this, but in her younger days in India she felt visually undressed by men continuously and this affected her later comfort level.

Don enjoys train travel immensely, while I've adjusted to it quickly, even memorizing some of the stops near the hotel so we have no trouble finding our station.

Going downtown we disembark at Churchgate, the end of the route, a huge station with a prominent police presence. One day we begin taking pictures inside the station, but a soldier waves his hand at me, saying "No pictures". Every station has a police or army presence, even before the 2008 attacks, I'm told. That was not the case in Delhi, however, and we were quite surprised this year to find soldiers entrenched behind sandbag bunkers in every metro station. A clever warning on the wall of a Mumbai station reads: "Unlike trains, terrorists do not arrive with an announcement. Be alert."

This time around I view India more through a writer's eyes; observing in this way is quite different from being simply a traveller. On the first trip, I took things in viscerally, now it's more of a creative journal keeping. The previous sense of overload is not present. Rather than believing "there's too much of everything," my frame of reference now is: "It just is." The amazing and the atrocious are still here, simply a part of this country of dichotomies. The vibrant energy and colourfulness, along with the complexity and elusiveness combine to draw visitors back.

Quiet interlude

It's Boxing Day and I remain at the hotel, regrouping after the activities of the past two days, while Don takes the train to downtown Mumbai for a self-guided walking tour. The time goes by quickly; I read, watch a bit of fuzzy TV, rest and order noodles from room service.

Our laundry, sent out by the hotel, is returned; we forgot to say no ironing, so drip dry pants and shirts have been ironed in a make work project. We pay extra for this, of course, but they do a very nice job and it provides the *dhobi wallah* (washerman) with extra income. Laundries in India never seem to lose anything and here in Mumbai a one and a half-inch square blue cotton tag is sewn onto every single garment to identify our clothes.

We heard an amusing laundry story in the Holy City beside the Ganjes River. A friend, walking by the river with her travelling companion, noticed some clothes drying on an enormous angled cement wall. "I hope they're not ours", said the young woman. "Oh no", replied our friend, "They wouldn't wash the clothes in the Ganjes". Then, a little farther along the ghat, what did they see but several pairs of pants and shirts belonging to them! After that I wasn't too keen on sending any more clothes out to be washed. Despite its pollution from germs and heavy metals, however, the Ganges is still blessed holy water with special properties.

Don returns after an enjoyable walking tour, consisting of several hours tramping around in the heat and humidity looking at old architecture. Since he's on his own he returns home in a second class train car, reliving his time in Calcutta thirty years ago. When he tried to board, the car was jammed to the doors with men, there was really no room for anyone else. A man stepped off the train for a moment to let Don climb aboard, then all the men pushed him inside. Don figured they were afraid this big old white guy might fall out onto the tracks if they didn't do something proactive!

Downtown Mumbai on Sunday

Downtown Mumbai
(Photo: Don Smith)

It's now Sunday, three days after Christmas. Leaving the hotel around eleven, we check in with Bronwen, calling more often during the holidays. Then ambling through the quiet Santa Cruz neighbourhood, we board the train for Churchgate station. Many people take Sunday as their day off, so it's a peaceful trip.

From the station a cab takes us to the famous Taj Mahal Hotel. Our driver is from Delhi; he's been driving in Mumbai for a few months, after the Japanese tour company he worked for in Delhi went out of business. Missing his wife, parents and three-year-old son, he plans to return home soon. As a tour guide it's his business to know the sights in Mumbai and he kindly suggests some places to visit.

The Taj is a heritage building, built in 1892, not as fantastic as the fables would have you believe, but quite beautiful. The hotel was Mumbai's first harbour landmark and had the first licensed bar in the city. For more than a century, it has played an intrinsic part in the life of Mumbai, hosting Maharajas, dignitaries and eminent personalities from across the globe.

I notice some well-dressed women sitting in the large rotunda foyer that's filled with comfortable easy chairs and enormous plants. Attached to the main gold-domed palace there's a new wing that houses boutique retail stores on its ground floor. The most attractive area of the hotel is a guests-only patio, with a large pool and a sitting area with tables and plants, where several people are relaxing.

Our plan is to have a meal here; the Australian woman in McLeod Ganj told me she always lunches at the Taj when she's in Mumbai and can afford it on her pension. We attempt to locate a restaurant, but find the Indian, Japanese and Chinese buffets rather expensive at 2000 rupees ($50).

By now though I need to eat and Don locates a Colaba restaurant in the guidebook, near Leopold. The doorman assures us it's only a five-minute walk, but I'm suspicious after so many negative experiences walking too far in the heat; in this instance the time estimate is accurate.

In a small, retro café, one of Colaba's originals, Don orders a non-traditional Sunday dinner of mashed potatoes, orzo pasta, tofu and veges, swimming in a tasty sauce, while I have pasta. For dessert there's excellent chocolate cake, but no coffee, their espresso machine is broken.

The temperature is comfortable later in the day, so we window shop for a while on the busy sidewalks, where the clothing stores that make up the bulk of the retail offerings all look the same to me. The Colaba neighbourhood resembles Haight Ashbury in San Francisco in many ways, funky and rundown, just beginning to become a bit gentrified.

Searching for a cab to return to the train station, Don finds that the first driver wants 200 rupees for an air con cab filled with cigarette smoke, so he walks away. We find a regular one for a good price and the driver drops us off at the station.

For the first time, our carriage is state-of-the-art, with silver and glass windows that slide up and down, clean working fans, an electronic printout of each station coming up plus a computer voice announcement, just like on the Sky Train in Vancouver. There are even ceiling vents for air- conditioning; we'll have to come back in the summer and check that out, says Don, (not!).

Half of the car is first class, the other half second, divided by a mesh barrier. Not many people are travelling in first class, but second is packed as usual. Someone back there is talking loudly and when I turn around to see what's happening I notice a little girl just inches behind me. She's watching, so I smile and wave, drawing the attention of the extroverted guy, who begins a repetitive chant of, "And how are you madam?" I grin and turn away, knowing if I respond in any way, a lengthy interchange will begin.

On the trip back, Don takes pictures of slums from the doorway of the moving train. We pass a street of small, rough looking houses; on the far side of it I notice two teenage girls walking down the street, wearing pristine-looking salwar kameezes.

Back at the hotel, I rest my neck, a bit swollen after two plus months spent bouncing around on buses, trains and cars. Perhaps I'll have an Ayurvedic massage in Goa.

I've not been at my best in Mumbai, a hot city of 20 million can be hard to handle. At times my judgmental behaviour has reared its head, as it does when I'm too hot, sick, overtired or otherwise uncomfortable. Smaller, quieter centres, with friendly residents appeal to me, places where people put their hands together in the traditional Hindu greeting of "Namaste" (greetings or good day), or the Tibetan one of "Tashi Delek" (blessings, good luck).

Someone in a local store here in Santa Cruz greeted me that way, but most people seem to have given it up in the cosmopolitan former Bombay. Staff in the upscale hotels we visited are very Western; I would hazard a guess that they've been told not to use the traditional greeting, although one did reply in kind when I wished him "Namaste" on Christmas Day. I miss these friendly interchanges that connect us to each other.

Our Santa Cruz neighbourhood
(Photo: Don Smith)

It's evening now and we take a stroll in the neighbourhood for some air and to stock up on snacks to last us until Goa, where there will be a greater selection of foods. Don's favourite corner store is on a street near the train station; there he buys the nuts and figs he loves so much and cheaper bottled water, I buy cookies. Shopping is done in small stores in India, we've not seen any supermarkets, but perhaps upscale suburban neighbourhoods have them.

It's the perfect time to stroll around, finally cool enough; the neighbourhood is attractive, a community of tall trees and quiet side streets. In fact, the leafy streets oddly remind me of summertime in Toronto, where I grew up. Many women are out alone this evening, without their men, some stroll along with other women. Moving on, we notice Hindu shrines placed at intervals along the street. An older, genteel-looking Indian woman is walking with a beautiful little girl, her granddaughter, no doubt;

they're leading a daschund, (my favourite dog, because our old dog Blackie was part daschund). I stop to admire the girl's lovely dress and the woman advises us to see the exhibition currently on at the yoga school. Not being in the mood at the moment, instead we buy a tiny ice cream cone from a street vendor, cost: six rupees, or 15 cents, then continue walking slowly back to The Legend with our bag of goodies. Our last evening in Santa Cruz has given us a chance to enjoy the community life that takes place when the city cools down. It's remarkably different in the evening, an air of calm has fallen over the neighbourhood, the feeling of relaxed energy is palpable, as the residents ease off after their work day. Tomorrow, Monday December 29, we move on to Goa in South India, our final destination.

Goa By the Sea

Benaulim Beach, Goa
(Photo: Don Smith)

Arrival

It's a short plane ride from Mumbai to Goa and the trip is uneventful. We're met at the small airport by the hotel driver and efficiently delivered to

Carina Beach Resort at the edge of town, motoring first along the highway, then through the narrow treed streets of Benaulim.

A winding driveway leads from the road to the attractive Portuguese colonial-style buildings that house close to 40 guestrooms. The setting is park-like, with multi-coloured flowering bushes and lofty palm trees.

The proper, but helpful desk manager, Natalia, gives us a brief orientation to the hotel and area. As the days pass I look forward to my interactions with her, she imparts much helpful information about the community. Natalia always wears Western clothing, but most of the other female staff prefer the simple cotton dresses with fitted bodices that are traditional to this Portuguese-influenced area.

Goa is our last stop, a vacation from travel, if you will, and we're both feeling ready to return home. As my energy flags both physically and psychically, I injure myself in small ways and the intuitive manager wonders if I'm homesick.

Natalia and the hotel owner have worked together for many years, first in his dental practice and now at the resort. Elfredo is quite formal in manner, at first this comes across as arrogance, but he is very knowledgeable and always willing to share information. We later discover him to be a very trusting man.

Our room is typical Goan style, plain with high ceilings and a ceiling fan; there's a view of the garden and pool from the balcony. The bathroom is spartan and has a very unusual shower, an older version of "on demand heating", a system originating in South America, in this case an insulated electric wire goes right into the shower head, this sounds dangerous but actually works well.

There's a problem with mosquitoes in the evening and we put DEET on our legs and feet before going to outdoor restaurants. During the day, tiny bugs, similar to North American *no see ums*, bite my thighs and ankles as I sit beside the pool, causing redness and itching, and I finally resort to DEET to deal with them also.

Health Canada advises travellers to take malaria drugs indiscriminately in all parts of India, while British medical site recommends using them only in moderate to high risk areas, a healthier prospect. Goa is moderate risk according to their colour-coded map; we arrive with Malarone pills but both the hotel owner and our waiter assure us, "There's no malaria here, you don't need pills".

Our plan now is to keep the expensive supply of medicine for a future trip, taken in a high dose it's beneficial for acute attacks of malaria. Visitors are less likely to get malaria than locals, provided they're not in the jungle or fields for extended periods of time, as their health level is generally higher. Dysentery is the bigger threat, offset by oral vaccine taken before leaving home.

A Rich Past

Originally a Portuguese colony, Goa is India's smallest state by area and fourth smallest by population, at just over one million people. Its coast is on the Arabian Sea, to the north is Maharashtra and to the south lies Karnataka.

Goa is well known for its 60 miles of fabulous sandy coastline, world heritage architecture and places of worship. Inexpensive beer, wine and liquor are also a draw. Panaji is the state's capital, while the historic city of Margao, where our hotel owner lives, still shows a strong Portuguese influence.

The state has an unusual history; it was ruled by a Buddhist emperor in third century BC and was home to many monasteries. The Portuguese conquered Goa in the early 16th century, holding it for 450 years, until 1961, when the Indian Army finally seized possession of it, after Portugal refused to cede it on India's independence in 1947.

While hot and humid most of the year, by May the temperatures are over 35 C, then the monsoons arrive in early June and last until late September. Winter is short, from mid-December to February. This is the first part of January and we experience temperatures of over 30 C at times during the day, hotter than usual, with about 20 C at night. The humidity is high and since Carina Beach Resort is a mile from the ocean, the cooling breezes do not reach us.

Foreign visitors enjoy Goa's warm climate in winter, and in the summer rainy season Indian tourists take their holidays. Tourism from abroad is down, the hotel staff tell us; the 2008-9 season saw 14,000 British tourists, while only 9,000 have arrived to date.

The second largest industry in Goa after tourism is inland mining; iron, bauxite, manganese, clay, limestone and silica are extracted. Agriculture is shrinking, but cultivation of rice, areca, cashew and coconut still provides many people with part-time work.

Fishing is also declining because traditional fishermen cannot compete with the mechanised trawlers; the industry still employs 40,000 people however.

Corporate fishing is a problem in the state of Kerala farther south also, and many men from both coastal areas work abroad in countries like Kuwait, sending money back to their families; it's an important source of cash inflow.

The literacy rate of well-off Goa is an astonishing 80 percent, 15 percent higher than the country as a whole, per the 2001 census. Two thirds of the residents are Hindu, a quarter Christian and there are some Muslims and a few Sikhs, Buddhists and Jains. The Benaulim area is predominantly Christian.

Konkani is the official language and the native one of two-thirds of the population here. Our resort owner and staff speak Konkani, Portuguese, Hindi and English fluently.

The Rhythm of Our Days

Pool at Carina Beach Resort
(Photo: Don Smith)

Although the setting is exquisite, I don't enjoy the first part of the vacation as much as hoped; it's taken almost a week to acclimatize due to the hot and humid weather. During our first few days here I've taken a break from recording experiences for the book.

An emerging feeling lessens my pleasure also; the thought that I've been away too long. I'm beginning to worry about my mother in her care home back in British Columbia; is she okay, is she dying? I have recurring dreams about her fading away. It occurs to me that the dreams are making their appearance because I'm concerned that I will not be there when my mother eventually does pass on.

More often than not our loved ones die when they are alone, perhaps their family members have stepped out of the room for a moment, or they choose to pass during the night (in fact this is exactly when my mother does ultimately leaves us).

Suddenly I "know", in that inexplicable way that my desire to get back home is an old, deeply buried regret because I was not present at the moment our newborn baby, Sarah, died in Sick Childrens' Hospital in

Toronto many years ago. I was recovering in another hospital, across the road. With this awareness, the worry about my mother dissipates instantly.

Most of us hold old traumas in our bodies; recognizing and writing about this has been a gift for me, an opportunity to revisit the regret and blame, this time in a very different way. Now I'm giving myself permission to let go.

With gut-wrenching tears and the use of Byron Katie's powerful question, "Is the belief that Sarah died alone true?", I've been able to process this old hurt to another level. The reality is that Sarah did not die alone, she was surrounded by compassionate caregivers and, most importantly, by loving angels.

Our days develop a rhythm; each morning begins with us and the mosquitos breakfasting on the lawn; they're sparser in the daytime, but still lurk in the damp shade close to the ground. Sometimes we walk before breakfast, when it's a bit cooler. Then Sheldon or one of the other waiters serves us a full meal of eggs, curd, fruit and coffee.

In the heat of the day our time is usually spent by the pool. There are no umbrellas on the pool deck and the sun filters through the partial shade; at first our skin burns, then adjustments are made, hats are worn, shirts pulled over bathing suit, and chairs located in the lee of the large building being constructed next door. As the days go by, the heat and our internal clocks slow us down to a pace that suits the bucolic atmosphere.

Some afternoons e-mails and blog posts are sent from the luxury of an air-conditioned travel agency in the centre of town. Experimenting with going to the beach at different times of the day, we discover that the mile walk down the hot, dusty roadway is best left to later in the day, until our hotel manager tells us of a shorter back route, along a sandy path.

Leaving the resort can be challenging, it's difficult to find an auto rickshaw on the outskirts of town. When it's time to come back, there are drivers lingering in town, waiting for fares, but by then it's usually cooler.

The town of Benaulim has many stores with clothing and souvenirs on offer; shopkeepers are friendly, but always push us to buy something, faced with fierce competition. Off the beaten track, away from the main street, there's a thriving residential area. We find the neighbourhood women quite friendly here, as in other places we've visited.

Once we actually get ourselves to the beach and settle under an umbrella with cold drinks in hand, it's an enjoyable experience. While relaxing at an outdoor restaurant one day, a Goan woman arrives, carrying an armload of cotton shirts and short skirts. I'm looking for white pants and a shirt; we engage in conversation and she tells me about her children and husband, who doesn't work much. The woman is quite the entrepreneur, warm and friendly, not too pushy, but I take everything with a grain of salt, enjoying our conversation while also mindful that her goal is the get the best possible price for her goods.

When the restaurant staff kick her off the property we sit down together closer to the water to look over the products. I purchase a white shirt after a tough bargaining session, sticking to the specific amount my intuition suggests.

The staff, having no other customers and being inquisitive sorts, want to know what I've paid for the shirt; they shake their collective heads when I tell them, saying that we should make the trip to the big Indian market, several hours and two bus rides away, to buy cheap clothes. Taking this trip in the heat for a couple of garments is about the last thing I'd consider doing, but two factors are at play in their minds; as a tourist I must want to buy, buy, buy, plus they want me to get what they consider to be a fair price, one they could afford themselves.

Carina Beach Resort serves excellent continental food and authentic Goan cuisine, with plenty of seafood, but dining out is a highlight of the day. Benaulim offers many choices in restaurants, a couple conveniently close by, with more on the beach.

One evening around five o'clock, taking the sandy path from the bottom of the hotel garden to the beach, we stroll along the shore for a while. Drawn to a funky old wooden diner, as the orange sun falls below the horizon and the ocean turns from pink to darkness, we enjoy freshly caught prawns and share our Indian beer.

Other times Pedro's, the original beach restaurant, opened in 1969, is our destination for lunch or dinner. A Norwegian couple at the hotel tell us they discovered it more than 20 years ago; the food's excellent, as predicted. Built far back on the sandy beach, Pedro's allows CD vendors to wander the restaurant while guests are eating, a tad bothersome.

Tonight it's a return trip to Malibu, a five-minute walk from Carina. The food is great and every Tuesday night they have live jazz-blues. This time our arrival is late and all the outside tables are taken; next Tuesday, our last night, an advance reservation will be made. An alternate restaurant close by, where we spent New Years' Eve, becomes our dining spot tonight. Good food but mosquitoes abound!

Around the Benaulim Neighbourhood

The Village of Vadie
(Photo: Don Smith)

Tuesday morning, we take a walk half a mile along the curving main road, in the opposite direction from Benaulim's downtown, to Jack's Corner, a much older residential area, formerly a tiny village called Vadie; (at first the locals don't know what we're saying, as they pronounce it 'Wodo'). Jane, a British guest at the hotel comes here often; there's always something to engage one's interest.

Vadie is a well-off community of brightly painted wooden houses, one bright purple; some are very large and have been turned into guesthouses and homestays. Many have tiny thatched barns in their backyard, where their animals are kept, close to home.

Pigs are not cooped up here and they wander freely in the neighbourhood; sometimes in fields or along the road, other times they're in someone's backyard. Curiously, the pigs of Benaulim have straight, instead of curly tails, and they wag them! Some dogs' tails, on the other hand, are curly. Cows do not wander the roads as in most parts of India, they remain in the fields and flocks of small white birds follow them around, picking up their droppings.

We've chosen Benaulim for our stay as it's a quiet part of Goa, with an older crowd of tourists and families. Colva, a few kilometres north, is much busier, especially during the Christmas and New Year's season. When we venture over there, Colva appears to be one long, dusty, treeless main street heading down to the sea, full of clothing stores and restaurants. It's so hot we don't stay long; my skin can't breathe properly because I've worn sun block for a change, and I'm sweating buckets, unusual for me. An amiable shopkeeper, originally from the state of Kashmir near the northern border of India, offers me a seat outside his store and we chat while Don seeks transportation for our return to Carina Resort.

We've never had problems with theft in India, but in this part of the world there are thieves who specialize in stealing women's purses. Natalia warns us not to carry passports or quantities of money around the neighbourhood, to lock them in our rooms or use the inexpensive safety deposit boxes provided. "Hold your purse close to your body", she tells me, demonstrating how I should carry my tiny shoulder purse.

But many unseasoned visitors ignore this wise advice; in denial, they persist in carrying large handbags, often with all their papers and large amounts of cash, not bothering to hold onto them properly. This makes them walking targets for the lazy thieves on motorbikes, who first target their prey, then turn around and race at high speed toward the women, tearing the purses from their shoulder as they pass them.

Visitors to Goa are usually British and Russian, but our hotel has mostly Europeans and a Swedish family at the moment. They prefer not to have Russian guests at the resort, Sheldon tells us. "This is a quiet place where everyone settles down early, and those particular guests keep their own schedule, returning late after imbibing vast quantities of alcohol, then sleeping long hours. They turn up for breakfast after mealtime is over. With no English, the waiters must resort to bringing the eggs out from the kitchen to show them what's on the menu."

The Paddekars

Peddekar Working
(Photo: Don Smith)

A team of coconut pluckers, or *paddekars*, arrive at Carina Resort, causing quite a buzz during the breakfast hour. Every three months they climb the coconut palms, up to 70 feet high, balancing themselves on wedges cut into each tree, knocking down the ripe coconuts and cutting off dead branches. It's a highly skilled and risky occupation.

New Delhi Television on-line reports:

> "With no safety gear on…with a swift series of spider-like maneuvers, he's at the top of the tree, slicing the nuts with a heavy blade tucked into his loincloth. One misstep and he would fall up to 100 feet to the ground."

Both guests and staff watch rapt as the pluckers chop at the trees; down below women place the coconuts in large baskets and carry them away on their heads, then drag the dead branches to a truck in the driveway.

> "The price of coconuts drops each day", Elfredo says; "no one knows why, the prices of other staples are rising, split peas for dahl cost five times what they did, tomato prices have also increased five times since the restaurant menu was costed."

There's a shortage of paddekars in many areas, I read in the Sunday paper, and pluckers must be brought in from the poor state of Bihar in the northeast. "The sons of coconut pluckers don't want to do that work", he says, "they want more prestigious, white collar jobs and consequently the profession will die out". "The caste-based division of labour is losing its grip on the society," says the local newspaper. This threatens the large export industry that sends oil, desiccated coconut, doormat fibre, milk, milk powder and mattresses out of the country. Goans themselves consume ten coconuts per week in each household.

Hobnobbing

Motoring the Highways & Byways
(Photo: Sheldon)

In an attempt to move out of my comfort zone, I suggest renting a motor scooter from Sheldon, our waiter, to tour the small villages in the neighbourhood. In my younger days I liked nothing better than a fast ride on the back of a motorcycle, but since then have been cautious physically, with the occasional aberration, such as the *spelunking* phase in West Virginia many years ago (spelunking is exploring caves).

Traffic is heavy on the main streets and it feels like we're going quite fast. The back roads are tricky as they often dead end, but eventually we manage to wind our way, at a comfortable pace, to Varka, the town to the south that converges with Benaulim.

Don suggests driving towards the beach and to our surprise there's a five-star hotel on the waterfront, The Ramada Caravel Resort. Uniformed guards at the security gate say, "Of course, you can go up for tea," without even glancing at our passports. The hotel is beautiful, featuring an expansive open atrium with cascading waterfall, artwork and comfortable seating areas. Most guests are Indian, here to attend a large corporate conference.

In a comfortable private seating area beside the bar, we enjoy coffee and mineral water near an open window that overlooks both garden and pools. Guests lounge beside pools and on lawns under palm trees, where every single coconut has been removed from the trees as a safety precaution. Almost as many uniformed pool staff are in evidence as visitors.

After the drinks, we go down one level, past the restaurant where staff are setting up lunch, and outside to the pool area. Older and respectable looking, we're usually allowed to wander around at will. Passing the pools, we walk through immaculate lawns and gardens, down a pathway to the beach, a three-minute walk. On the way we notice quite a few signs in Russian, and presume the Caravel must have Russian-speaking staff. At the beach, the only place to sit is at the bar, so we gaze out at the water for a few moments, then turn back towards the hotel.

The motor scooter is available to us for a few more hours, so we take our time riding back to Benaulim, winding our way through beach communities and avoiding busy roads; adjusting to this mode of transport, I'm beginning to have fun.

Back in Benaulim, we discover a hidden café, behind a small yellow hotel in the middle of the main thoroughfare. The owner, a French woman, serves incredible hummus and stuffed peppers, and tells us she also has a part-interest in a vineyard in India.

There is another luxury hotel worth seeing farther south, called The Leela, the woman relates, Bill Clinton stayed there in 2008. It's decor is much more interesting according to her, so we decide to check it out another day.

Back at Carina Resort we watch the construction of the four-story hotel next door. Some of the beautiful trees abutting our pool area have been cut down, Elfredo tells us. At times the building necessitates clamour, but nothing even close to the noise level at a Western job site, as most of the work is low tech, labour intensive manual tasks. Men and women transport supplies up the stairs to the top of the building; the women, saris tucked up to avoid tripping, carry bricks in baskets placed atop their heads, stabilized by a hard cotton ring underneath.

Many condos are also being built in the neighbourhood, most over the two-story bylaw. The community is taking the builders to court over this, resulting in many unfinished buildings with rebar sticking out of them. A similar situation is occurring in Mumbai, I read, where one builder must remove several stories from the top of a building. Other condos here are complete, but stand empty due to lack of both renters and buyers.

Bugs that go bzzz in the night

Anticipating a good night's sleep after a busy day of touring, we retire; a lengthy thunder and lightning storm strikes in the night, lasting from two in the morning until five, causing a massive power outage all over the Benaulim area. Within minutes our room begins to feel like a sauna without the whirling fan.

Normally the upper windows are opened at night, once the lights are turned off, to let some fresh air in; the movement of the fan keeps the mosquitos away. Tonight, even though it's pitch dark, they come round in short order. Since going back to sleep is impossible, I wave my Chinese fan around to keep the bugs away, then after a few minutes, jump out of bed, walk straight to the shower and drench myself head to toe.

More comfortable now, using a battery operated headlamp, I read in bed, moving the fan slowly to and fro. Don is enjoying the porch in the dark, he says there are no mosquitos out there. I don't believe him.

Interview with Elfredo

Elfredo, who built and owns Carina Beach Resort, has agreed to an interview about caste in Goa and in India in general, a subject he's familiar with.

"It's all about caste," Elfredo remarks. Even though Portuguese missionaries carried out mass conversions to Christianity in Goa from the 16th century onward, the devotees retained their Hindu caste practices. As a boy, he learned the South Indian categories of caste; Brahmins, Sadors, Kunbis and Sudras, the caste above Dalits. Only Brahmins, like our host, were allowed to attend school and occupy the high positions of doctors, lawyers and priests at that time.

"People of the other three castes did not attend school, for the most part, so although they were able to earn a living farming, as paddekars or as fishermen, they were backwards," Elfredo explains. "Now everyone goes to school, there's no differentiation between castes. Back then a Brahmin boy would never be allowed to marry outside his caste, if he did, the couple were cut off and disinherited. The situation in South India has changed, sometimes Brahmins marry into Sudra families."

After years of neglect, the Indian government now calls Sudras, Dalits and other lower castes, "scheduled castes", Elfredo says, making them equal in law and giving them special privileges, such as preferred university admission. Members of scheduled caste are admitted to university with 50 percent, while Brahmins like his son require 95 percent to get in.

Elfredo goes on to say that in present day Goa, no one talks about caste, they talk about class, and that depends on education and jobs. I mention the article about well-educated, higher class men applying for jobs as railway porters; Elfredo agrees that it's all mixed up now, "Before there weren't enough educated people, now there's too many and not enough jobs for 500 million people."

The more traditional north and the relaxed south are like two distinct countries in many ways, one of these being marriage customs. Ninety percent of couples choose their partner in Goa, Elfredo tells me. "The boys and girls meet and fall in love at college; it's rare for parents to arrange marriages now. Our outlook is completely different because of the Portuguese influence, even in dress and food."

He agrees that marriage is not straight forward in the north; it's a mixture of arranged and non-arranged marriages. Some young people there still conform to their parents' wishes; he gives the example of his daughter's university friend from Lucknow, Uttar Pradesh, near Nepal. This young woman dated at university, but upon returning home she was told by her parents that she must marry someone they chose. "It doesn't matter if she likes the person or not," Elfredo says; "she has to get married."

Despite their freedom, South Indian couples are still "committed to being the good son or daughter." Elfredo tells an interesting story about his son, studying medicine in London. On every visit home, families came to talk about marriage; he would see their daughter, then say no. Finally his parents confronted him, "Why are you meeting those girls if you are not interested? Be frank with us." "I've met another doctor, a Spanish woman," was his reply. "I want to marry her." Elfredo and his wife told their son they would not interfere; if he thought he'd be happy with a girl from Barcelona, he should go ahead.

This story has a happy ending; the whole family went to Barcelona last year for a civil marriage, then her family came to Goa for the religious one.

When I mention that 80 percent of the poor in India are Dalits, Elfredo responds that after 60 years of Indian independence, the Dalits are still very poor because of corruption; although the government has many schemes to help, the money does not reach the right people, he says. "If the government gives me one kror rupees (about a quarter million dollars) to help 50 families, before it reaches the poor in Bihar state, half the money has disappeared."

Crooked politicians can buy the votes of ignorant people, whereas this doesn't work with well educated ones. This is where Elfredo's rebel persona comes out. "If a politician promises me 1000 rupees ($20), saying 'Vote for me', I will tell him, 'You'll either get four smacks from me', or, 'I'll vote for whoever I want', or, if I'm smart enough, I'll accept the money and still vote for whoever I want!"

He agrees with Deepti that they don't necessarily want the Dalits lifted up. "They're needed to do the scut work. They want them to remain as they are, then when they help them, they're almost venerated," he passionately states.

We end our time together with Elfredo's final thoughts on the caste system in Goa:

"It's dying and we're glad. We're all human beings with a body and a soul; we can't differentiate a person because he belongs to a particular caste. To be born to this or that family is a coincidence. I could have been born there and been treated as a down-caste. I don't treat anyone that way".

The Leela Hotel

On a very hot day, two days before our homeward trip, we travel by auto rickshaw to Mobor, twenty minutes away, to visit The Leela Kempinski Goa Hotel, as it's officially called. Fellow Carina guests, a respectable retired British couple, were recently denied entry to the hotel, so we call ahead to ask if we can come for tea. The hotel receptionist says "You can come, but bring your passports."

On arrival at The Leela's gate, the guards are not interested in our passports, waving them away and phoning ahead to notify front door security that we're on our way. Strolling leisurely up the long, tree-lined driveway, then through the property, we admire the opulent grounds. As we near the hotel, security guards come towards us, asking, "Where have you been? We've been looking for you," demonstrating just how tight security is here. They're satisfied with our explanation and indicate that we should proceed to the security checkpoint, where all bags, cameras and sundry items go through a rolling baggage check, like at the airport. It makes sense that a former United States president and the Dalai Lama would choose this location for meetings.

Spread over 75 acres, The Leela, described as eco friendly, consists of a main complex, cottages perched on lagoons, several golf courses, pools and

Mobor Beach. Rustic bridges, waterfalls cascading over large boulders and an enormous kidney-shaped pool with a waterfall at one end complete the picture.

More elegant than the more conventional Ramada Caravella, The Leela is eye-catching both inside and out, its decor described as "a blend of South India's temple traditions and Portuguese heritage." In the spacious marble lobby are flowing water pools, intricately carved wood and metal Indian and Buddhist sculptures, even live musicians playing tabla and sitar. My favourite sculpture is a four-armed bronze goddess in a carved wooden display case, against a background wall of bright red fabric; I believe she is Shakti, the Great Mother.

The Leela Kempinski Goa offers guests a choice of 200 hundred rooms, suites or villas. Being a curious man, Don asks the desk clerk for a quote and discovers that prices range from 9,000 to 20,000 rupees per night, (150 to 350 dollars), high for India, but surprisingly low for this level of luxury.

As we stroll down the cement walkway towards the beach, guests are being driven around in golf carts by staff. "They're lazy," we say judgmentally, then realize later that they're smart to ride in this heat.

Mobor Beach is smaller than the Ramada's. A narrow walkway runs along the high tide line and guests lounge nearby under coconut palms and umbrellas. It's low tide, and the waves are high today. Vendors are not allowed on the property, but as soon as guests begin their trek towards the water, they're approached repeatedly to buy goods; the staff and security guards can do nothing about this once guests are off hotel property.

The beach dining room is set up for lunch, so the staff ask us to sit at the open air bar for a drink. We settle comfortably under the thatched roof for a rest and a cool beverage. On the walk back, I notice a sign that says Leela Hotels are located all over India; in Kerala to the south, Udaipur, Mumbai, Bangalore, Delhi, plus new ones in the planning stage. From the pictures, I suspect this Goan one is the most beautiful.

We amble back down the long driveway to the gate, where our auto rickshaw driver patiently awaits us to drive us back to Benaulim for lunch on the beach.

Last Memories of Goa

The last evening in town; our table at Malibu Restaurant is beside the lovely flower garden, not too far from the band. There's no problem with mosquitoes, the few coils spread around help.

The band is smooth, they either play often or practice a lot. On the drum set of the lead singer/drummer there's a stamp that says "Johns Hopkins University." This interesting detail may explain his delightful accent when he sings jazz standards; very precise English pronunciation with a lilting Indian overlay. After one long set lasting an hour and a half, there's a break, then more music; we stay for the first round and part of the second.

Unfortunately I can't eat my planned meal of fresh calamari; I overdid the fried foods at lunch, a meal of french fries and garlic prawns by the pool. Don has a large red snapper with a salad, while I settle for vegetable chow mein.

Awakening around seven-thirty the next morning, we climb out of bed for a final, short stroll in Vadie. It's hot and humid already, so the walk is a short one. The temperature cooled for a few days, but has now risen again; clearly winter is not here yet.

After our breakfast I'm back in the room packing, when I hear several planes fly overhead, a new experience around here. I wonder aloud if we notice them because we have flying on our minds, then Don reminds me that sounds carry depending on the wind direction. If the wind has in fact changed, winter may really be arriving.

The trusting nature of Indians never ceases to amaze me. Here at Carina Beach Resort a much larger sum of money is at stake than previously, with other vendors. Since this place is a medium-sized, relatively upscale resort, the assumption was that credit cards would be accepted, but they have proven to be too much trouble and expense for the business, so it's now a cash-only venue.

Elfredo is not concerned. "Don't stress yourself at all; you're on vacation. Send the money when you get home." We're very touched that this kind man would allow us to leave his resort and return to Canada owing him 40,000 rupees (over $700) for our 16-day stay.

Appreciating the offer, but preferring to clear the bill up, Don manages to withdraw the maximum on his debit card at a bank over two days, enough to cover the bill with a little left over.

Our plan is to leave Carina Resort at six o'clock this evening for an eight-thirty flight to Delhi, arriving there at eleven p.m. A driver will deliver us to the familiar Prince Polonia Hotel, where we'll spend a restful night before our overnight flight home tomorrow. But things are to turn out quite differently from what we've expected.

Carina Beach Resort in the Evening
(Photo: Don Smith)

What Happened Next

An uneasy journey

On the thirteenth of January we say goodbye to the staff who have taken such good care of us during our two-week stay, and leave Carina Beach Resort around dinnertime for our flight to Delhi. As the taxi winds its way through small towns enroute to the highway, we soak in the magnificent scenery one last time.

The plane takes off as scheduled at eight-thirty and the trip is uneventful until we near Delhi. Forty-five minutes outside the city, the pilot comes on the loudspeaker with a curious announcement, "There's fog around the Delhi airport," he says, then, "*I'm keeping my fingers crossed* that we'll be able to land and will keep you posted." His particular choice of words does not inspire confidence in any of the 150 people on board. Twenty minutes later he tells us the plane will not be allowed to land in Delhi, as the minimum legal visibility requirement for this medium-sized plane cannot be met.

Each winter, air traffic in North India, especially in busy Delhi, is disrupted as haze engulfs the entire region. The type of radar equipment and lack of staff training at this airport mean more disruptions than in some places such as London, England. Once the threshold for landing or takeoff has been reached, as this evening, all activity ceases.

Our plane is diverted back to Jaipur, the closest airport. Didn't like the city all that much the first or second time round and here we are again! I have a fleeting vision of holing up in the Hotel Madhuban for a cozy night's sleep (the best thing about Jaipur), however, no room offer is forthcoming, and we must reach Delhi in plenty of time for our overseas flight. Coaches will be provided to take passengers there, we're told.

Staff at the Prince Polonia in Delhi say their driver is already at the airport waiting, but he will be contacted and sent home. On arrival, we pay for the driver's time, but the hotel kindly waives our room charge.

The Jaipur airport is busy; it takes a while to locate our luggage and the waiting buses. By now it's eleven p.m., everyone is tired and the ground crew doesn't seem to have much information. Confusion reigns as a group of ten men from our plane complain about the situation; one puffed up bully shouts loudly at the innocent staff. By the time we reach the line of buses all are close to capacity; our seats are the worst possible, behind the rear wheels.

Long distance bussing is done at night, when there's less congestion. The roads between Jaipur and Delhi are astonishingly bad, even the main ones. Our passage is slow as the skilled driver cautiously manoeuvres the vehicle through the dense fog.

As the back of the bus springs up and down, I'm thrown into the air and dropped down again every few minutes. Don has fifty pounds on me, so he remains seated. Fortunately my memory foam travel pillow absorbs much of the neck impact as I'm slammed back onto the seat.

The vehicle becomes quite cold and we pull a heavy wool blanket over our legs, hoping it's bug-free. Surprisingly, I doze a bit between midnight and seven thirty, when we arrive at the Delhi airport.

On this impromptu journey there are no scheduled stops for passengers, only for the driver and his relief at a truck stop. Most male passengers leave the bus, but a European woman stops me in the aisle, saying it's pitch dark and there's nowhere to pee. As usual, I've sipped only a little water enroute, nonetheless the last hour is quite uncomfortable. As I write this my body relives the tension of the bus ride, but my great love for India propels me through these occasional rough experiences.

Passengers are dropped off at the International terminal, then the bus moves on to the domestic one. Fortunately there's a washroom available outside the security perimeter, so no awkward explanations or delays are necessary.

The cab driver we engage speaks enough English to communicate with us and is familiar with the location of Paharganj. Despite this, plus explicit directions in Hindi from the Prince Polonia front desk, he must stop and ask a couple of men on the street for its exact location.

Wherever you go there you are…again

Not sure what it is about me and buses; whether I want to or not, I'm repeatedly faced with long distance bus trips and their attendant trials and tribulations. Part of the challenge of travel in developing countries I suppose.

At this point a permanent moratorium on long bus or train rides has been declared by myself and Don concurs. My plan for reaching McLeod Ganj, Dharamsala next time involves neither buses nor trains; the one-hour flight from Delhi to an airport close to the mountain village is inexpensive if booked ahead.

In *The Dance of Seventeen Lives*, the author recalls flying into the Dharamsala area during the winter. Initially pleased to discover that the monk beside him was the Dalai Lama's brother, he soon wished he was seated elsewhere, for as the blustery flight progressed, the poor monk, apparently afraid of flying, kept up a repetitive mantra of "Maybe today we'll all die", unnerving all around him.

Paharganj in Winter

Finally, we arrive at the hotel and are checked in quickly. We're now ensconced in a cosy corner room, overlooking a side lane that's gated at night.

Some guest rooms are closed as room renovations and a revamp of the wholesale store below is still underway. During the day there's some construction noise, but it's not a problem as our room is far enough away, at the opposite corner of the building. We're just happy to be settled in this familiar home away from home.

Delhi looks and feels like a different city in mid-January. People walk around with scarves over their heads and huddle around street fires to warm up. Air comes down from the Himalaya Mountains and with the added fog, a temperature of 10 degrees C feels much colder than it normally would.

To give you some idea of how damp it is, towels cannot be left in the unheated bathroom and extra pillows come to us from the storage room feeling wet. A small electric heater makes the small bedroom fairly cozy, however.

A blanket of haze covers North India each winter, caused by cold air moving south, combined with pollution and moisture from the irrigation canals. Delhi and other northern cities are hardest hit, and this winter is worse than usual. Levels have increased tenfold over 50 years, and scientists are concerned that changes in cultivation and irrigation patterns, over-cultivation of rice, and even efforts to plant trees and boost forest cover may be worsening the situation.

Our room has been freshly painted, and the new bathroom has a tub with a shower, although the plastic is so thin it feels like it will break when you stand in it. The toilet does not flush, so I ask the staff to take a look at it; they come upstairs immediately and do a simple repair. (We've become used to defective bathrooms in both McLeod Ganj and Udaipur, but in this big city hotel things run more efficiently).

After a well-earned nap, we leave our room to take a stroll around the bazaar a block away. The sun is warm, raising the temperature to a balmy 15 degrees C for a few hours in midday.

When we're not out on the street, people-watching from the balcony is a fascinating pastime, as many tableaus unfold below our second floor corner perch, which looks down on both the street and the private laneway. It's surprisingly quiet, especially at night, just one street back from the main Paharganj market. At the moment, however, voices rise up from the street. Indian men walk by in groups, a tourist couple passes, the young woman holding the arm of her middle-aged partner, not cool in Northern India, where most visitors respect the non-touching in public custom.

The side lane is an attractive residential street, at times crowded with parked cars. A sidewalk sleeper sits on the curb outside a large white house with stylish architecture; kneading dough in a small bowl, he later cooks chapatis over a tiny open fire. Six women come down the lane wearing salwar kameez suits, scarves tightly wrapped around their bodies and over their heads for warmth, as it's mid-afternoon now and the air is becoming chillier. The mixed colours of their clothing brighten up the otherwise dull day, as they walk along chatting animatedly with each other. A woman and her two small children stand beside the shoe repair man as he sews a shoe by hand in his tiny kiosk next to the gate of the laneway.

In front of the hotel a beggar carrying a baby walks down the street, while one of the irritating map sellers tries to flog his wares to tourists. He stalks a woman; she can't seem to get rid of him, perhaps she's too polite, new in town likely.

Four boys about ten or eleven years old have piled onto the tiny ride-on tractor by the curb for a joyride. The woman talking to the shoe man comes running; she slaps one boy and is about to throw a chunk of brick at them, but they run away, darting at high speed down the lane. Suddenly I realize that the woman and her family are homeless; what appears on the surface to be a rather violent reaction to the boys' mischief making is a natural, visceral response to the possible loss or damage of a precious object. Now, squatting at the curb, the mother cooks dinner for her family of five over a tiny wood fire framed by a handful of bricks, in appearance like a miniature barbecue. Afterwards they collect the ashes from the fire; everything is useful here.

An auto rickshaw and a van driver stand patiently outside the hotel waiting for customers. A vendor sits beside two large mounds of coal, piled in the street not far from the door of the hotel; several men carry their coal purchases in pails over their arms, taking it home for cooking and heating.

Brij's cargo rickshaw has been moved around the corner, just inside the gate to the lane, away from its place of prominence at the front door of the hotel. The entire entrance to the hotel has been shifted from outside the building to the inside, as it was encroaching on city property. The beautiful four-foot statues of Ganesh, the elephant god and Haniman, the monkey god, still flank the door, but without their Plexiglas cases now.

Many other businesses in the city were also ordered to move their stairways off city property, in preparation for the Common Wealth Games in ten months. Additionally all above ground wiring in Delhi is being buried, to make the city more attractive for visitors, a mammoth job over this short time period.

Last day

We have one day to enjoy Delhi. The taxi is ordered for midnight for the flight to Hong Kong at four a.m. Downstairs we encounter Brij; the on-going remodelling means his presence in the hotel is more evident. No longer hidden in his basement office, where we first met him two years' ago, Brij is now located in the main floor craft store, where products are sorted for shipment and sold to hotel guests and others who wander in from the street. Only yesterday I discovered that the prices in the shop are wholesale. The store no longer stocks clothes; however, I buy some attractive leather change purses for friends, a leather elephant bank for a baby present and gorgeous green drop earrings for myself.

We decide to re-visit Old Delhi; after a short metro ride, we take an auto rickshaw to Chawri Bazaar Road, the main street of the community, then climb the steep stairway to the Jama Masjid Mosque's imposing red sandstone entrance. Here we're turned away because noon is the time for Muslim congregational prayers; we've picked the wrong day and time to arrive. Foreigners are allowed in this afternoon, we're told.

Jama Masjid is the main mosque of Old Delhi and the largest and best-known in India. Completed in 1656, it was commissioned by a Mughal Emperor and constructed by the same man who built the Taj Mahal. The mosque is close to 300 feet long and 90 wide; its roof is covered with three domes of black and white marble and gold, flanked on either side by two high minarets, each with 130 steps. Twenty-five thousand worshippers can fit in the courtyard, accessed by flights of stairs through three entrances that are also home to food stalls, shops and street entertainers. One of the three approaches, the eastern one, has 774 steps.

Terrorist explosions struck Jama Masjid in April, 2006, deliberately planned for Friday, the Holy Day; 13 people were injured, but the building itself was not harmed. Again in September of 2010, two Taiwanese tourists were hurt sitting in a parked bus, near the gate three entrance.

Ellen in Old Delhi Market
(Photo: Don Smith)

The Old City is inhabited predominantly by Muslims, whose traditional lives revolve around work and the mosque, much as they did a century ago. After leaving the mosque we walk down Chawri Bazaar Road and tour the narrow lanes of the markets for a couple of hours. The neighbourhood is medieval looking except for the odd modern touch such as the criss-cross of electrical wires above the streets. Some shops are closed on Fridays but there's enough going on to make our window shopping fulfilling.

The main thoroughfares are difficult to cross, but once across one finds peace in the back lanes amongst the tiny shops and the delicious smells of home cooking. Shoppers can buy anything here from books, clothes and shoes to electronic and consumer goods and exotic spices.

There are very few tourists in Old Delhi in the winter, and we see no women in the streets today, unlike last October, when many women were out in public, wearing a more modest dress than their Hindu sisters.

With no plan in place, without even the Delhi pages of our guidebook, we wander the maze of look-alike lanes, unable to find the popular restaurant from our last visit, or locate another suitable looking café. Muslim cuisine is heavy on meat and it's best to be cautious about what and where one eats so close to travel time. Both hungry and tired from our trek around the bazaar, we make a decision to return to Paharganj.

Back on the main street we meet an unusual bicycle rickshaw driver. This man is 65 years old, with excellent English, acquired while working for Mother Teresa in his hometown of Calcutta, where he transported clothing for poor people. Here in Old Delhi there's lots of tourist business for someone who can interact with Western customers, as most drivers' English is limited or non-existent. We're deposited by him at the nearest metro station, a different one this time, and travel the few stops back to our hotel.

Paharganj, View from Balcony
(Photo: Don Smith)

We bid adieu to Paharganj by climbing four flights of stairs to an open deck tourist restaurant in the middle of the square; from this lofty perspective there's a great view of the neighbourhood activities taking place below. Relaxing in the sun, we're served good Western food by a young Nepalese woman. In keeping with a pattern established in 2007, my ritual last meal in India is a delicious pizza. I like to think of it as my re-entry meal.

After lunch we stroll around the community then walk down the wide street that runs off the square to the post office to try and trace the box mailed home in early December. The parcel hasn't reached Gibsons, BC yet; it will take a minimum of one month to reach Canada, an employee advises us, but later in the day Don finds that Alan has written to say the parcel is in our house awaiting us.

We've had good luck sending and receiving parcels between India and Canada, though there's always risk involved. Our friend Dolma received only one of two pairs of shoes sent to her in McLeod Ganj by an American friend; the following year we do have trouble when I unthinkingly send several Olympic T-shirts there in two unregistered packages.

Enroute to Canada

Our taxi arrives on schedule and the drive to the airport is speedy at this late hour. We're processed at Indira Ghandi airport using a new, quick check-in procedure. After a short time in the pre-boarding waiting room, we're ushered onto the plane at the appointed time.

International flights require 200 metres minimum for takeoff, our pilot tells us, a 25 metre reduction made last November by Civil Aviation. Fewer flight delays were expected this winter consequently, but this hasn't been the case with the heavier fog.

As the 4 a.m. takeoff time approaches, we're told that visibility is fluctuating; it's fine for a few moments, then deteriorates. The pilot advises he has chosen to keep the plane on the runway on standby, ready to take off when a window of opportunity arises.

The hours tick by as we wait, and he periodically thanks us for our patience. As 7 o'clock rolls around, the crew serves a choice of either an Indian or an Asian breakfast, then the passengers settle in again. My ability to sit this long without feeling stir crazy surprises me.

As daylight begins to arrive, visibility improves, and sometime between eight and eight-thirty the control tower clears us for takeoff to Hong Kong. The flight is uneventful and the plane arrives there in under six hours. It's now seven at night in Hong Kong, but with the zone changes we don't yet realize this, knowing only that the connection for the flight to Vancouver will be tight.

Cathay Pacific employees holding signs meet and walk with us to another area of the airport, where other personnel inform us that our flight to Vancouver left an hour and a half previously. There will be a layover in Hong Kong until early the next evening. Not many people on the Delhi to Hong Kong flight were going on to Vancouver, so the plane was not held. The staff have booked us onto the same flight twenty-four hours later and vouchers are provided for the overnight stay at the airport hotel.

The Regal Airport Hotel is colossal; its 1100 rooms are rented by the night, during daytime hours only, or in four-hour segments for traveller layovers. The only hotel in the airport, it's connected to the passenger terminal of Hong Kong International by an enclosed, air-conditioned link bridge.

Initially, we can't enter our assigned room, the key card is coded incorrectly; we drag our weary bodies down the long corridors and back to the registration desk. When finally inside, we find ourselves in a large, modern bedroom, and the staff are very attentive to extra requests such as special pillows.

Unfortunately, security regulations forbid us to access our luggage; it remains checked and will be put on the plane tomorrow night. Another lesson in being a good traveller, a basic one that slipped our minds; always include a change of clothes in your carry-on, especially underwear, along with toiletries and medications. I've packed everything but a clean shirt, so I spot clean the long-sleeve black jersey I've been wearing and blow it dry with the hotel hair dryer.

The complimentary hotel room, priced at upward of $300 a night, comes with vouchers for three buffets meals; dinner, breakfast and lunch, at the Café Aficionado, one of the facility's six restaurants. With each meal there's an enormous selection of hot and cold food; neither of us can do justice to it the first night, being so sleep deprived.

We retire early and sleep well, except for a three a.m. wakeup call to phone Vancouver; our friends must be informed that although our plane will, in fact, arrive on time tomorrow, we will not be on it! Expensive e-mails have also been sent from the hotel to both them and our daughter, but we don't completely trust that mode of communication.

The next day, well rested, we thoroughly enjoy our breakfast and lunch buffets, sampling small amounts of a variety of dishes. Almost everything imaginable is on offer, fish of every description, more meat than we choose to eat, pasta, plenty of vegetables and salads, even an ice cream bar for dessert.

At the hot buffet I recognize the chef's accent as West Coast North America and initiate a conversation with him. He's from Portland, Oregon, and has cheffed at the Vancouver Regal Hotel; it truly is a small world.

In between meals we relax in our room and take a walk around the periphery of the hotel, choosing not to go into Hong Kong; there's not quite enough time and we don't feel like rushing. We realize the delayed flight out of Delhi and the consequent missed Hong Kong to Vancouver flight are a gift in disguise and quite enjoy breaking up the trip in the luxury of this five-star hotel.

Finally it's evening, and we board the plane for Vancouver to discover that it's only two-thirds occupied, as there's been a repetition of the fog problem in Delhi and many passengers have missed this flight.

At the outset our seatmate is a young woman, an accountant who is immigrating to Canada with her parents, to join her brother in Surrey, BC. After a short while she moves to the other side of the plane to sit with them and we spread ourselves and our belongings over five seats, enjoying the comfort of travelling a long distance in a partially full plane. Don is so well rested he doesn't sleep at all during the entire 10 plus hour flight and I nap only briefly. Entertaining movies and television shows make the time pass quickly.

Our friends and our daughter meet us at the Vancouver airport for a happy reunion. It's lovely to see them, however our main focus is on reaching home. They deliver us to Horseshoe Bay ferry terminal in West Vancouver. On the boat we encounter the same neighbour who picked us up on arrival back on the Sunshine Coast from India in 2007; he and his daughters drop us off right at our door. Arriving home relatively refreshed after an extensive international voyage is officially a first for us.

EPILOGUE

Past and Present Align

A year and a half after our time in India, I finally ask my friend Alma Anderson, a professional psychic, for a reading about McLeod Ganj. There was no urgency around this, part of me has been enjoying the anticipation of what I feel certain will be an enlightening reading. Alma is the right person for this work because for many years she has had Tibetan spirit guides.

Channellers receive information in energetic patterns from spirits; they then process this into easily understood messages. (From *Spirit Speak* by Ivo Dominguez Jr.).

My friend, Judith Onley has given me permission to use the definition of channelling given to her by US, the large group soul she works with:

> "Channeling is a gateway between the physical and non-physical realms facilitated through a human being willing to speak the words for all to benefit from the teachings and wisdom of the higher realms of enlightenment."

As mentioned earlier, I have consulted Alma on and off over many years, and the information she has brought forward has been a support on my spiritual journey. Usually I come with specific questions or concerns that she addresses; her guides also offer messages they feel are important.

Many people born in the hippy generation, the late 1940s and early 1950s have an affinity for the Eastern part of the world, and I am no exception. My psychic abilities were enhanced in the spiritual atmosphere of McLeod Ganj and the channeling process with Alma serves to validate what I sensed from that first day in Bhagsu.

When Alma tunes into McLeod Ganj she sees a lot of light, much more light than darkness. "It could be wonderful if people were ready, or scary if they weren't." Mcleod Ganj is a safe place for foreigners, primarily due to the presence of the Dalai Lama, I'm told.

There's still some violence there, I tell her, for who could forget the image of the murdered woman in the tree from *An Indian in India*. Alma checks this out and says that McLeod Ganj is 85 percent amazing and 15 percent weird; one could become almost depressed there or pick up strange energy. There are not as many robbers or other bad people as in some other places, she is told. "They're telling me that people who are very bad could have an instant transformation there."

"Anything you buy or are gifted with in McLeod Ganj will remain as a *talisman* for a long time (something with magical or protective powers); sometimes the energy never wears out. It's unbelievable," says Alma, not one easily impressed. "A client brought me a scarf from the Dalai Lama and I feel his energy when I wear it."

My research indicates that Tibetan Buddhist roots in the Dharamsala area are very old, stretching back to the eighth century. As I knew viscerally, Alma affirms that McLeod Ganj is a very important place for me and that I have spent a number of lifetimes in this part of Himachal Pradesh state. "You've been both male and female, Tibetan and Indian. One life span as a British soldier may be the most important one." This is unexpected because I resonate with the Tibetans. Alma senses that the place affected me profoundly during that lifetime in the late 1800s or early 1900s. She cites Rudyard Kipling's description of the delirium produced by the sun in India, "Only mad dogs and Englishmen go out in the noonday sun." "In that lifetime, you go through great mood swings; it's almost like the place caused you an addiction. You didn't like it, didn't really want to be there, but you wouldn't leave," she says.

I tell her that the latest visit to McLeod Ganj affected me very strongly, in a positive way, and that being away from there was painful for a long time; the feeling is fading now, but it's taken almost two years.

In that soldier life I was not a nice person, and treated people like servants, apparently. "Be sure to offer something when you return there; you owe a little bit from that past life."

Immediately before this I was a very poor Indian woman, a *sadhvi* or female sadhu, someone who formally gives up, or renunciates, all worldly goods and family. "You are sitting on the ground dressed in orange; it's almost like your job is simply holding the space for others," Alma says. I remark that I view this as part of my role in this lifetime, as a healer, bodyworker, life coach and counsellor. (The concept has been part of my vocabulary for many years, holding the space for someone means being calmly and fully present, creating a safe container for them while they sit quietly, tell their story, explore their feelings, do whatever they need to do.)

"You were a Tibetan temple teacher, mostly male, many times in McLeod Ganj," Alma reports, "going through some amazing evolution and participating in incredible rituals that accelerated your soul's progress. Tune into rituals when you're there, they still have some of them," she advises.

These lifetimes were a very long time ago, a time when there was no death, I'm told, when some souls moved through a portal into another

287

dimension. Doing some research, I discover that this involves raising the frequency of the physical body into Light instead of going through physical death. The idea of portals is now being researched as a future possibility. In theory the potential exists to create a pathway to other worlds, quantum scientists say.

At this point Alma begins to feel a bit dizzy, uncommon for a seasoned psychic, because the energies coming through are so powerful. "I'm impressed, but they say it's no big deal," Alma humorously relays. "McLeod Ganj was a portal and may still be; you've been a *gatekeeper* in a few lifetimes (someone who helps people move to other dimensions.)" She pulls a tarot card and it's The Magician.

She goes on to say that I belonged to the same group soul as the people around me. This was at a time "before the Garden of Eden" when humans did not have individual souls. (I know animals share group souls, but was not aware humans had.) "Does this group soul include Don, myself, Dekyi, Khenrab and perhaps some Tibet Hope Center folks?" I inquire, and receive an affirmative reply.

"The Tibetan culture never forgot what the other dimensions are like and how to transcend between them, the way we have; they do not need to remember, the continuity is there," Alma's guides tell her.

"Many people who spent time in McLeod Ganj (back then) ascended to a different frequency; some, like you, did not complete their tasks, so you're back on earth. I'm being told that you're coming to some really important work now. My guides have been telling me for some time that magic is coming back to our culture," Alma relays.

Many others have been speaking and writing about the changes our culture is undergoing, as the vibration of the planet and everyone on it rises. Martha Beck's new book, *Finding Your Way in a Wild New World*, is about using magic and modern day shamanistic tools to manifest a life that is abundant in all ways.

Suddenly Alma surprises me by saying, "I don't know who I'm talking to…I'm talking to *The Book of Records* right now." (The *Akashic Records* are believed to be a sort of library that exists on another metaphysical plane, containing the collective thoughts and consciousness of all people and of the universe, past, present and future.)

"Why did the white people forget?" I ask. "It's for your own good," *The Akashic Records* tell me.

What comes next will be a key point of the channelling session for me: "When we reach a level of consciousness where death, war and murder are viewed, not as black and white, negative or positive, that's when we start to remember." Cultures such as Mexican or Thai do not think in the linear way that we do, Alma tells me.

I'm cautioned not to push myself when back in McLeod Ganj, to feel that I must do certain things; (I did that during the last trip; Alma must be picking up on that). "Not all magical places are easy." "Do less when you're there and be sure to take your *Rescue Remedy*" (a homeopathic remedy from the Bach Flower line). Because I'm quite psychic according to Alma, I could run into problems if not protected, experiencing overshadowings; this is when a spirit appropriates a person's consciousness to a greater or lesser degree, she explains.

Alma also reminds me to take my digital recorder on the next trip as I will be channelling while there. I received a significant amount of impressions on the last trip, both while awake and asleep, next time the work will be enhanced.

I describe my plan to interview Tibetan women during my next visit, a change from the numerous men I worked with last time. My book will juxtapose interviews with North American and Eastern women, contrasting their experiences. "Some are ancient souls," Alma says, "but others are more like prima donnas."

We conclude the session with Alma affirming that McLeod Ganj is one of my spiritual homes. (It did not have the same effect on Don, although he has had powerful experiences there in past lives, she explains.) "It's definitely a place that will speed up your evolution; it could never be forgotten, because it activated part of your energy system."

CONCLUSION

We've been home for a while now, and on the surface my life hasn't altered all that much. Underneath I'm a changed person. I'm more in touch with the essence of who I am. I've seen the incredible beauty and magic of India, heard the stories, felt the pain of the Tibetan exiles, seen the poor Dalits begging and cleaning up others' refuse for a living.

In Dharamsala I answered a spiritual calling. There I found another of my homes. Each and every place visited offered a vast variety of experiences and opened my eyes to different ways of living.

Travel and volunteering introduced me to new possibilities and taught me how to live a more holistic life, connected to spirit more of the time, a life closer to my ideal.

For a long time after the 2007 trip, I longed to be back in India, perhaps as much for the opening of heart and mind as for the intensity of exotic places. I have brought this back with me into my life.

Winston Churchill, writing about Russia, called it "…a riddle, wrapped in a mystery, inside an enigma…" this metaphor suits India also. I have swallowed the India experience whole and surrendered to it.

During my time in the country I often struggled to comprehend a culture I have no frame of reference for. Now I realize that to expect to understand the culture with such brief exposure is to demand the impossible. Certainly we learn more on each successive visit, but can only ever relate to India from our own personal perspective.

One must adjust to being home after an extended time in a developing country. *Reverse culture shock* is more challenging to most than the initial culture shock experienced on arrival.

Lisa Napoli, author of *Radio Shangri-La*, speaks of her return to Los Angeles after her own transformational experience in Bhutan; she has given me permission to quote her: "It was all too easy...too flat, colourless... I couldn't just go back to a world of work, leisure, and consumption. But I fought the tendency to think another location, other people, another world, would be better and yet to accept that the way I'd been living wasn't right for me anymore. The answers would follow in due time."

This is very similar to the way I feel. Travelling offers the possibility of beginning to look at life anew, to alter the way we view the world and our place in it. Then we incorporate that fresh worldview into our daily living in the West; that is when the personal work really begins.

I realized after the first trip to India that although travel and volunteering is now a necessary and important component of my life, I cannot live it waiting for a few months in India or some other developing country every couple of years. So I formed an intent to develop an engaging and rich life here at home, in this community we live in, as well as to enjoy my time abroad, one that incorporates the spiritual components of giving service and that segues into my life of travel and volunteering.

Sponsoring Tibetans in exile to come to our home community as part of a Canadian government initiative is one way we can help others, while also bringing our life at home and our travel and volunteer experiences full circle.

I'm aware of spirit most of the time now in small ways; from the flowers I gaze at outside the door of my writing studio, to the enormous coniferous trees growing in the neighbourhood, to the blue herons who make their appearance on occasion as I take my daily walk along the beach.

Over the past decade India's changes have been greater than most countries in the world. We're so fortunate to have the privilege of spending time in this unusual country, at a crossroads between the 20th and 21st centuries, before she becomes less recognizable. For me there was a strong, immediate connection to India, as if we've always been friends. I doubt I'll ever be past the point of learning, and India will continue to transform me in many ways. She will draw me back, until I'm very, very old; then my travels will be through my imagination as well as my connection to lifelong friends there. For now Don and I will continue to travel and to volunteer, in India again, and Uganda, where we will help our Ba'hai friends in their work. These experiences offer us the possibility of refreshing ourselves anew in body, mind and spirit. My spirit longs to add another chapter to the story.

ACKNOWLEDGEMENTS

I am very grateful for the skilled editing and marketing assistance of Jill Crossland and for her generosity and high level of commitment to making this book everything it could be.

Thank you to Suzanne Doyle-Ingram for your technical assistance, proofreading and marketing expertise. Your unstinting efforts are much appreciated.

To Don my partner and travel companion thank you for taking this journey with me. While I recorded my experiences in words Don used his camera and it struck me as we put the book together how perfectly those photographs fit into the chapters. Thank you for your help with the maps.

Alma; your psychic reading added extra richness to the book. Thank you.

Finally, the ongoing support of my daughter Bronwen and other family and friends helps me believe in my writing.

AUTHOR'S NOTE

The names of some monks and other Tibetans have been changed to protect the individual or their family or in cases where I was not able to contact them for permission.

ABOUT THE AUTHOR

Ellen Besso is a Holistic MidLife Coach and Author who helps women uncover their passions, find new directions in life, live abundantly as caregivers and put spirituality into practice in their daily lives.

Ellen trained as a Life Coach with Dr. Martha Beck, author of Finding Your Way in a Wild New World and monthly contributor to O, The Oprah Magazine. Judith Duerk, author of A Circle of Stones was Ellen's mentor for a number of years. Ellen also studied and worked as a Trager bodywork practitioner and is a meditator in the Kriya yoga tradition.

Her calling is to mentor and assist women on their journey of discovery with inspirational coaching, groups, books and articles. Ellen's 25 years of experience as a life coach, counsellor and social worker and as a midlife woman, mother, caregiver and spiritual seeker make her uniquely qualified to guide and support women. Her first book, Surviving Eldercare: Where Their Needs End and Yours Begin, chronicles her pilgrimage with her mother who had Alzheimer's and provides a body, mind, and spirit approach to caregiving.

In 2007, 2009 and again recently, Ellen's spiritual pursuits took her to India, where she and her partner travelled and volunteered, tutoring Tibetan refugees in Dharamsala, India; Ellen looks forward to returning to India in the future.

An Indian Sojourn – One woman's spiritual experience of travel and volunteering is a memoir about her time in India. It is the second book in Ellen Besso's MidLife Maze Series.

Made in the USA
Charleston, SC
07 June 2013